Demystifying eResearch

Understanding means simplifying.

—Jacques Bertin, *Semiology of Graphics*

DEMYSTIFYING eRESEARCH

A Primer for Librarians

Victoria Martin

LIBRARIES UNLIMITED

AN IMPRINT OF ABC-CLIO, LLC
Santa Barbara, C   Colorado • Oxford, England

Copyright © 2014 by ABC-CLIO, LLC

All rights reserved. No part of this publication may be reproduced, stored in a
retrieval system, or transmitted, in any form or by any means, electronic, mechanical,
photocopying, recording, or otherwise, except for the inclusion of brief quotations in a
review, without prior permission in writing from the publisher.

Library of Congress Cataloging-in-Publication Data

Martin, Victoria, 1961–
　Demystifying eResearch : a primer for librarians / Victoria Martin.
　　pages cm
　Includes bibliographical references and index.
　ISBN 978–1–61069–520–6 (pbk.) — ISBN 978–1–61069–521–3 (ebook)
1. Internet research. I. Title.
ZA4228.M37　2014
001.4′202854678—dc23　　　　　　2014024061

ISBN: 978–1–61069–520–6
EISBN: 978–1–61069–521–3

18　17　16　15　14　　　1　2　3　4　5

This book is also available on the World Wide Web as an eBook.
Visit www.abc-clio.com for details.

Libraries Unlimited
An Imprint of ABC-CLIO, LLC

ABC-CLIO, LLC
130 Cremona Drive, P.O. Box 1911
Santa Barbara, California 93116-1911

This book is printed on acid-free paper (∞)

Manufactured in the United States of America

Contents

Preface

Demystifying eResearch: A Primer for Librarians, as captured in the subtitle, is intended as a start-up guide to eResearch and how eResearch pertains to the library community. Technical descriptions of the software and computing technologies related to eResearch are outside of the scope of this book (there are many specialized works that address this task). Nor does this book offer a comprehensive view of eResearch. Instead, the book takes the broadest possible approach to the complex topic of eResearch by surveying its core themes and concepts and clarifying key points of tension that surround it in easy-to-read and simple language. It provides the reader who has little or no experience in the area of eResearch with a clear understanding of what eResearch is, how it impacts a library's mission, services, and collections, and how librarians can contribute to eResearch activities at their parent institutions and other research communities. Key terms are defined and explained. Relevant library initiatives and best practices are described. Essential resources and readings are suggested. The book also identifies requisite skills and emerging work requirements and recommends training and professional development opportunities for those librarians who might be expected to repurpose themselves or expand upon their existing competencies to meet the challenges of working in the eResearch environment. This combination of conceptual overview of eResearch coupled with a description of specific resources and real-world examples of eResearch activities within the library community is designed to quickly increase the reader's level of competence with regard to eResearch and their awareness of the current state of eResearch librarianship.

The book is intended for both novice and experienced librarians who have an interest in expanding their understanding of eResearch and how it impacts the libraries where they work. Although its primary audience is librarians and information professionals, this book can also serve as a useful reference resource for anyone else who is interested in eResearch or whose work involves answering questions about eResearch. It can also be used to support introductory graduate courses in the research process, eScience, research data management, scholarly communication, and collaboration, and digital curation.

Acknowledgments

I would like to acknowledge the support of the University Libraries at George Mason University granting me research leave to work on this book. I would also like to acknowledge the assistance of several people who contributed to the writing of this book, including: Douglas Hernandez, reference and instructional support specialist at Mercer Library, George Mason University, for assisting me with information search and citation verification; Barbara Ittner, managing editor at Libraries Unlimited/ABC-CLIO, for helping me in the process of editing and providing suggestions for improving my manuscript; Emma Bailey, senior production editor at Libraries Unlimited/ABC-CLIO, for her prompt, helpful responses to my questions; and N. Magendra Varman, associate program manager at Lumina Datamatics Ltd., for his infallible guidance during the book production process. A special thank you goes to my husband James, my proofreader extraordinaire, for his patience and support while I shepherded this book through its development.

Some material in this book appears in a chapter I authored titled "Developing a Library Collection in Bioinformatics: Support for an Evolving Profession," which appears in *Library Collection Development for Professional Programs: Trends and Best Practices*, edited by Sara Holder, copyright © 2013, IGI Global (http://www.igi-global.com). This material is used by permission of the publisher.

Introduction

The practice of eResearch is rapidly being adopted in many disciplines, from the sciences to the humanities. It has diverse characteristics, operates in different contexts, and is becoming increasingly distributed across multidisciplinary and multi-institutional research collaboration efforts. Even though at least some knowledge of eResearch is becoming an expected area of competency for librarians, eResearch librarianship is still a relatively new and not yet well-defined field. While most librarians may be familiar with the terms eResearch and eScience (which are sometimes used interchangeably for the same concept), they are not always familiar with the concepts themselves and thus might find them intimidating. This book aspires to offer a strong, yet accessible, overview of the eResearch concept and how it pertains to libraries and library services.

The book has two parts, which are further divided into chapters. Each chapter introduces a new topic, includes key term definitions, explains core ideas, offers specific examples of relevant resources, and, when appropriate, provides a historical overview of the topic. Endnotes and a list of suggested resources on the topic are included at the close of each chapter. The book concludes with a glossary and a subject index.

Part I offers an overview of eResearch by defining and explaining:

1. Key terms and concepts such as the difference between eResearch and traditional research practices
2. Research data and characteristics and types of research data
3. Research data formats and naming conventions
4. Research data documentation and metadata
5. Data management and preservation
6. Data management planseResearch-enabling technologies such as Grid computing, the Internet, cloud computing, visualization, the Social Web, and Virtual Research Environments

7. Internet-based tools for scholarly communication; exploration of new publishing models and peer-review processes; and dissemination and preservation of research results and discoveries

8. Researchers' attitudes toward technologyeResearch practices across various disciplines

Although computational tools and research methodologies for conducting eResearch were initially used in science domains, these tools and methodologies are beginning to support data-intensive research across all other disciplines as well. Part I bridges the concept of eResearch to other fields, including the social sciences, the arts, and the humanities, and explores the growing interdisciplinary nature of current research practices.

As the research process becomes more computerized and increasingly distributed across larger-scale, multidisciplinary, and multi-institutional collaborations, eResearch support is becoming a key component of many libraries' services and collections. This presents a paradigm shift for libraries on many levels and requires new strategies for research support and significant development of library infrastructure. Part II discusses how eResearch affects nearly every aspect of the library's functions, collections, and services and how it impacts the library's mission. Part II also describes how libraries can be positioned to work more effectively in an eResearch environment and suggests potential eResearch activity areas such as assistance with data management plans, data curation, teaching good data practices to researchers, and providing research consultations on authorship and copyright. Even though many librarians already have applicable skills to work effectively in the eResearch environment, at least some additional training is essential to apply their traditional knowledge and strengths in new ways to competently work with eResearchers. Part II identifies the needed skills and competencies for librarians who are working, or planning on working, with eResearchers; explores the opportunities for them to acquire any additional skills and knowledge they need to perform their role in support of eResearch; and suggests training and professional development opportunities that would qualify librarians to better address the unique challenges of managing data. Part II also describes prominent eResearch initiatives and programs such as those taking place at the Massachusetts Institute of Technology (MIT), Cornell University, Purdue University, and Johns Hopkins University as well as those taking place at smaller institutions.

Even though the material in each chapter can stand on its own with minimal context from the other chapters, readers without the background knowledge of eResearch are recommended to read this book in a linear fashion, chapter by chapter. Alternatively, readers with specialized areas of interest might choose to go directly to a specific chapter that interests them.

List of Acronyms

AAAS	American Association for the Advancement of Science
AAUP	Association of American University Presses
ACH	Association for Computers and the Humanities
ACRL	Association of College and Research Libraries
ADA	Americans with Disabilities Act
ADHO	Alliance of Digital Humanities Organizations
AJAX	asynchronous JavaScript and XML
AI	artificial intelligence
ALA	American Library Association
ALLC	Association for Literary and Linguistic Computing
ALS	Alliance Library System
APA	American Psychological Association
APC	article processing charge
API	application programming interface
ARL	Association of Research Libraries
ARPA	Advanced Research Projects Agency
ARPANET	Advanced Research Projects Agency network
ASCII	American Standard Code for Information Interchange
AWS	Amazon Web services
BIRN	Biomedical Informatics Research Network
BMC	BioMed Central
CAL	computer-aided learning
CC	Creative Commons
CCBY	Creative Commons Attribution License
CERN	Conseil Européen pour la Recherche Nucléaire (European Council for Nuclear Research)
CI	cyberinfrastructure
CIBER	Center for International Business Education and Research
CIC	Committee on Institutional Cooperation

CISE	Computer and Information Science and Engineering program
CLIR	Council on Library and Information Resources
CNI	Coalition for Networked Information
CRM	customer relationship management
CSCW	computer-supported cooperative work
CSV	comma-separated value
CTO	chief technology officer
CUL	Cornell University Libraries
D2C2	Distributed Data Curation Center
DARPA	Defense Advanced Research Projects Agency
DCC	Digital Curation Centre
DCEP	Data Curation Education Program
DCI	Darwin Core Initiative
DCMI	Dublin Core Metadata Initiative
DDI	Data Documentation Initiative
DH	digital humanities
DHQ	*Digital Humanities Quarterly*
DHSI	Digital Humanities Summer Institute
DigCCurr	Digital Curation Curriculum
DIL	data information literacy
DLF	Digital Library Federation
DMP	data management plan
DMPTool	data management planning tool
DMS	Data Management Services
DNA	deoxyribonucleic acid
DOAJ	Directory of Open Access Journals
DOE	Department of Energy
DOI	digital object identifier
DRM	digital rights management
EBI	European Bioinformatics Institute
EC2	elastic compute cloud
EGI	European Grid Infrastructure
EML	ecological metadata language
ESI	E-Science Institute
FEDORA	Flexible Extensible Digital Object and Repository Architecture
FITS	flexible image transport system
GAC	graduate academic certificate
GEOSS	global earth observation system of systems
GIS	geographic information system
GPS	global positioning system
GSLIS	graduate school of library and information science
GSM	global system for mobile communications
GWAS	Genome-Wide Association Study

HASTAC	Humanities, Arts, Science, and Technology Advanced Collaboratory
HCI	human-computer interaction
HCIL	Human-Computer Interaction Lab
HDFS	hadoop distributed file system
HPC	high-performance computing
HTC	high-throughput computing
HTML	hypertext markup language
HTRC	HathiTrust Research Center
HTTP	hypertext transfer protocol
IaaS	infrastructure as a service
IATH	Institute for Advanced Technology in the Humanities
I-CHASS	Institute for Computing in Humanities, Arts, and Social Science
ICPSR	Inter-University Consortium for Political and Social Research
ICT	information and communication technology
IDC	International Data Corporation
IDEF0	integration definition for function modeling
IDP	International Dunhuang Project
IEEE	Institute of Electrical and Electronics Engineers
IIS	Information and Intelligent Systems
IMLS	Institute of Museum and Library Services
IP	Internet protocol
IPEDS	integrated postsecondary education data system
IPR	intellectual property rights
IPUMS	integrated public use microdata series
IR	institutional repository
IT	information technology
JHU	Johns Hopkins University
JHUP	Johns Hopkins University Press
JISC	Joint Information Systems Committee
JPEG	Joint Photographic Experts Group
LB21	Laura Bush 21st Century Librarian Program
LC	Library of Congress
LEAD	Linked Environments for Atmospheric Discovery
LIS	library and information science
LLAMA	Library Leadership and Management Association
LO	learning object
LOD	linked open data
LOM	learning object metadata
LOR	learning object repository
MA	master of arts
METS	metadata encoding and transmission standard
MIT	Massachusetts Institute of Technology
MLA	Modern Language Association

MLIS	master of library and information sciences
MODS	metadata object description schema
MOOC	massive online open courses
MPP	massively parallel processing
MVE	modular visualization environment
NASA	National Aeronautics and Space Administration
NCBI	National Center for Biotechnology Information
NCES	National Center for Education Statistics
NCeSS	National Centre for e-Social Science
NCRR	National Center for Research Resources
NDL	National Digital Library
NDLP	National Digital Library Program
NDLTD	Networked Digital Library of Theses and Dissertations
NEH	National Endowment for the Humanities
NIH	National Institutes of Health
NIST	National Institute of Standards and Technology
nM	nanoManipulator
NoSQL	Not Only SQL
NSF	National Science Foundation
OA	open access
OAI	Open Archives Initiative
OAPF	open access publishing fund
OASPA	Open Access Scholarly Publishers Association
OCA	Open Content Alliance
OCLC	Online Computer Library Center
OCR	optical character recognition
OCS	open conference systems
OECD	Organization for Economic Co-operation and Development
OER	open educational resources
OGSA	open grid services architecture
OJS	open journal systems
OPUS	Online Publications at University of Stuttgart
P2P	peer-to-peer
PaaS	platform as a service
PDA	personal digital assistant
PDF	portable document format
PDL	Perseus Digital Library
PhD	doctor of philosophy
PI	principal investigator
PKP	Public Knowledge Project
PLoS	Public Library of Science
PMC	PubMed Central
PMC	post-masters certificate

PNS   post-normal science
PREMIS   preservation metadata: implementation strategies
PURL   persistent uniform resource locator
RB   research blogging
RDF   resource description framework
REDCap   research electronic data capture
RLUK   Research Libraries UK
RSS   Originally used for RDF site summary; now stands for really
             simple syndication
QA   quality assurance
QC   quality control
R&D   research and development
RDM   research data management
RLUK   Research Libraries UK
S3   simple storage service
SaaS   software as a service
SADT   structured analysis and design technique
SBE   social, behavioral, and economic sciences
SCB   Society for Conservation Biology
SDI   spatial data infrastructure
SHERPA   Securing a Hybrid Environment for Research Preservation
             and Access
SLA   Special Libraries Association
SNS   social networking site
SOA   service-oriented architecture
SPARC   Scholarly Publishing and Academic Resources Coalition
SQL   structured query language
STM   science, technology, medicine
TCP   transmission control protocol
TD   transdisciplinarity
TEI   Text Encoding Initiative
TR   transdisciplinary research
UCLA   University of California at Los Angeles
UK   United Kingdom
UNICORE   Uniform Interface to Computer Resources
UNT   University of North Texas
UP   university press
UPCC   University Press Content Consortium
URI   uniform resource identifier
URL   uniform resource locator
URN   uniform resource name
U.S.   United States

VLE	Virtual Learning Environment
VRE	Virtual Research Environment
W3C	World Wide Web Consortium
WCMC	Weill Cornell Medical College
WCS	Worm Community System
WLCG	Worldwide LHC Computing Grid project
WWW	World Wide Web
XML	extensible markup language
ZVI	Carl Zeiss digital microscopic image format

Part I

eResearch Defined and Explained

1

What Is eResearch?

eRESEARCH VERSUS TRADITIONAL RESEARCH: DIFFERENCES AND SIMILARITIES

The ultimate purpose of research, including eResearch, is the creation and dissemination of new knowledge. In the process of creating this new knowledge, researchers often find themselves looking for the same information, or data, again and again (i.e., "re-searching") and then interpreting this information in their attempt to answer a specific question or to solve a specific problem. Research findings are then shared with other researchers and the public through formal and informal methods of scholarly communication, and they become the foundation for further advancements in research that contribute to new knowledge for the benefit of mankind.

The difference between traditional research and eResearch lies not in *what* is happening, but rather in *how* the research is conducted, communicated, and preserved. While many traditional research activities take place in a laboratory setting (in the sciences), or during interpersonal communication (in the social sciences), or in an archive (in the humanities), eResearch activities, as the e-prefix suggests, take place in a Web-based environment.[1] Information and computational technologies (among them, the Internet being the most widespread and influential) have transformed the way in which researchers collect, analyze, share, and preserve data, and how they conduct literature research, publish research results, communicate with the audience, and maintain formal and informal networks with their peers. These activities involve the use of novel tools and techniques and require on the part of the eResearcher a mastery of new knowledge and skills.

Although eResearch practice is often discipline and project dependent, a successful eResearch enterprise generally involves the following features that emphasize the collaborative, technology-based, multidisciplinary, and geographically distributed nature of eResearch:

- Computerization of the research process
- Development of virtual collaborative environments designed to facilitate research
- Creation of distant collaborations of individual researchers or research teams, often international and interdisciplinary in scope
- Scholarly communication among geographically distributed researchers enabled through Web-based formal and informal communication tools

eResearch, however, neither replaces traditional research nor competes with it. Even though it fundamentally alters the ways in which researchers carry out their work, communicate, share, and preserve discoveries that result from their research, the task of eResearch is to support and enhance the research process and contribute to its ultimate goal, which is the creation of new knowledge.

eRESEARCH: DEFINITION

Providing a single authoritative definition of eResearch is a challenging task. There is little agreement in the literature on exactly what eResearch means. These definitions depend upon the context in which the term is used as well as upon an individual author's perspective on what eResearch is and what it is not. Some definitions of eResearch emphasize the ultimate impact of advanced information technology on the research process as a major characteristic of eResearch; some focus on an expected outcome of the research process (faster, better, cheaper); and some are tied to a particular discipline or project that have and use discipline-specific language around the subject. To confuse matters further, the terms eResearch and eScience are sometimes used interchangeably for the same concept. There are also other synonyms of eResearch used in published literature, such as cyberinfrastructure, cyberscience, cyberscholarship, e-scholarship, e-infrastructure, electronic research, digital scholarship, and "computer supported cooperative science" (Jirotka, Lee, and Olson 2013). Furthermore, there is no consensus on how the term should be spelled: e-Research, e-research, eresearch, and eResearch.

Appelbe and Bannon (2007) argue that a definitive meaning of eResearch is impossible and, instead, that there are "useful characteristics of eResearch projects that can distinguish the degree to which a particular project might be promoted as eResearch" (Appelbe and Bannon 2007, 83). They also argue that eResearch is characterized not as much by the *use* of information technology in the research process but rather by researchers' *reliance* on information technology, such as hardware, software, networks, and human resources.

In his last talk to the Computer Science and Telecommunications Board on January 11, 2007, Jim Gray, a distinguished American computer scientist and Turing Award winner, described eScience as a "transformed scientific method." He called it "the fourth paradigm" and "a fourth branch of science" (the first three branches are theoretical, experimental, and computational sciences) that unifies theory, experiment, and simulation. He argued that eScience is a data-intensive science (as opposed to the experimental, theoretical, and computational scientific paradigms) and a new way of doing research that requires a new model for conducting scientific inquiry (Gray 2009).[2]

Although the definition of eResearch is still a matter of some debate, the underlying theme in all these definitions is the collaborative, data-driven, networked nature of the research practice. Common to all definitions is the notion that eResearch refers to the use of information and computing technologies such as the Grid computing, the Internet, cloud computing, visualization software, and scholarly communication and collaboration online tools that support every aspect of the research process.

A unifying definition of eResearch as a profound change in every aspect of the research process across all disciplines—from the conception of a research project (hypothesis) to methodology design and data collection, analysis, and finally to publication and archiving of research results—is yet to be developed. Even though this ambiguity might at times be confusing, it reflects the evolving state of eResearch. To avoid an overly complicated definition, but the one that pinpoints the fundamental aspects of eResearch and accommodates the diversity of perspectives, disciplines, and experiences, this book adopts the broad definition provided by Nicholas Jankowski in *e-Research: Transformation in Scholarly Practice*. According to Jankowski, "e-Research" is "a form of scholarship conducted in a networked environment utilizing Internet-based tools and involving collaboration among scholars separated by distance, often on a global scale" (Jankowski 2009, 207).

eRESEARCH VERSUS eSCIENCE

Since the 1990s, researchers, scholars, and funding agencies have paid particular attention to the application of advanced computational and information technologies in scientific research. This trend enabled the mobilization of large-scale resources for the further development of new paradigms in the sciences, ultimately leading to the creation of a cyberinfrastructure for research in the United States, the eScience program in the United Kingdom, and e-Infrastructure within Europe and elsewhere.

The term "e-Science" originated in the United Kingdom in 1999.[3] John Taylor, then director general of the Office of Science and Technology in the UK, is credited with coining this term that he defined as "the large scale science that would increasingly be carried out through distributed global collaborations enabled by the Internet" (National E-Science Centre 2014). Malcolm Atkinson, Director of the UK's e-Science Institute and National E-Science Centre, interpreted eScience more broadly as "the systematic development of research methods that exploit advanced computational thinking" (Research Councils UK 2014). In these definitions, as elsewhere, eScience is commonly perceived as "Big Science" that is interdisciplinary, data-intensive, and collaborative, often associated with large national or international projects and done at major research facilities. The examples of such "Big Science" projects are the TeraGrid (https://www.xsede.org/tg-archives), the Biomedical Informatics Research Network (BIRN) (http://www.birncommunity.org/), and the Linked Environments for Atmospheric Discovery (LEAD) project (http://d2i.indiana.edu/leadii-home).

The focus of eScience then, as now, was on the physical and biological sciences often said to be characterized by a "deluge" of data where large volumes of data, too large for traditional labor analysis and often requiring the expertise of researchers from multiple disciplines to be analyzed, were processed with the aid of Grid computer networks, resulting in the creation of new research methodologies and even new disciplines such as astroinformatics.

While the eScience characteristics outlined above originated in and evolved to a greater degree in the sciences, the initial characterization of eScience as being restricted to the "hard sciences" is now giving way to a broader, more diverse interpretation and can be gathered together under the term of eResearch. In this context, eResearch extends eScience's remit to all disciplines referring to the use of distributed resources across multiple domains to conduct research with the following key features: data-driven, technology-based, multi- and interdisciplinary, and collaborative. Across all disciplines, research activities are now being enhanced and even revolutionized by the wide adoption of eScience tools, such as high-performance and cloud computing, storage and visualization tools, and dissemination of research results through the Internet; and eScience methodologies, such as identification of patterns and trends from the mining and analysis of data and collaborative problem-solving. eResearch projects, like eScience projects, might be as data intensive, technology-based, multi- and interdisciplinary, and collaborative as eScience projects. Researchers in all fields are recognizing that the solutions to global problems—such as climate change and increasingly rapid spread of contagious diseases, among others—will not likely be solved by isolated disciplines, but rather by collaboration between the science and "non-science" fields. Although the awareness of and sensitivity to the diversity of existing disciplinary cultures, research styles, and practices is important, eResearch bridges the concept of eScience to all fields of scholarship without privileging specific disciplines and thus marks a shift of attention toward exploiting a wide variety of information and communication technologies in any research activity.

While the terms eScience and eResearch are not yet fully defined and have considerable overlap, eResearch is not simply an extension of eScience, even though it extends eScience practices to other disciplines. eResearch is a broader concept taking into consideration not only global computational science projects, but any research activity performed digitally at any scale. Furthermore, the concept of eScience is broadening to encompass nonscience disciplines such as the social sciences and humanities. These developments open up avenues for mutually beneficial collaboration between different research disciplines and, coupled with the use of advanced digital technology, will continue to "diffuse" disciplinary boundaries and foster breakthrough research.

RISKS AND CHALLENGES OF eRESEARCH

New ways of conducting research also present risks and challenges. Although both eResearch and traditional research face a few common demands, such as the complexity of the research process itself or mandatory compliance with funders' research regulations, some demands are unique to eResearch. As the research process is being increasingly supported by technologies that enable small- and large-scale research collaborations, these technologies bring with them their own complications. Among them are limited network and storage capacity, access to and sharing of research data collections along with related networking and computing resources, integration with developing cyber-infrastructure, and long-term user support for collaboration across disciplinary, institutional, and geographical boundaries. Curation of massive digital data sets and preserving them for future reuse can also be problematic because of the sheer volume of research data that is being generated as well as the wide variety and complexity of digital data types and formats. Furthermore, the rapid pace of technological advances challenges the continuity of access to digital data that tends to become obsolete more quickly than data recorded on paper.

Although eResearch efforts are driven, to a great extent, by technological developments, eResearchers also face a number of nontechnological challenges, including legal, ethical, interpersonal, and interdisciplinary ramifications. Since data is one of the major drivers of eResearch, it should be no surprise that some of the most significant challenges to successful eResearch projects are related to data protection, confidentiality, access, use, and reuse. There is contentiousness between the risks in exposing research data and the pressure to make research data openly available as an integral part of the research record. Dealing with sensitive data, such as crime data or health data, and how others may use this data in the future is another concern. It is not always an easy task to determine who has rights to access sensitive data, and what data must be protected during collection and investigation and safely discarded after its use. A number of legal requirements apply to the collection and management of research data, particularly where research involves human subjects, as well as ethical require-ments for responsible conduct of research, especially where research involves using live animals.[4]

Another challenge is posed by the emergence of eResearch collaborations and what Cohen (2010) calls an "ethics of collaboration." eResearch is a complex social process involving credibility, interpersonal trust, and accountability. When multiple distributed interdisciplinary research teams are collaborating on a research project, it is crucial to identify who authored what and when and how the products of collaboration will be reviewed for tenure and promotion. In addition, new modes of scholarly communication present challenges to researchers, from the complexity of open access pub-lishing to the controversial nature of social media as a means of communica-tion in various aspects of research.

Communication issues may also arise within interdisciplinary and international collaborative efforts due to the methodological variability of diverse disciplines, the need for creating and maintaining a shared vision on eResearch projects, issues of power and hierarchy, and barriers of language and culture within multinational teams.

Although these challenges have no easy answers, they indicate the growing vitality of eResearch and its capacity for catalyzing significant transformation of research methods and practices. Understanding these challenges, and bal-ancing them against the risks and rewards of eResearch, is one of the keys to conducting effective research projects.

NOTES

1. According to *The Oxford Dictionary of New Words: A Popular Guide to Words in the News*, the prefix "e" ("electronic") means "in machine-readable form; existing as data which must be read by a computer" (Tulloch 1996, 98–99).

2. The term "science" is often used as a generic synonym for the term "research," particularly a basic and systematic research. Similarly, some authors use the term "eScience" as a synonym for "eResearch." In this book as well as in other works, the term eResearch is used in a manner akin to eScience, in that it describes a research methodology rather than a discipline-specific scholarship.

3. In the United States, the term *cyberinfrastructure,* which is often used inter-changeably with the term eScience, was first coined by a National Science Foundation Blue-Ribbon Committee "to reflect how the traditional modes of scientific research ... are being enhanced and even revolutionized by the integrative capabilities of high-performance computers, storage and visualization tools for very large data-sets, digitally enabled sensors and instruments in the environment, virtual organiza-tions for collaborative problem solving, and interoperable suites of software services and tools that seeks to resolve complex problems of analyzing massive spatial datasets" (Atkins 2003).

4. Some professional societies representing particular disciplines publish guidelines for the ethical and responsible conduct of research on their websites—for example, the

American Psychological Association (APA) (http://www.apa.org/research/respon-sible/index.aspx) and the Society for Conservation Biology (SCB) (http://www.conbio.org/about-scb/who-we-are/code-of-ethics/).

WORKS CITED

Appelbe, Bill, and David Bannon. "eResearch—Paradigm Shift or Propaganda?" *Journal of Research and Practice in Information Technology*, 39, no. 2 (2007): 83–90. http://ws.acs.org.au/jrpit/JRPITVolumes/JRPIT39/JRPIT39 .2.83.pdf (accessed February 28, 2014).

Atkins, Daniel. *Revolutionizing Science and Engineering through Cyberinfrastructure.* Report of the National Science Foundation Blue-Ribbon Advisory Panel on Cyberinfrastructure, National Science Foundation Publication NSF0728. Washington, DC: National Science Foundation, 2003.

Cohen, Matt. "Design and Politics in Electronic American Literary Archives." In *The American Literary Scholar in the Digital Age,* edited by Amy Earhart and Andrew Jewell. Ann Arbor: University of Michigan Press, 2010.

Gray, Jim. "Jim Gray on eScience: A Transformed Scientific Method." In *The Fourth Paradigm: Data-Intensive Scientific Discovery,* edited by Tony Hey, Stewart Tansley, and Kristin Tolle, xvii–xxxi. Redmond, WA: Microsoft Research, 2009. http://research.microsoft.com/en-us/collaboration/fourthparadigm/ 4th_paradigm_book_complete_lr.pdf (accessed February 28, 2014).

Jankowski, Nicholas W., ed. *e-Research: Transformation in Scholarly Practice.* New York: Routledge, 2009.

Jirotka, Marina, Charlotte P. Lee, and Gary M. Olson. "Supporting Scientific Collaboration: Methods, Tools and Concepts." *Computer Supported Cooperative Work (CSCW)* 22, no. 4–6 (2013): 667–715. doi:10.1007/s10606-012-9184-0.

National E-Science Center. *Defining e-Science.* http://www.nesc.ac.uk/nesc/define .html (accessed February 22, 2014).

Research Councils UK. http://www.rcuk.ac.uk/ (accessed February 22, 2014).

Tulloch, Sara. *The Oxford Dictionary of New Words: A Popular Guide to Words in the News.* Oxford: Oxford University Press, 1996.

SUGGESTED READINGS

Bent, Moira, Pat Gannon-Leary, and Jo Webb. "Information Literacy in a Researcher's Learning Life: The Seven Ages of Research." *New Review of Information Networking* 13, no. 2 (2007): 81–99. doi:10.1080/13614570801899983.

Borgman, Christine. *Scholarship in the Digital Age: Information, Infrastructure, and the Internet.* Cambridge, MA: MIT Press, 2007.

Dutton, William H., and Paul W. Jeffreys, eds. *World Wide Research: Reshaping the Sciences and Humanities.* Cambridge, MA: MIT Press, 2010.

Hey, Anthony, Stewart Tansley, and Kristin Tolle. *The Fourth Paradigm: Data-Intensive Scientific Discovery.* Redmond, WA: Microsoft Research, 2009. http://research.microsoft.com/en-us/collaboration/fourthparadigm/4th_paradigm _book_complete_lr.pdf (accessed February 25, 2014).

Hine, Christine, ed. *New Infrastructure for Knowledge Production: Understanding E-Science.* Information Science Publishing, 2006.

Jankowski, Nicholas W. "Exploring E-Science: An introduction." *Journal of Computer-Mediated Communication*, 12, no. 2 (2007): 549–62.
Jankowski, Nicholas W., ed. *e-Research: Transformation in Scholarly Practice*. New York: Routledge, 2009.
Weller, Martin. *The Digital Scholar: How Technology Is Transforming Academic Practice*. London: Bloomsbury Academic, 2011.

2

Understanding Research Data

Data is only useful to the extent that we can both find it and make sense of it.

—Ian Foster (2011, 29)

DEFINITIONS OF DATA

Although "data" is a commonly used term within the eResearch community, the term itself is used inconsistently. Its meaning depends on the context, in which the question is asked, or the discipline, within which research is being conducted.

The *Oxford English Dictionary* defines data as "related items of (chiefly numerical) information considered collectively, typically obtained by scientific work and used for reference, analysis, or calculation" (OED Online 2013). In computer science, data are defined as information that can be processed by a computer (Pfaffenberger 2003). The *McGraw-Hill Dictionary of Scientific and Technical Terms* states that data are "a general term for numbers, letters, symbols, and analog quantities that serve as input for computer processing" (McGraw-Hill 2013, 548). *A Dictionary of Epidemiology* defines data simply as "a collection of items of information" (Porta 2008). In less formal situations, some people refer to everything created in a digital form or converted to a digital form as "data."[1]

A broad attempt to define data was undertaken by a Critical Delphi study, Knowledge Map of Information Science, conducted in 2003–2005. The study, involving 57 prominent scholars from 16 countries, aimed to explore the theoretical foundations of information management. Published as a series of four articles, the study documented at least 130 definitions of data, information, and knowledge (Zins 2007a, 2007b, 2007c, 2007d). Such a variety of definitions, even among leading information science professionals, suggests that there is considerable flexibility in usage of the term data.

WHAT ARE RESEARCH DATA?

Despite this ambiguity regarding the definition of data, research data commonly refer to raw material obtained by researchers during the course of their work for the purposes of producing and validating original research results. This definition highlights the three important characteristics of research data: *when* data are obtained, *what* they consist of, and *why* they are used. According to these characteristics, research data can be regarded as "situational" because the same material can be research data for some people but not others, and the same material can be research data for a person at some point in time but not at some other time. Likewise, data can be obtained by a researcher for one purpose but used by other researchers for a different purpose (University of Edinburgh 2014).

Data are at the heart of research. Discovering, accessing, generating, manipulating, interpreting, and presenting data, be it through experiment, observation, simulation, surveys, or some other means, are the key activities in the research life cycle, and much of a researcher's time and effort is devoted to them. Researchers also spend a substantial amount of time and energy on discovering the preexisting data that may complement or modify their research objective.

Even though raw research data are valuable in their own right (for example, they can serve as a backup for a theory or form the basis of new research), these data, no matter how valuable, are of no use to people unless they are interpreted. As Kock, McQueen, and Corner (1997) observed, "a piece of data becomes information or knowledge only when it is interpreted by its receiver" (71). Once raw data are interpreted—i.e., organized, analyzed, or assigned some meaning—they become information that, in turn, is transformed into knowledge, which can be then transformed into wisdom (Ackoff 1989). Thus research data may be viewed as the foundation from which information, knowledge, and wisdom are derived. One of the special tasks of eResearch is to interpret data and allow information to emerge from data that could then be transformed into knowledge and wisdom and consequently be used by other researchers, educators, and, ultimately, humankind (Anderson and Kanuka 2003).

DIVERSITY OF RESEARCH DATA

Research data come in many varied formats and can be numerical, descriptive, visual, auditory, or tactile. It can be collected as observations, text, images, sounds, numbers, symbols, computer program results, measurements, or experiences that are independent of context, analysis, or observer. Research data can also be discipline-specific, e.g., Flexible Image Transport System (FITS), or instrument-specific, e.g., Carl Zeiss Digital Microscopic Image Format (ZVI). Information about how, when, where, and by whom the data were collected or generated and with what tools is considered to be a special kind of data (also known as *metadata*, or data about data).

Various authors have attempted to identify types of research data based on data origins, methods of collection, or collection purpose. Floridi (2005) identified five types of data: (1) primary data (obtained by the researcher through a first-hand experience); (2) secondary data (gathered by other researchers); (3) metadata (data about data); (4) operational data (collected from a process whose primary purpose is not merely the generation of the data); and (5) derivative data (resulted from processing or compiling primary data). Allan (2009) categorized three types of data: (1) not-repeatable (through an observation); (2) repeatable (through an experiment); and (3) calculated (through a computer simulation). Thessen and Patterson (2011) divided data into two main types: (1) observational (an object or event witnessed by an observer), and (2) processed (obtained through the processing of raw data).

With regard to data origins, research data are broken down into two broad categories: primary data and secondary data. The difference between primary and secondary data is similar to that between primary and secondary information resources. Primary data are always original and refers to data being collected or obtained by the researcher from first-hand experience, for example, during a personal interview or a field study. Secondary data refer to data gathered and recorded by other researchers or agencies, for example, from a book or an existing data set. Secondary data are obtained prior to (and for purposes other than) the project at hand but may be useful addressing a research problem currently under investigation. Government agencies are one of the principal sources of secondary data, although secondary data may also come from nongovernment organizations or individuals. While secondary research data may be less expensive and less time-consuming to generate, it has several drawbacks: it can be obsolete, or collected in such a way that it does not answer the research question of the user, or does not completely fit the research question.

Research data can be collected or generated in many different ways. With regard to data collection methods, data can be grouped into the categories of technology-assisted or manual recording of observations (e.g., weather measurements), computer simulations (e.g., traffic analysis), experiments (e.g., random surveys for sociological purposes), and record keeping (e.g., government or business records). Data can be generated via filed or laboratory instrumentation; sensor networks, satellites, and even cell phones.

Data can exist in hardcopy, such as field notes, or in computer-readable (or digital) form, such as text, image or sound files, websites, databases, or data sets.[2]

Data in the form of hard copy can be stored in desks or file cabinets; digital data may reside (typically in multiple versions and in several places) on an individual researcher's computer, an institutional data storage facility, a laboratory server, or a digital data archive. Increasingly, research data are becoming an important end product of scholarship, complementing the more traditional role of scholarly publications.

RESEARCH DATA LIFE CYCLE

The data life cycle describes the stages that data progress through during the research process that result in the creation of new knowledge. A typical research data life cycle has eight phases:

1. Planning
2. Data collection
3. Data quality assurance and control (QA/QC)
4. Metadata creation
5. Data preservation
6. Data discovery
7. Data integration
8. Data analysis

Even though in every phase of the data life cycle, the researcher collects or generates new data arising from experimentation, observation, or investigation, these phases are not always sequential.

THE DATA DELUGE OR "BIG DATA"

> The sheer volume of information that is now being produced, and expected to be produced in the future, is a cause for concern. Researchers fear that there will be too much data to handle, process, or even look at.
> —Robin Williams et al. (2009)

The phenomenon of production of digital data at an astonishingly rapid and vast scale, nicknamed as "data deluge" or "big data," has been widely reported in literature (Bell, Hey, and Szalay 2009; Carlson 2006; Gershon 2002; Hey and Trefethen 2003; Marcum and George 2010).[3] A study by the International Data Corporation (IDC) indicated that the world has created a staggering 1.8 zettabytes of information and that the world's information is doubling every two years (Gantz and Reinsel 2011). What distinguishes data deluge from data flow in the past is not just its vast volume, but also its diversity (the sources and types of data being collected) and its velocity (the speed with which the data flow through the networked systems).

In addition, these data may have different structures, may be heterogeneous, or may be completely unstructured (e.g., multimedia and text documents).[4]

The massive amounts of data that eResearchers can generate with modern instrumentation coupled with the speed in which they can be accessed and analyzed are one of the greatest challenges for conducting research in the twenty-first century. It is changing the nature of research in fundamental ways and presents both advantages and disadvantages for researchers. The ability to access and analyze raw data using supercomputers makes it possible for researchers to discover order and patterns in data that, in the past, had been "too great, slow or complex for the human eye and mind to notice and comprehend" (Markoff 2011, D1). On the other hand, the world of eResearch is awash in such great quantities of digital data that they are often too large to be processed using traditional data processing techniques.

The phenomenon of "data deluge" has dramatically impacted nearly every scholarly discipline. "Big science" fields[5] such as physics and astronomy have constructed tools and distributed digital libraries and data repositories to manage and share the enormous volumes of data generated by linear accelerators, sensor networks, satellites, space stations, seismographs, and other instrumentation. A new generation of technologies has emerged to address processing large data sets such as MapReduce framework, including Hadoop Distributed File System (HDFS), NoSQL (Not Only SQL) data stores, MPP (Massively Parallel Processing) databases, and in-memory database processing systems. In the life sciences, "high-throughput computational techniques, also known as 'omics,'[6]have produced such a vast quantity of complex biological data that specialized software tools [have been] designed by experts in the field to facilitate the interpretation and analysis of this data. ... Worldwide online [biological] databases (such as GenBank (http://www.ncbi.nlm.nih.gov/genbank/) and Protein Data Bank (http://www.rcsb.org/pdb/home/home.do) were created, offering scientists the opportunity to access a wide variety of [biologically relevant data]" (Martin 2013, 271).

Social scientists work with large data sets of demographic, economic, and other information generated from social media, sensor networks, administrative and customer service records, private sector data, Internet search activity, crowdsourcing systems, and surveys, among others. Econometric analysis depends heavily on computational interpretation of large data sets and might be considered the precursor to today's "big data" social sciences. Furthermore, many eSocial science research projects are dealing with large sets of historical sociological data such as raw census data, labor and occupancy records, membership rosters, and maps. For example, the Philadelphia Social History Project at the University of Pennsylvania studies historical, economic, social, and demographic landscape of Philadelphia in the nineteenth century.

Even though computational technology has been used in humanities research to a lesser extent than in the sciences and social sciences, where it is more typical to rapidly accumulate and share high volumes of data and use data-intensive applications, the humanities researchers have begun to work with large digital datasets also, particularly in archaeology, where the scale of data collection and the potential for computational analysis might be considered analogous to "Big Science" projects (Schnapp 2012). These "Big Science" projects that Schnapp (2012) calls "Big Humanities" projects involve data-intensive, large-team collaborative efforts that can take several years to realize. Examples include HASTAC (Humanities, Arts, Science, and Technology Advanced Collaboratory) (http://www.hastac.org/); the Digging into Data Challenge project (http://www.diggingintodata.org/), funded by several international agencies; and the TextGrid project (https://www.textgrid.de/en/home/), a Germany-based consortium of several academic communities in philology, linguistics, art history, and musicology.

DATA MANAGEMENT

The challenge researchers are facing today is not only in vast amounts of available data, but also in legal and ethical challenges around the management and preservation of data, particularly data that contain—or can be used to deduce—sensitive information about living persons, for example, banking and tax information or information about health and sexual behavior. In this age of the "data deluge," researchers are responsible not only for the integrity of research data they collect or generate, but also for the safety, security, and usability of that data. The processes used to manage data are known as data management. Good data management facilitates the responsible conduct of research and is a value-added process by which data can be made discoverable, identifiable, accessible, and comprehensible over the long term, sometimes long after the research project that produced that data has been completed. For example, researchers might continue to work with some or all of their data after their project has been finished, or other researchers could reuse that data at a later time for some other purpose. Good data management ensures that data are stored, preserved, made available for reuse, or discarded, according to legal, ethical, and funders' requirements.

To be usable and useful for the research community, data need to be managed from the point of creation onward. Because of the increasingly interdisciplinary nature of eResearch, data reuse can sometimes lead to breakthrough research. To better enable data reuse, researchers increasingly rely on good data management that requires them to decide and document what formats to use for collecting and storing their data, what metadata to use in describing it, who owns the data, who can access the data and when, what the data may be used for, and for how long they will be made available. Data that are poorly managed might need to be collected again, which in some cases, such as with observational data, might be impossible to accomplish.

In the context of eResearch, where data are produced chiefly in digital form and inherently depend on the speed with which the computer technology advances or becomes obsolete, the data can become inaccessible or, in the worst-case scenario, completely lost. Digital files can also get corrupted or accidentally discarded. Good data management might help combat the obsolescence of the data as well as enable the survival of data and maximize the data's accessibility and understandability.

DATA DOCUMENTATION AND METADATA

To ensure that research data are usable over the long term, it must be well documented and described. Data documentation refers to the records that provide information about the data. Examples of data documentation types include laboratory and field notebooks, information about equipment settings, codebooks, methodology reports, data files, models, algorithms, scripts, questionnaires and test responses, audio and video tapes, models, artifacts, specimens, samples, photographs, slides, films, methodologies, and workflows. Codebooks are a data documentation type, commonly used in the social sciences. The purpose of codebooks is to provide details regarding the structure, contents, layout of a data file, and other factors associated with data quality. The documentation formats vary from handwritten notes, computer files, or webpages.

Another form of data documentation is metadata. Metadata (often defined as "data about data") describe all aspects of data and software components used for the collection or creation of data. According to the Cyberinfrastructure Council of the National Science Foundation (2007), metadata add relevance and purpose to data and enable the identification of similar data in different data collections.

While data documentation is intended to be read by humans, metadata are usually meant to be computer-readable. In the increasingly digitized research environment, the use of metadata (compared to data documentation itself) becomes particularly important.

Metadata are commonly broken into three broad categories:

1. Descriptive metadata (include a project title, author's name, abstract, description of the research goal and scope, and keywords);
2. Administrative metadata (include information relevant to archiving and preservation such as rights management, access control, file formats, and usage requirements);
3. Structural metadata (describe how different components of data relate to each other).

Typical research metadata describe:

- What data consist of
- Who created, collected, or generated the data

- What data formats were used
- When and where the data were collected
- Where the data were stored
- How the data were processed, assured, and analyzed
- Why the data were collected or generated

Various discipline-specific metadata standards have also been developed to ensure accurate description and consistency in the content and format of metadata over the long term. Dublin Core Metadata Initiative (DCMI) (http://www.dublincore.org/), one of the most common metadata schemes, developed a vocabulary of 15 properties that describe a wide range of data. These properties, all of which are optional and can be used in any order, include basic ("core") information about data: title, date, type, rights, creator, subject, source, description, publisher, contributor, format, identifier, language, relation, and coverage. Some metadata standards are developed for specific disciplines. For example, Darwin Core Initiative (DCI) (http://rs.tdwg.org/dwc/index.htm) facilitates the sharing of biological diversity metadata; Ecological Metadata Language (EML) (https://knb.eco informatics.org/#tools/eml) is developed for the ecological and environmental studies; the Data Documentation Initiative (DDI) (http://www.ddi alliance.org/) aims to create an international standard for describing data from the social, behavioral, and economics sciences. These standards ensure that research data can be discoverable, identifiable, and retrievable. They also facilitate later interpretation and reuse of data.

DATA MANAGEMENT PLANS

Good data management can further be facilitated by a series of documented procedures and policies known as a data management plan. A data management plan describes data generated, collected, or used for a research project, and how that data will be obtained, managed, stored, accessed, and shared during and after a research project. This can help other researchers understand the data and the purpose for which the data was originally collected or generated.

Major research funders, among which are the National Science Foundation (NSF), National Institutes of Health (NIH), and National Endowment for the Humanities (NEH), now require explicit Data Management Plans (DMPs) as part of research proposals and requests for funding. For example, the current NSF policy states that as of January 18, 2011, all NSF research or grant proposals "must include a supplementary document of no more than two pages labeled 'Data Management Plan'" (National Science Foundation 2014). Under this policy, a researcher must submit a data management plan as a supplement to a research or grant proposal.[7] Although the format, coverage, and specific requirements vary by funder, a typical data management plan must address the following components:

- Types of data (such as samples, observations, models, physical artifacts, laboratory specimens, or survey results)
- Data format (such as text, images, database files, or multimedia) and naming conventions
- Methods for data processing (such as workflows, software, or algorithms)
- Metadata content and standards (such as DCMI, EML, or DDI)
- Policies for access, sharing, and future reuse, including the policies related to privacy, confidentiality, security, intellectual property rights, and ethical conduct of research
- Plans for long-term storage, archiving, and preservation of data
- Anticipated budget and how the costs will be paid

In addition to creating data management plans, researchers must ensure that the publicly funded research data are made freely available to other researchers and to the public, unless there are privacy or safety concerns that prevent free data sharing. This open data management policy, along with other policies, is part of a broader effort to promote open access to publicly funded research. Some private and government organizations such as the Howard Hughes Medical Institute, the National Institutes of Health, and the World Bank require researchers to deposit their data collected using public funds in freely accessible repositories.

DATA MANAGEMENT TOOLS

Numerous data management tools exist worldwide. They are designed to facilitate research data management and offer seamless solutions for enabling data discovery, acquisition, citation, use, and reuse. For example, a collaboration of research organizations, including DataONE and the Smithsonian Institution, developed an online data management planning tool—the DMPTool (http://dmp.cdlib.org/)—to assist researchers in meeting the requirements for data management plans. The DMPTool provides researchers with ready-to-use customizable data management plan templates intended for specific research sponsors. It provides step-by-step instructions for writing data management plans and allows researchers to edit, save, share, print, and download their data management plans. Since its release in October 2011, the DMPTool has generated great interest among the research and library community and has won a number of prestigious awards, including the Larry L. Sautter Golden Award for Innovation in Information Technology (http://blog.dmptool.org/2012/07/06/sautter-award/) and the Library of Congress's Top 10 Digital Preservation Developments of 2011 (http://blogs.loc.gov/digitalpreservation/2012/01/

top-10-digital-preservation-developments-of-2011/). Given the success of the first version of the DMPTool, its creators have released the DMPTool version 2 (DMPTool2) that expands the tool's feature set and improves its utility for researchers.[8]

DataUp (http://dataup.cdlib.org/) is another valuable tool that facilitates research data management. Created by the California Digital Library in partnership with Microsoft Research Connections and the Gordon and Betty Moore Foundation, DataUp allows researchers to organize their tabular data, describe them using standard metadata, and archive them in a digital repository. The tool comes in two open-source forms: an add-in operating within Microsoft Excel, and a Web-based application that allows users to upload tabular data to the Web-based tool in either Excel format or comma-separated value (CSV) format.

DATA PRESERVATION

While proper data management of primary research data is essential to fulfill the requirements of the responsible conduct of research, proper data preservation is also crucial. Primary research data must be preserved in order to be valuable, over time, to other researchers and the public.

Data preservation typically encompasses the deposition of research data and metadata in a data center that can be associated with a research sponsor, a government organization, a library, or a home institution. These data centers have potentially greater longevity, more continued funding, and more stable data management and preservation than individual research, thus making the data more widely accessible in the long term.

There are many advantages to depositing data in a data center or a public data repository. Data centers and repositories assign to data digital object identifiers (DOIs) so that the data can be identified and cited. They create metadata to describe the data and facilitate data curation and sharing. Some repositories also provide tools that allow researchers to "interact" with their data or, when necessary, assist with the migration of their data to up-to-date formats. For example, DataONE (http://www.dataone.org/), a multi-institutional, multinational, and interdisciplinary collaboration funded by the U.S. National Science Foundation, provides long-term archiving of biological, ecological, and environmental data and supports data access, integration, and analysis capabilities. In addition, it offers researchers user-friendly tools for data visualization and analysis and includes a search tool, ONE-Mercury (https://cn.dataone.org/onemercury/), for finding data held by any of the DataONE member nodes and a collection of best practices for data management throughout the data life cycle. ONEShare repository, directly connected to DataONE's network of repositories, was created specifically for the data management tool DataUp. It allows researchers to deposit their tabular data and metadata directly into the ONEShare repository from within the tool and thus enables seamless data archiving within the researcher's current workflow.

DATA SHARING

The advantages of data sharing have inspired much discussion since release of the National Academy of Sciences publication *Sharing Research Data* (1985). Data sharing means free access to raw data, such as facts, numbers, texts, images, or ideas, including the raw data that have not been published or deposited into a data center or repository. Funders such as the U.S. National Institutes of Health (NIH)[9] and the National Science Foundation (NSF)[10] mandate sharing of data from research. Many scholarly journals make sharing research data a requirement for publication. For example, a condition of publication in the journal *Nature* is that "authors are required to make materials, data and associated protocols promptly available to others without undue qualifications. Data sets must be made freely available to readers from the date of publication, and must be provided to editors and peer reviewers at submission, for the purposes of evaluating the manuscript" and that submission of data sets "to a community-endorsed, public repository is mandatory" (Nature Publishing Group 2014). Another example is the Public Library of Science (PLoS), which, starting December 2013, requires authors submitting to PLoS journals "to make all data underlying the findings described in their manuscript fully available without restriction, with rare exception" (Public Library of Science 2014). Publicly available data sets are valuable to diverse user communities, including scientists, educators, students, and policy makers. They can also be useful for engineering research, for example, to assess instrumentation based on its past or expected performance.

As the size and diversity of data continue to grow, sharing of data becomes challenging. As a result, cloud computing services, such as those provided by Amazon and Microsoft, have become a popular solution for storing, processing, and sharing data. In addition to enabling a convenient on-demand access to a shared pool of customizable computing tools and resources, cloud computing offers other benefits such as cost effectiveness, faster implementation of features, flexible provisioning of resources, and a pay-as-you-go service. (Cloud computing is discussed in more detail in Chapter 3.)

ONLINE DATA COLLECTIONS

Some researchers might have access to data sets from their own institutional repositories. These ready-to-use data collections allow researchers to utilize, re-purpose, and manipulate data instead of gathering or generating their own raw data, which can be a tremendous time- and energy-saving tool.

In addition to these institutional repositories and commercial data repositories that charge fees for access to their data sets, many ready-to-use data collections are freely available online. Below is a sample of freely available secondary data set collections.

A. Data collections from organizations and government agencies:
- Bureau of Labor Statistics: "Databases, Tables and Calculators by Subject" http://www.bls.gov/data/
  Provides data of the demographic and labor force characteristics.
- Data.gov
  http://www.data.gov
  Serves as the catalog for data collections generated by the U.S. government categorized into raw data, data tools, and geodata.
- Integrated Public Use Microdata Series (IPUMS)
  http://www.ipums.org
  Includes detailed U.S. Census information going back to 1850, international data sets, and American Community Surveys from 2000 to 2008.
- Organization for Economic Cooperation and Development (OECD) Data Lab
  http://www.oecd.org/statistics/datalab/
  Provides free access to statistical data sets.
- UNData
  http://data.un.org/
  Provides access to worldwide health, education, industry, and demographic statistics as well as data on key global indicators.
- World Bank Data
  http://data.worldbank.org/
  Provides access to data sets including economic and data indicators from countries around the world as well as historical data as far back as the early 1960s.

B. Data set collections assembled from various sources
- Amazon Public Data Sets
  https://aws.amazon.com/publicdatasets/
  Includes Census information, genome data sets, and data culled from Wikipedia, Securities and Exchange Commission, and the Freebase.com data project.
- Inter-University Consortium for Political and Social Research (ICPSR)
  http://www.icpsr.umich.edu/icpsrweb/landing.jsp
  Maintains and provides access to social science data sets, including data collections in education, aging, criminal justice, substance abuse, terrorism, and other areas.

C. Data set collections created through mashups[11]
- Google Earth
  http://www.google.com/earth/index.html
  Includes worldwide geographical data. Features 3D realistic imagery of places around the globe.

- Google Fusion Tables
  http://www.google.com/fusiontables/Home/
  Allows you to manipulate and visualize data with charts, timelines, maps, and other visualization tools.

- Google Books Ngram Viewer
  https://books.google.com/ngrams
  A graphing tool that extracts selected "Ngrams" (letters, words, or phrases in eight languages) and generates graphs that allow the user to analyze patterns and frequency of words and phrases in books from the Google Books digitization project.

- Google Public Data
  http://www.google.com/publicdata/directory
  Provides publicly available data from organizations and academic institutions worldwide and allows researchers to visualize these data using graphs, charts, and maps.

Recently, data integration services are transforming data discovery on the Web from multiple lists' search results into tools that provide answers to factual questions. For example, Wolfram Alpha (which calls itself a "computational knowledge engine") (http://www.wolframalpha.com/) "computes" the answers to a wide range of factual questions by utilizing data from Web definitions, numbers, facts, graphics, and other data.

NOTES

1. The English term "data" comes from the Latin translation of Euclid's work titled *Data* (from the first Greek word in the book, *dedomena* ["given"]), a collection of 94 propositions that discuss the nature of "given" information in geometrical properties. *Wikipedia*, http://en.wikipedia.org/wiki/Data_%28Euclid%29 (accessed February 23, 2014).

2. Some other types of data include "hard data," "dark data," "dated data," "little data," "open data," and "Linked Open Data (LOD)." "Hard data" usually refers to "hard facts" that cannot be refuted. "Dark data" refers to data that have not been properly documented, described, stored, or published and thus are likely to become irretrievable and, eventually, lost for researchers and other potential users. "Dated data" means obsolete data that are no longer useable. "Little data" refers to data produced by small research groups working on projects of a year or two in length. "Open data" is *data that can be freely used, reused, and redistributed by anyone*. The mass of appropriately annotated data that can be accessed through the Internet is referred to as "Linked Open Data (LOD)."

3. While defined in various ways, "big data" refers to data sets whose size is so large that traditional tools and techniques to manage and analyze data are no longer valid and new approaches need to be developed. While some studies claim that John Mashey, the chief scientist at Silicon Graphics in the 1990s, was the originator of the term "Big Data" (even though there are no scholarly papers to support the

attribution of the term to him), other studies argue that the credit for coining the term must be shared among several scientists (Diebold 2012).

4. The first mention of the term "deluge of data" is found in a 1954 National Tele-metering Conference (*The Complete Papers and Discussions of the 1954 National Telemetering Conference*, NTC, 1954). However, the first mention of the popular phrase "data deluge" appeared in NASA SP 385, which published the Proceedings of the 1958 Symposium on Flight Flutter Testing. W. M. Whitney—listed as a "Contributor" from JPL (Jet Propulsion Laboratory)—gave the introduction, and presented a section on the "data deluge." While the conference took place in 1958, it was published in 1962. The Proceedings can be accessed on the HathiTrust Digital Repository at http://catalog.hathitrust.org/Record/000074504.

5. The term "big science" was coined by Alvin Weinberg in 1961. "Big science" is typically characterized by large-scale international, collaborative efforts and stand-ardization of processes and products. "Little science," on the other hand, typically focuses on local research problems and works in small teams. Price in his canonical work *Little Science, Big Science* (1963) argued that the difference between little science and big science lies not in the size of research projects, but in the maturity of science as an enterprise.

6. The neologism "omics" refers to the study of collections of molecules, biological processes, or physiological functions and structures as systems.

7. In addition to other requirements, the National Science Foundation has mandated that data management plans will be subject to peer review and must be reviewed "as an integral part of the proposal, coming under Intellectual Merit or Broader Impacts or both, as appropriate for the scientific community of relevance" (National Science Foundation 2013).

8. The DMPTool is based on DMPonline, a Web-based tool designed by the United Kingdom's Digital Curation Centre (DCC) for creating and exporting data management plans (https://dmponline.dcc.ac.uk/).

9. "NIH Data Sharing Policy and Implementation Guidance," https://grants.nih.gov/grants/policy/data_sharing/data_sharing_guidance.htm.

10. NSF Data Sharing Policy, https://www.nsf.gov/bfa/dias/policy/dmp.jsp.

11. In Web development, a mashup is a website, or Web application, that combines content from different resources or services into a single website or application.

WORKS CITED

Ackoff, Russell L. "From Data to Wisdom: Presidential Address to ISGSR, June 1988." *Journal of Applied Systems Analysis* 16 (1989): 3–9. doi:10.1002/9781444303179.ch3.

Allan, Robert N. *Virtual Research Environments: From Portals to Science Gateways.* Oxford: Chandos Publishing, 2009.

Anderson, Terry, and Heather Kanuka. *E-research: Methods, Strategies, and Issues.* Boston: Allyn and Bacon, 2003.

Bell, Gordon, Tony Hey, and Alex Szalay. "Beyond the Data Deluge." *Science* 323, no. 5919 (2009): 1297–98. doi:10.1126/science.1170411.

Carlson, Scott. "Lost in a Sea of Science Data." *Chronicle of Higher Education* 52, no. 42 (2006): A35.

Cyberinfrastructure Council, National Science Foundation. *Cyberinfrastructure Vision for 21st Century Discovery.* 2007. http://escience.caltech.edu/work shop/CI_Vision_March07.pdf (accessed February 23, 2014).

Diebold, Francis X. "On the Origin (s) and Development of the Term 'Big Data.' " *Penn Institute for Economic Research, Pier Working Paper 12-037.* 2012. http:// economics.sas.upenn.edu/sites/economics.sas.upenn.edu/files/12-037.pdf (accessed February 23, 2014).

Floridi, Luciano. "Is Semantic Information Meaningful Data?" *Philosophy and Phenomenological Research* 70, no. 2 (2005): 351–70. doi:10.1111/j.1933 -1592.2005.tb00531.x

Foster, Ian. "How Computation Changes Research." In *Switching Codes: Thinking through Digital Technology in the Humanities and the Arts,* edited by Thomas Bartscherer and Roderick Coover, 16–37. Chicago: University of Chicago Press, 2011.

Gantz, John, and David Reinsel. "Extracting Value from Chaos." *IDC iView,* June 2011, 1–12.

Gershon, Diane. "Dealing with the Data Deluge." *Nature* 416, no. 6883 (2002): 889– 91. doi:10.1038/416889a.

Hey, Anthony, and Anne E. Trefethen. "The Data Deluge: An E-science Perspective." In *Grid Computing: Making the Global Infrastructure a Reality,* edited by F. Berman, A. Hey, and G. Fox, 809–24. Hoboken, NJ: Wiley, 2003.

Kock, Nereu F., Robert J. McQueen, and James L. Corner. "The Nature of Data, Information and Knowledge Exchanges in Business Processes: Implications for Process Improvement and Organizational Learning." *The Learning Organization* 4, no. 2 (1997): 70–80. doi:10.1108/09696479710160915.

Marcum, Deanna B., and Gerald George, eds. *The Data Deluge: Can Libraries Cope with E-science?* Santa Barbara, CA: Libraries Unlimited, 2010.

Markoff, John. "Digging Deeper, Seeing Farther: Supercomputers Alter Science." *New York Times,* April 25, 2011. http://cns.iu.edu/docs/news/20110425 _NYTimes.pdf (accessed February 28, 2014).

Martin, Victoria. "Developing a Library Collection in Bioinformatics: Support for an Evolving Profession." In *Library Collection Development for Professional Programs: Trends and Best Practices,* edited by Sara Holder, 269–89. Hershey, PA: IGI Global, Copyright © 2013. This material is used by permission of the publisher.

McGraw-Hill Dictionary of Scientific and Technical Terms. New York: McGraw-Hill, 2002.

National Science Foundation. "NSF Data Management Plan Requirements." 2014. https://www.nsf.gov/eng/general/dmp.jsp (accessed March 31, 2014).

National Science Foundation. "Proposal Preparation Instructions." January 2013. http://www.nsf.gov/pubs/policydocs/pappguide/nsf13001/gpg_2.jsp (accessed February 23, 2014).

Nature Publishing Group. "Availability of Data and Materials." http://www.nature.com /authors/editorial_policies/availability.html (accessed February 24, 2014).

OED Online. "Data, *n.*" Oxford University Press, 2013. http://www.oed.com/view/ Entry/296948?redirectedFrom=data (accessed January 3, 2014).

Pfaffenberger, Bryan. *Webster's New World Computer Dictionary.* Indianapolis, IN: Wiley Publishing, 2003.

Porta, Miquel, ed. *A Dictionary of Epidemiology*. Oxford: Oxford University Press, 2008.

Price, Derek J. de Solla. *Little Science, Big Science*. New York: Columbia University Press, 1963.

Public Library of Science. "Data Access for the Open Access Literature: PLOS's Data Policy." http://www.plos.org/data-access-for-the-open-access-literature-ploss-data-policy/ (accessed March 22, 2014).

Schnapp, Jeffrey. "The Short Guide to the Digital Humanities." In *Digital Humanities*, edited by Anne Burdick, Johanna Drucker, Peter Lunenfeld, Todd Presner, and Jeffrey Schnapp, 121–36. Cambridge, MA: MIT Press, 2012.

Thessen, Anne E., and David J. Patterson. "Data Issues in the Life Sciences." *ZooKeys* 150 (2011): 15–51. doi:10.3897/zookeys.150.1766.

University of Edinburgh. *MANTRA: Research Data Management Training*. http://datalib.edina.ac.uk/mantra/ (accessed February 23, 2014).

Weinberg, Alvin M. "Impact of Large-Scale Science on the United States." *Science* 134, no. 3473 (1961): 161–64. http://www.jstor.org/stable/1708292 (accessed March 14, 2014).

Williams, Robin, Graham Pryor, A. Bruce, S. Macdonald, W. Marsden, J. Calvert, M. Dozier, and C. Neilson. "Patterns of Information Use and Exchange: Case Studies of Researchers in the Life Sciences." *Research Information Network*. http://www.rin.ac.uk/our-work/using-and-accessing-information-resources/patterns-information-use-and-exchange-case-studie (accessed February 9, 2014).

Zins, Chaim. "Classification Schemes of Information Science: Twenty-eight Scholars Map the Field." *Journal of the American Society for Information Science and Technology* 58, no. 5 (2007a): 645–72. doi:10.1002/asi.20508.

Zins, Chaim. "Conceptions of Information Science." *Journal of the American Society for Information Science and Technology* 58, no. 3 (2007b): 335–50. doi:10.1002/asi.20507.

Zins, Chaim. "Conceptual Approaches for Defining Data, Information, and Knowledge." *Journal of the American Society for Information Science and Technology* 58, no.4 (2007c): 479–93. doi:10.1002/asi.20508.

Zins, Chaim. "Knowledge Map of Information Science." *Journal of the American Society for Information Science and Technology* 58, no. 4 (2007d): 526–35. doi:10.1002/asi.20505.

SUGGESTED READINGS

Ackoff, Russell L. "From Data to Wisdom: Presidential Address to ISGSR, June 1988." *Journal of Applied Systems Analysis* 16 (1989): 3–9. doi:10.1002/9781444303179.ch3.

Pryor, Graham, ed. *Managing Research Data*. London: Facet Publishing, 2012.

3

eResearch-Enabling Technologies

The computing technology has become an indispensable tool, almost an extension of the e-researcher's body.
—Benjamin Bederson and Ben Shneiderman (2003)

While this book does not address the complex technical issues with technologies that enable eResearch, it does recognize that some understanding of this domain is important for information professionals. For this reason, this book takes a broad approach to the description of technologies assuming that those readers who are interested in learning more about them will consult other publications, including those titles suggested at the end of this chapter.

A great variety of eResearch-enabling technologies exists that provide an enhanced and more effective research environment for scholarship in all disciplines. These enhancements: (1) enable better collection, access, processing, and management of data so that scholars can focus on research discoveries; (2) allow individual researchers and research teams to collaborate more effectively across time and distance; and (3) provide wider and more rapid knowledge dissemination through online scholarly communication channels. Since eResearch is still an emerging paradigm, the technologies that enable it will continue to evolve also. Researchers will experience an advancement and refinement of tools and services they use, both proprietary and open source, that will become increasingly virtual and more user-friendly and simplified so that the scholars can concentrate more on research tasks at hand than on operating the interface.

THE INTERNET AS PLATFORM FOR eRESEARCH

The Web, like the Internet, is designed to let users communicate with other users without seeing the machinery that makes the system work.
—Tim Berners-Lee (1996, 77)

Reference resources commonly define the Internet, or the Net for short, as a worldwide system of interconnected computer networks that communicate with one another using a shared set of standards and protocols such as the standards for TCP (Transmission Control Protocol) and IP (Internet Protocol). The TCP and IP standards, supported on both UNIX operating systems and personal computer operating systems, allow digital data packets to be sent and received across networks and provide flexible flow control and reliable transmission of these data streams. The computers connected over the Internet this way can send and receive all kinds of information such as text, images, sounds, video, and computer programs (Henderson 2009; Muller 1999).

The creation of the Internet was preceded by its precursor ARPANET, a project initiated by the Advanced Research Projects Agency (ARPA) of the U.S. Department of Defense in 1969. ARPANET is considered the first packet switching network designed to support the sharing of computing facilities among computer scientists and engineers.[1] From this initiative, a variety of research networks began to evolve, including the National Science Foundation's (NSF) NSFNET in the United States, and the research network across Europe called GEANT. From its origins in a military environment as a research project, the Internet eventually grew into an essential tool for educational and research organizations and has gradually made its way into businesses, homes, and schools around the world.[2]

The success of the Internet was, however, limited until 1989, when Tim Berners-Lee, named by *Time* magazine as "one of the 100 greatest minds of the 20th century" (Niemann 2004), and Berners-Lee's peers at the European Organization for Nuclear Research (CERN),[3] invented a new document format—HTML (hypertext markup language)—and a new accompanying document retrieval protocol—HTTP (hypertext transfer protocol). Together, HTML and HTTP enable users to link one hypertext-formatted document to another document, which can be on different computers anywhere in the world. This invention transformed the Internet into a cross-referenced database of interlinked documents allowing people to navigate through links and view pages through their Internet browsers. (This is why such documents are referred to as being "hyperlinked.")

After trying out several names for their invention, including "The Information Mine," "Mine of Information," and "The Information Mesh," Berners-Lee and his team named it the World Wide Web, also known as WWW, W3, or simply as "the Web." Even though the Web is not synonymous with the Internet, it is nowadays the most prominent aspect of the Internet. Originally intended as "a personal information system and a tool for groups of all sizes, from a team of two to the entire world" (Berners-Lee 1996, 69), the Web has become a major global technological force that, at the present time, connects hundreds of millions of computers and mobile electronic devices through high-speed wired and wireless networks and allows people around the world to make routine use of computing and information resources through a Web browser, enabling such activities as email, information search, social networking, and photo sharing.

The high adoption rate and widespread popularity of the Web, however, have raised concerns about the lack of the right protocols, guidelines, and standards for the Web that would ensure the Web's continued evolution and interoperability. To address this concern, the World Wide Web Consortium (W3C) (http://www.w3.org/) was formed in 1994. Based at the Massachusetts Institute of Technology (MIT) in Cambridge, Massachusetts, and at the National Institute for Computer and Automation Research in France, and initially established in collaboration with CERN (where the Web originated), W3C is led by Berners-Lee, who described the W3C's mission as follows: "To lead the World Wide Web to its full potential by developing protocols and guidelines that ensures long-term growth for the Web" (W3C 2014). In addition to developing protocols, standards, and guidelines for the Web, W3C also serves as an open forum for discussion about the Web and is involved in software design and education outreach.

Since its advent, the Web has progressed through three generations—from Web 1.0 to Web 3.0—and is in the process of transitioning to Web 4.0 and Web 5.0. Web 1.0 (otherwise known as the Read Only Web, according to Berners-Lee) was intended for publishing hypertext documents, which later included multimedia objects. The Read Only Web provided limited user interaction and collaboration capabilities and only enabled users to search for information in those documents and read them on the screen.

Web 2.0, also known as the Social Web, introduced an interactive element into the Web that emphasized user-generated content and user interactions. Tim O'Reilly, who is being credited for creating the term Web 2.0 in 2004, defined Web 2.0 applications as services that get better the more people use them (O'Reilly 2006). These applications allowed users to easily publish and edit information online, share it with other users, and create social networks based on shared interests, views, and other common criteria.

Web 3.0, also known as the Semantic Web or the Web of Data, refers to the W3C's vision of the Web of linked data that would make Web content machine-readable. It aimed to fill the gap between a machine-readable language and human language so that computers and people could work in cooperation (Berners-Lee, Hendler, and Lassila 2001). The idea was that the Semantic Web would combine human and artificial intelligence to enable data to be linked from one source to any other source and to be understood by computers so that people could easily find and integrate information over the Internet.

Web 4.0, or the Symbiotic Web, is still an emerging idea and has not yet been thoroughly defined or fully realized. It is envisioned as a human-machine symbiosis based on wireless communications (mobile devices or computers) that will have "the ability to connect people and objects anytime, anywhere in the physical and virtual worlds" (Kambil 2008, 57).

Similarly, Web 5.0 is a novel and more advanced concept that is difficult to define precisely at this time. It is being imagined as a futuristic Sensory-Emotive Web that would move the Web "from an emotionally flat environment to a space of rich interactions" (ibid). The dream behind the Sensory-Emotive Web is to enable humans and computers to interact with each other and that computers will be able to "read" human emotions based, for example, on the changes in their facial expressions or physiological symptoms such as heart rate.

Although the Internet itself does not add a significant intrinsic value to the quality of research, as observed by Anderson and Kanuka (2003), the use of the Internet for research purposes provides some of the most critical benefits to the facilitation of the research process and the way research is conducted and disseminated. These benefits include:

- *Increased access to data and data management tools.* The popularity of the Web has led to an abundance and diversity of online research data—from processed data (such as scholarly publications) to unprocessed data (such as collections of raw data)—that researchers can locate and access from their institution's workstations, home computer, via mobile technologies, and through a wide range of platforms including publishers' websites and social networking sites.

- *Enhanced scholarly communication.* The Internet provides innovative support for traditional types of scholarly communication, including the digitization of print books, journals, and fragile or degraded ancient documents, and a promotion of new publishing models such as open access publishing.

- *More rapid access to information resources and scholarly literature.* The Internet, with its global reach, provides new ways to disseminate information and research results more rapidly and widely. Web-based scholarly materials such as electronic journals that are highly regarded by researchers across most disciplines as the main research resource can be accessed quickly and conveniently via the Internet from office or home (or wherever researchers happen to be working). Furthermore, electronic journals are usually available on the Internet weeks before they are available in print, which is particularly important in the sciences and medicine where currency of content and expediency of access are often crucial.

- *More effective collaboration among research teams and across disciplines.* Because the Internet spans both the geographical and temporal barriers, it enables researchers to collaborate on projects without traveling long distances or coordinating local time differences.

- *Cost-effectiveness.* The Internet reduces the cost associated with data collection, processing, storage, and archiving as well as the cost of timely
  access to research literature (for example, via open access journals). This
  factor is particularly important for underfunded or unfunded researchers
  or for those researchers who work abroad, especially in developing
  countries (Menon 2002).

In some research areas, such as studies in the social and behavioral sciences,
the Internet data collection provides a greater sense of confidentiality than the
traditional paper-and-pencil data collection methods. For example, when conducting research involving sensitive subject matters such as addiction or attitude
toward sexuality, or when involving research participants from the specialized
or stigmatized populations such as people with STDs or with mental disorders,
the Internet allows scholars to study research subjects without having the
research subjects be physically present at a certain geographical location or at
a certain time. Further, the use of the Internet reduces the possibility of human
error as well as makes it easier to correct errors when they occur (Hewson
et al. 1996; Menon 2002; Subramanian et al. 1997).

The specific examples of Internet-enabled eResearch services and tools include:

- Fedora, the Flexible Extensible Digital Object and Repository Architecture
  http://www.fedora-commons.org
  An open source, digital object repository system that allows for long-term
  storage and retrieval of data and metadata.
- MyNetResearch
  http://www.mynetresearch.com/
  An online portal that enables users to find and collaborate with other
  researchers around the world. Provides e-collaboration tools such as Literature Search and Citation Analyzer, Journal Selection Guide, Research
  Methods Adviser, Conference Selection Guide, Grants Program Locator,
  Online Survey Manager, and Bibliography Creator.
- Public Library of Science (PLoS)
  http://www.plos.org/
  An open access publisher committed to making scientific and medical literature a freely available public resource. Currently publishes seven online
  peer-reviewed open access journals. Provides the ability for readers to rate
  and comment on, and to have discussion threads about, published articles.

GRID COMPUTING

The purpose of computing is insight, not numbers.
—Richard Hamming (2012, v)

The concept of the Grid as a geographically distributed computing platform
for a large-scale resource sharing and data storage facilities (known at the

time of its creation as "metacomputing") was originated in the early 1990s when a number of major test-beds, such as CASA (Collaborative Adaptive Sensing of the Atmosphere), were deployed (Bote-Lorenzo, Dimitriadis, and Gómez-Sánchez 2004; Magoulès 2009; Plaszczak and Wellner 2006).[4] The term "Grid," used as an analogy for other infrastructure grids, such as the electrical power grid, first appeared in 1999 in the book *The Grid: Blueprint for a New Computing Infrastructure*, edited by Ian Foster and Carl Kesselman. The authors defined a computational grid as "a hardware and software infrastructure that provides dependable, consistent, pervasive, and inexpensive access to high-end computational capabilities" (Foster and Kesselman 1999, 18). In the subsequent publication *The Anatomy of the Grid: Enabling Scalable Virtual Organizations*, this time coauthored with Steve Tuecke, Foster and Kesselman expanded their concept of the Grid and described it as "flexible, secure, coordinated resource sharing among dynamic collections of individuals, institutions, and resources" (Foster, Kesselman, and Tuecke 2001, 200). Even though the concept of the Grid has evolved over the years and other definitions have emerged in scholarly and popular literature, the influential definitions by Foster, Kesselman, and Tuecke, who are regarded as "the fathers of the Grid," are still being widely cited.[5]

Standard Grid technologies, such as those based on the Open Grid Services Architecture (OGSA) that define a common, standard, and open architecture for Grid-based applications, are generally less understood than the Internet technologies because of their perceived technical complexity and barriers to access such as the perception that Grid computing technologies are restricted to grand-challenge applications or being available chiefly to researchers affiliated with corporations or academic institutions (Fernandes 2008). Despite these perceptions, Grid computing has gained prestige and popularity in the research community due to its ability to aggregate diverse and geographically distributed computing resources and address problems that cannot be easily solved on a single computer (Hey and Trefethen 2003; Magoulès 2009; Stanoevska-Slabeva and Wozniak 2010).

Even though the Grid has primarily been utilized for supporting high-performance computing, it has also been successfully used for research purposes such as supporting data-intensive knowledge discovery applications. The Grid's middleware software, a set of mediating services between the operating system and applications that "hides" the technical complexity of the underlying operating system from the user, makes it easier for researchers to perform their tasks. Researchers, especially those working in such computationally intensive disciplines as bioinformatics, climate dynamics, genomics, and computational neuroscience, use Grid technologies to access, collect, and process large amounts of data (and consequently synthesize new information and knowledge from these data). Specifically, data grids that have emerged as "a specialization and extension of the 'Grid' " (Chervenak et al. 2000) allow researchers, especially in a multi-institutional environment, to share the computing power, resources, and storage capacity. Data grids also assure a secure access to large datasets and allow the subsequent data management. The Biomedical Information Research Network (BIRN) (http://www.birncommunity.org/) and the Southern California Earthquake Center (SCEC) (http://www.scec.org/) are notable examples of data grids.

Knowledge grids further expand the capabilities of data grids by providing knowledge discovery and knowledge management services—data categorization, ontologies, knowledge sharing, and workflow development. Built upon the standard grid technologies and using such knowledge-based methodologies as data mining, intelligent software agents, and mathematical modeling, knowledge grids allow researchers to generate and manage sophisticated knowledge discovery applications designed as workflows that allow users to take advantage of Grid services and resources. Discovery Net (http://www.discovery-on -the.net/), a project funded by the EPSRC under the UK e-Science Programme, is an example of a Grid-enabled knowledge discovery service.

Peer-to-peer (P2P) grids and access grids are other popular trends in research computing and collaborations. Based on Grid technologies, P2P grids, such as Our Grid (http://www.ourgrid.org/index.php) and JXTA (https:// jxta.kenai.com/), enable a group of computers to form self-organized and self-configured peer groups that can collaborate without the need of a centralized management infrastructure.

Access grids, envisioned as "workspaces of the future" (Stevens, Papka, and Disz 2003), are designed to support real-time meetings, demonstrations, and presentations among remote participants via a set of computer-mediated resources. For example, AccessGrid.org (http://www.accessgrid.org/) offers resources and software for shared virtual workspaces as well as provides recommendations for room layout and the use of technical equipment.

The initial success of using the Grid computing for scientific an engineering research has led to the establishment of prominent national- and international-scale infrastructures, including:

- The European Grid Infrastructure (EGI)
  http://www.egi.eu/
  Provides researchers in academia and industry in different European countries with round-the-clock access to computing resources regardless of geographic location.
- The Globus Project
  https://www.globus.org/
  An open source software effort that allows users to share computing power, databases, and computing resources across multiple independent domains. The Globus Project developed the Globus Toolkit (http:// toolkit.globus.org/toolkit/) that was named the "most promising new technology" by *R&D Magazine* (2002), called a top-10 "emerging technology" by *Technology Review* (2003), and awarded a Chicago Innovation Award by *The Sun-Times* (2003).

- Legion
  http://legion.virginia.edu/
  A project at the University of Virginia that allows the users to access data
  and resources and collaborate on research projects through virtual work
  spaces.
- Open Science Grid
  http://www.opensciencegrid.org/
  Originally intended for facilitating data analysis for the Large Hadron
  Collider (LHC). Supports data analysis for researchers and computer
  scientists around the world.
- TeraGrid
  https://www.xsede.org/tg-archives/
  A project funded by the U.S. National Science Foundation (NSF) in 2001
  and operated through 2011. Provided researchers in molecular bioscience,
  earth science, mathematics, neuroscience, and other science disciplines
  with a large computing infrastructure.
- UNICORE (Uniform Interface to Computer Resources)
  http://www.unicore.eu/
  Enables uniform access to various hardware and software platforms and
  organizational environments and supports secure access to distributed
  resources.
- The Worldwide LHC Computing Grid project (WLCG)
  http://wlcg.web.cern.ch/
  Formerly the Large Hadron Collider (LHC) Computing Grid designed by
  CERN. One of the world's largest computing grids, connecting over 170
  computing centers in 36 countries.

The concept of the Grid as a core infrastructure for scientific research has
gradually given way to a broader view of the Grid as a wide range of computing tools and services that support industrial and commercial applications as
well as research in "nonscience" disciplines. For example, cloud computing
technologies that represent an advancement from grid computing are being
appreciated by researchers for their relative ease of use and implementation.
There is an ongoing discussion among the scholars on whether the common-
ality between the grid and cloud technologies and the benefits of simplicity
and cost effectiveness of cloud computing will make the Grid obsolete. Even
though this question is still unanswered, the combination of new technology
trends and research advances continue to transform the research enterprise
and are at the heart of a new approach for conducting research.

FROM GRID TO CLOUD

Cloud is about how you do computing, not where you do computing.
—Paul Maritz (Data Center Quotes 2014)

With the advent of cloud computing in 2002 by Amazon (and later expanded by Google, Microsoft, Yahoo, Salesforce, and Zoho), new opportunities became available to organizations, researchers, and individual users (Nayak and Yassir 2012). Even though cloud computing, and the associated cloud data management, is a heavily used term in scholarly and popular literature and media, there is still no consensus on what constitutes a "cloud" and what cloud computing exactly is and what it is not.[6] Furthermore, different communities working with the cloud computing technology might have different views of what cloud computing is and thus may emphasize different aspects of cloud computing rather than reflect the entire concept. For example, industries and companies may be incentivized by cost savings and energy consumption efficiencies; researchers may be enticed by the increased access to data and data storage capacities; libraries may be looking to cloud computing for powering their core automation applications through cloud-based services; individuals may be interested in taking advantage of free social networking, photo sharing, and email offerings.

Among the most highly cited definitions of cloud computing is the definition released by the National Institute of Standards and Technology (NIST) in 2011. NIST has defined cloud computing as "a model for enabling convenient, on-demand network access to a shared pool of configurable computing resources (e.g., networks, servers, storage, applications, and services) that can be rapidly provisioned and released with minimal management effort or service provider interaction" (Mell and Grance 2011, 7).

The NIST's definition summarizes the key elements of cloud computing—from the principal characteristics to the service models—all captured in a single sentence. According to NIST, cloud computing must have the following five principal characteristics:

1. On-demand self-service—i.e., providing computing services for users "as needed automatically without requiring human interaction with each service provider" (ibid.)

2. Broad network access—i.e., supporting various types of network platforms such as computer workstations, mobile phones, laptops, tablets, and personal digital assistants (PDAs)

3. Metered service—i.e., providing a pay-as-you-go service

4. Elasticity—i.e., enabling the users to increase or decrease the computing resources they need depending on the load

5. Resource pooling—i.e., enabling consolidation of different types of computing resources

The NIST's definition also classifies a wide variety of services provided by the cloud computing into the three major service models that are available to research institutions, enterprises, and individual users. These service models, often referred to as "SPI model" (i.e., software, platform or infra-structure as a service), are:

1. *Infrastructure as a Service (IaaS).* IaaS delivers computing resources and services, such as virtual machines, storage, hardware, and software, and bills users on a pay-per-use basis. Some of the most high-profile IaaS operations are Amazon's Elastic Compute Cloud (Amazon EC2) (http://aws.amazon.com/ec2/) and Amazon's Simple Storage Service (S3) (http://aws.amazon.com/s3/). Amazon EC2 enables users to access virtual computers and pay for resources by the hour. Amazon C3 allows customers to store large amount of data accessible from anywhere with Internet connection.

2. *Platform as a Service (PaaS).* PaaS provides a platform service in which consumers can create their own applications that will run on a cloud computing platform. The Google App Engine (http://cloud.google.com/appengine/) and Microsoft Windows Azure (http://www.windowsazure.com/) are good examples of PaaS. The Google App Engine provides a series of APIs (Application Programming Interfaces) and an application model that enables the customers to use additional services built on the Google platform such as Gmail, BigQuery, and Datastore. Microsoft Windows Azure provides compute, storage, and infrastructure management services.

3. *Software as a Service (SaaS).* SaaS allows the customer to acquire a software application that is customarily provided through the Web without needing to purchase the platform to run that software application. Google Docs (http://docs.google.com/) and Google Calendar (https://www.google.com/calendar/) are examples of free SaaS implementations. Salesforce.com (www.salesforce.com) is an example of a commercial SaaS implementation that provides CRM (Customer Relationship Management) services online.[7]

Even though the NIST definition has not changed noticeably since its early adoption in 2011 and is still being cited as an authoritative formalized definition of cloud computing, the list of features of cloud computing, such as its deployment models, continues to expand. For example, the Cloud Security Alliance expands the NIST's definition by describing several deployment models of cloud computing, which include:

• Public Cloud (available to the general public)
• Private Cloud (available for individual organizations)
• Community Cloud (shared by several organizations with common concerns)
• Hybrid Cloud (the combination of two or more clouds—private, community or public) (Corrado and Moulaison 2011; Nayak and Yassir 2012).

The cloud computing–enabling technologies are produced by the convergence of at least two technological trends: the Internet (including Web Services, Web 3.0, and Service Oriented Architecture [SOA]) and Grid computing.[8] By converging these two technologies, cloud computing strives to adopt their key strengths by offering organizations and individuals more cost-effective ways to use Web services for their computing needs than the Internet and Grid computing could have offered when used separately (Abah and Ogwueleka 2013).

While the Grid and cloud computing have a similar mission—to increase reliability and flexibility of computing while reducing its cost—they differ in several technical respects such as the means of utilization, the scale, the usage patterns, compute and security models, and virtualization. Virtualization, as some authors argue, is perhaps the principal distinction between the Grid and cloud computing because cloud computing achieves a higher virtualization level than Grid computing by allowing one server to perform several computing tasks simultaneously (ibid.).[9]

Although on the surface the concept of cloud computing appears to be overly technical and complicated, it can be described more simply as a technology trend in which computing resources are delivered on demand to anyone with an Internet connection on a pay-per-use basis. In this context, clouds can be viewed as computers that are networked anywhere in the world with the availability of paying for the services used in a pay-per-use manner, meaning that just the resources that are being used will be paid for.

Recognizing the potential of cloud computing for helping cut the federal Information Technology budget, President Barack Obama hired Patrick Stingley (nicknamed as "Cloud Czar") as the first chief technology officer (CTO) of the Federal Cloud Initiative (2009). Before returning to the government as CTO of the Bureau of Land Management, Stingley prepared a development plan for a federal cloud computing capability and described how cloud computing aligned with the Federal Enterprise Architecture Framework. To further harness the benefits of cloud computing, the U.S. government has instituted the Cloud First policy that took effect in 2011. This policy required all agencies to secure cloud computing options before making any new investments and to either migrate to cloud computing or "justify" why they did not do so (Kundra 2011).

While still relatively new, cloud computing has already emerged as a successful computing infrastructure for supporting eResearch, especially in such data-driven disciplines as physics, biology, and Geographic Information Systems (GIS). These disciplines often deal with large data sets, sometimes under several owners, and require a substantial amount of computing resources to perform large-scale research and the construction of complex computational models to solve scientific problems. Traditionally, researchers addressed these needs by using the Grid technology, which, however, is not as "elastic" as cloud computing and may also be difficult to set up, maintain, and operate. Furthermore, smaller research teams or individual researchers could not always afford to create and operate grid infrastructures.

Cloud computing is a low-cost solution to the researchers' needs that addresses some of the Grid computing challenges. It offers the researchers a wide array of inexpensive online services on a pay-per-use basis—from computing services to data storage. These services not only cover specific research needs, but can also be released back into the "pool" when no longer needed. Cloud computing also "shifts the responsibility to install and maintain hardware and computational services away from the customer . . . to the cloud vendor" (Rosenthal et al. 2010, 342), a commercial cloud service provider. Cloud vendors can also provide access to datasets (e.g., census data), data repositories (e.g., GenBank), programming services (e.g., Windows Azure), specific applications (e.g., BLAST), and service platforms (e.g., Google App Engine). In addition, researchers no longer need to rely on laptops or removable media for data storage that can be easily damaged, lost, or stolen (Aymerich, Fenu, and Surcis 2008; Nayak and Yassir 2012). For these and other reasons, cloud computing as "primarily a new *business* paradigm" rather than "a new *technical* paradigm" (Rosenthal et al. 2010, 342).

New cloud computing platforms such as Amazon's MapReduce (http:// aws.amazon.com/elasticmapreduce/) and Dryad (http://datadryad.org/) enable researchers to process and store vast amounts of data without major restrictions regarding data formats. In Amazon's Simple Storage Solution (S3), users can also store as much data as they need as well as provision a server in just a few clicks using Amazon's Elastic Compute Cloud (EC2). Amazon's "sneakernet" service (http://aws.amazon.com/importexport/) addresses the problem of transferring large amounts of data into its cloud. The cloud can also serve as an accessible repository for documentation—for example, Hightail (formerly called YouSendIt) (https://www.hightail.com) as well as the source of productivity applications such as the presentation software SlideRocket (http://www.sliderocket.com/). New cloud-based informal communication models are also gaining popularity among researchers, for example Cloudworks (http://cloudworks.ac.uk/), that allow the authors to blog their unfinished manuscripts or presentations and gain feedback from other users. Other notable cloud-based applications that support eResearch include:

- Aneka
  http://www.manjrasoft.com/manjrasoft_downloads.html/
  A Manjrasoft Pty Ltd. PaaS application that acts as a framework for building customized applications and deploying them on either public or private cloud.[10]

- Box
  https://app.box.com/
  A cloud-based storage and content-sharing system for businesses and individuals. Up to 50 GB of storage is free for individual accounts.

- Dropbox
  http://www.dropbox.com/
  A free cloud-based storage system that allows for easy sharing of documents, images, videos, data, and datasets from a computer, through a website, or mobile phone applications.

- Globus Online
  http://www.globus.org/
  Allows for moving large quantities of data from one place to another.

- Incommon
  https://incommon.org/
  Provides "services in federated identity management to its members—institutions of higher education, federal agencies, research organizations, and corporations with affiliations with higher education in the United States and abroad" (Research.gov 2014).

- Office Web Apps
  http://office.microsoft.com/en-us/web-apps/
  Allows anyone with an Internet connection to access, work on, and share Office documents.

- Spanner
  https://cloud.google.com/products/app-engine/
  Google's data management system that distributes data at global scale and supports distributed transactions and offers access to it as part of its Google App Engine.

Another important feature of cloud computing, from which researchers can benefit, is that it equips them with the technical infrastructure that is needed for working collaboratively across geographic, institutional, and disciplinary domains. Cloud-based research collaboration makes it possible to reach the scholars dispersed geographically in any part of the world. In addition, cloud computing allows the researchers to disseminate their research results to a global community more rapidly through formal and informal scholarly communication venues and thus potentially impact the lives of many people, especially in the health and biomedical sciences where the timeliness of research discoveries might be crucial, both for the researchers and for the patients.

While the interest in cloud computing solutions is growing, concerns are also being voiced about the issues introduced through the adoption of this new computing model. According to the *2012 Strategic Security Survey: Pick the Right Battles*, top concerns with regard to cloud computing include: malware infection via malicious links, managing and enforcing security, and "preventing data breaches from outside attackers." (The 44-page report is available for download freely with registration at http://www.informationweek.com/.) Other frequently raised concerns are reliability, data security, privacy, ownership, network speed, and inflexibility in switching from one cloud provider to another (Androutsellis and Spinellis 2004; Nayak and Yassir 2012). Because reliability is a key requirement that ensures continuous access to a computing service, one of the most serious concerns is the reliance of cloud computing on network connectivity, especially when the cloud infrastructure is under heavy loads, or when there is a possibility of a cloud provider going out of business. The data ownership ambiguities, particularly where the confidentiality of data is concerned, raises the questions of who owns the data placed in the cloud and what rights the researcher and the cloud provider have regarding the data deposited in the cloud. The lack of certain flexibility for a user to switch from one cloud provider, known as a "lock-in" phenomenon, is largely due to the fact that different cloud providers may offer different service models. There are also inherent to the Web security concerns in depositing sensitive research data into a cloud environment.

The wide availability and the ease of use of cloud computing creates risks as well as opportunities. A thorough evaluation of this technological trend for research purposes might help circumvent the risks of cloud computing and reveal that the advantages of cloud computing might be greater than its disadvantages for some research fields than for others. This question warrants a deeper investigation, which is beyond the scope of this book.

VISUAL EXPLORATION: MAKING THE INVISIBLE VISIBLE

> Words make division, pictures make connection.
> —Otto Neurath (1936, 19)

Researchers and educators have a long tradition of using visual exploration as a means of graphical representation of data and concepts. Simple visualizations, such as standard graphs, maps, and diagrams, have been an indispensable technique in research and education for centuries because they could often illustrate data and communicate ideas more readily than numerical or textual representations. Visualizations have also been traditionally used during the hypothesis-generation process, especially when little was known about the data or when the exploration goals were "vague" (Keim 2002).

Technological innovations have enabled the creation of increasingly more sophisticated, dynamic, and highly interactive computer-based visualization tools, also known as "information visualization" (Bederson and Shneiderman 2003; Shneiderman 1996; Spence 2007). Along with the related but more mature scientific visualization, information visualization supports the further advancement of the visual exploration methodology that has become a vital component of eResearch in all disciplines.[11] These visualizations play the role of a mediator in the process of human-computer interaction and allow researchers not only to derive insight from large and disparate types of data and recognize trends and patterns in these data, but also to communicate complex ideas to their peers faster and more effectively than could standard graphs or diagrams of the past (Jankowski 2009; Keim 2002).[12]

Robert Spence, who is recognized as one of the pioneers of information visualization, defined visualization as "a software system, usually involving a visual display, which allows a user to interact with and change the view of some data with a view to forming a mental model of that data" (Spence 2007, 237). Because the creator and the viewer are able to get directly involved in the process of visual exploration and gain control over the computer-based applications through the use of interactive visualization tools, the confluence of the "brain-eye system" with the computational capacities of modern technology has made today's visual exploration more powerful and more meaningful (Bederson and Shneiderman 2003).[13] Molecular modeling, medical imaging, space exploration, archaeological reconstruction, geospatial cartography, and visual representation of statistical data are all examples of visualizations that help researchers gain understanding and insight into complex research problems.

Even though computer-supported visualizations have been part of experimental and theoretical eResearch since the earliest days of computing, the term "visualization" gained recognition only in 1987 after publication of the National Science Foundation's report *Visualization in Scientific Computing* (known as the McCormick Report). The McCormick Report prompted the launch of several visualization software systems, such as MVEs and apE, and provided an initial impetus for an emerging discipline of scientific visualization whose aim was to employ computational means to visualizing scientific problems (McCormick, DeFanti, and Brown 1987).[14] As computer-based visualizations became more pervasive in the research environment, further technological developments, especially the rise of the World Wide Web as a visualization platform, led to the creation of more advanced but also more publicly available visualization tools, ranging from Web-based applications to mobile touch devices that can be applied to solving complex problems in every research field.[15]

Many Eyes (http://www.many-eyes.com/), created by the Visual Communication Lab (part of IBM's Collaborative User Experience research group) and launched in 2007, is one example of how Web-based visualizations can be made accessible to a broad public. In addition to being a visual exploration platform, Many Eyes also serves as a medium of collaboration intended to "democratize" visualization technology. The site allows anyone with access to the Internet to upload their own data or data from other sources, choose a visualization format for those data, and share the result with other users who can post comments on those visualizations. Striving to reach the largest possible audience by "fostering a democratic deliberative style of data analysis," the creators of Many Eyes modeled their service on such popular, publicly available sites as Flickr and YouTube that made Many Eyes one of the most popular Web-based visualization tools (Viégas et al. 2007, 1121).

Another example of information visualization available to a broad public is the work of the Gapminder Foundation created by a Swedish researcher, Hans Rosling, and his team in 2005. Gapminder World (http://www .gapminder.org/), formerly Trendalyzer, a free software for statistical data, aims to enable "inter-active animation of development statistics in enjoyable and understandable graphic interfaces" (Rosling, Rosling, and Rosling 2005, 523). Interactive animation of the development trends in such areas as population, health, and economics creates animations that "not only reach and please the eyes, but that also transform statistics into understanding, i.e., goes beyond the eye to hit the brain" (Rosling, Rosling, and Rosling 2005, 522). Acquired by Google in 2007, Gapminder became part of Google Visualization Application Programming Interfaces (APIs) that any person can use to visualize their own statistical data. In addition to the possibility of exploring statistical data, Gapminder also offers a series of video clips ("gapcasts"), in which Rosling himself narrates the graphic animations. Gapcasts are also available on YouTube and in iPod versions.[16]

In the biological sciences, data visualization is an important and daily research activity that often requires more specialized applications. Blast2GO (B2G) (http://www.blast2go.com/), an interactive Java desktop application for bioinformatics research, provides numerous functions for the novel sequence data annotation, as well as management and statistical analysis of annotation results, and emphasizes visualization as an important component for optimizing the research performance. Through the use of statistical charts, data coloring, and combined graphs, the B2G's visualization function helps researchers monitor, understand, and analyze the entire annotation process. This user-friendly application has no technical requirements other than an Internet connection.

Anatomy TV (https://www.anatomy.tv/), published by Primal Pictures Ltd., is an example of a visualization tool created for an academic audience as a medium for Computer Aided Learning (CAL) that aims at making education more accessible and effective. Anatomy TV, a subscription-based 3D graphical human anatomy software, allows health science educators, students, and practitioners to explore, navigate, and manipulate virtual 3D models of a human body (using real anonymized patient Computer Tomography [CT] datasets) as well as to focus on specific anatomical structures and label and to annotate these structures with text, image, or video. For easier use, Anatomy TV does not require any special hardware and can be deployed to a regular personal computer.

Even though larger and faster displays and more powerful user controls have enhanced the potential of visual exploration for eResearch, visualization is still "solely a human cognitive activity" (Spence 2007, 5). It is the activity in which technology amplifies cognition by exploiting the advantages of human visual processing while compensating for cognitive deficiencies such as limited working memory (Card, Mackinlay, and Shneiderman 1999; Tory and Moller 2004a). The effectiveness of visual exploration (as well as of any research activity) still largely depends on "human factors" such as personal, social, and cultural characteristics of the user and the user's goals, preferences, values, and attitudes (Tory and Moller 2004a).

RESEARCHERS' ATTITUDES TOWARD TECHNOLOGY: PERCEPTIONS, CHALLENGES, AND FRUSTRATIONS

> The key issue in technological innovation lies not within technology itself but among its potential users—whether they possess a clear vision of opportunities that permit wise choices about what to pursue and what to prevent.
> —Carolyn Lougee (1994, 148)

As eResearch-enabling technologies are taken up in routine research practice, the question arises whether these technologies enhance the research practice or oversimplify it. Several studies, mainly using surveys and interviews, have examined researchers' use of and attitudes toward technology (Carpenter et al. 2010; Kroll and Forsman 2010). These studies revealed that researchers, while being reticent to immediately accept new tools and techniques (especially the ones that take time to develop facility with) as a more efficient means for realizing research goals, are still using a variety of digital technologies that are either provided by their institutions or selected by researchers themselves. However, the studies indicated, digital technologies are being seen as secondary to the actual research activities and perceived as a supplement to well-established research practices, rather than a replacement for them. New Web-based and other tools and applications are normally used if they can be easily absorbed into existing research work practices and avoided if they challenge traditional and conservative research working practices. As Bulger et al. (2011) found, "scholars use what works for them, finding technologies and resources that fit their research, and resisting any pressure to use something just because it is new" (p. 7).

There are distinctions between how different types of researchers seek information and use information technology. According to Bent, Gannon-Leary, and Webb (2007), a researcher's learning life goes through several stages that reflect the differences in the researcher's information needs and information-seeking behavior. The authors called these stages the "seven ages of research," which are:

1. Masters' students
2. Doctoral students
3. Contract research staff (CRS)
4. Early career researchers
5. Established academic staff
6. Senior researchers
7. Experts (Bent, Gannon-Leary, and Webb 2007, 85)

Even though the specific types of technological applications employed by researchers often depend on the discipline, research task, and the characteristics of an individual user, the researchers' appreciation of the many benefits of the World Wide Web is still prevalent (Carpenter et al. 2010; Kroll and Forsman 2010).[17]

The four generations of Web-based technologies, from Web 1.0 to Web 4.0, whose ease of use and a relatively shallow learning curve are being appreciated by busy researchers, provide benefits to researchers in every discipline.[18] The Web-based technologies are being widely used for various purposes: information and literature searches, accessing specialized databases and software applications (many of which are freely available on the Web), as a channel for scholarly communication, and as a means for finding and establishing collaboration opportunities. Other research benefits of the Web as reported by researchers include:

- Worldwide availability
- Ease of use
- Convenient access to digital content such as scholarly publications, data and information resources
- Data sharing
- Awareness of forthcoming research funding
- Increased likelihood of making themselves and their research visible to other researchers
- Increased opportunity for social networking with other scholars, within and outside of their area of expertise
- Learning about who is doing related work
- More rapid and efficient dissemination of research results

While technology affords many benefits to researchers, it also introduces a few challenges. Some of the most obvious challenges are the researchers' reliance on network connectivity, ownership ambiguities, and user privacy and security. One of the greatest areas of frustration expressed by researchers, however, is their concern that because of the constant development of technology, the valuable body of their older work in the form of data sets and documents recorded on outdated media or in obsolete formats would become inaccessible after a certain period of time. Some have stated that they would rather redo a previous work than try to retrieve it.

"Information deluge" and "cognitive overload" also appear to be a source of confusion rather than motivation for some researchers. Being insufficiently trained or informed to be able to fully embrace the latest technological innovations or take advantage of the expertise of knowledge mediators, such as librarians, they are challenged by the growing number and complexity of available tools and resources. Navigating the Web and finding useful, accurate, and authoritative online information requires fundamentally new searching skills as well as research skills (Anderson and Kanuka 2003). Identifying, locating, and learning how to use emerging technologies is also a time-consuming task for researchers who have a tremendous pressure on their time. Expertise and knowledge about these resources, and how to use them, are usually passed on by word of mouth to novice researchers by more experienced peers. Other sources of frustration reported by researchers include the need to outsource statisticians to conduct analysis of large text documents and data sets, a cumbersome process of entering, storing, and manipulating literature citations via citation management software such as EndNote, Reference Manager, RefWorks, and, more recently, Zotero.

These findings raise important questions about the correlation of technology and research. What seems critical is the importance of evaluating technologies not only in terms of their impact on research outcomes and productivity, but also in terms of their impact on individual researchers who use them. Even though the recent advancements in the field of Human-Computer Interaction (HCI) are promising, the goal of making technology even more "researcher-friendly" may take longer to achieve.

NOTES

1. ARPA changed its name to DARPA (Defense Advanced Research Projects Agency) in 1971. It changed it back to ARPA in 1993, and back to DARPA in 1996.

2. ARPANET was moved beyond the military community in the mid-1970s under the Internet name. ARPANET's first "killer application" was electronic mail (e-mail) released in 1972.

3. CERN is a French spelling of the European Council for Nuclear Research (*Conseil Européen pour la Recherche Nucléaire*).

4. The I-Way project, presented at the International Conference for High Performance Computing in 1995, and that linked together 11 experimental networks for one week, is considered to be the first computational Grid.

5. Foster has emphasized the importance of distinguishing the difference between "a grid" as a collection of networked computers acting together as a single megacomputer, and "*the* Grid" as an infrastructure for advanced computing. In his 2002 article *What is the Grid? A Three Point Checklist* (coauthored with Kesselman and Tuecke), Foster outlined the key features that characterize "*a grid*." They are:

- Coordination of resources that are not subject to centralized control
- The use of standard, open, general-purpose protocols and interfaces
- Delivery of nontrivial qualities of service

He further explains that "*the* Grid vision requires protocols (interfaces and policies) that are not only open and general purpose but also *standard*. It is standards that allow us to establish resource-sharing arrangements dynamically with *any* interested party and thus to create something more than a plethora of balkanized, incompatible, non-interoperable distributed systems" (Foster 2002).

6. Scholars are still unsure who coined the nebulous term "cloud" and when this occurred, but many agree that the name was inspired by the cloud symbol that often

represents the Internet in flow charts and diagrams and used a metaphor for the Internet where the cloud is "located."

7. The list of the service models included in the NIST definition is not comprehensive. There are other cloud computing service models, such as data as a service, communication as a service, monitoring as a service, and files as a service (Jennings 2010; Yang et al. 2011). As cloud computing continues to evolve, the landscape of service offerings will likely change also.

8. Some authors argue that cloud computing has evolved out of Grid computing and is the foundation for cloud computing (Abah and Ogwueleka 2013; Foster et al. 2008).

9. For a thorough comparison between grid computing and cloud computing see Foster et al. (2008) and Stanoevska-Slabeva and Wozniak (2010).

10. Even though Aneka started as a Grid initiative in 2006, it then rapidly emerged as a PaaS for cloud computing (Vecchiola, Pandey, and Buyya 2009).

11. While scientific visualization (also referred to as visual data analysis) focuses primarily on three-dimensional physical objects such as molecules, the human body, or the earth, Information Visualization deals primarily with abstract, nonspatial data such as discovering trends and patterns, and identifying interrelationships of various parameters/relationships among variables.

12. Ben Shneiderman, professor in the Department of Computer Science at the University of Maryland and founding director of the Human-Computer Interaction Lab (HCIL), together with his associates at the HCIL, has played a key role in the creation of a new field of study—Information Visualization—which emerged in the mid-1990s from research in computer science, human-computer interaction, visual design, business, and cognitive psychology. Another notable HCIL's project was its collaboration with the Library of Congress on designing user interfaces and organizing the content of the National Digital Library (NDL). Currently, the journal *Information Visualization* (http:// ivi.sagepub.com/) is dedicated to presenting recent research in the discipline.

13. Different authors have attempted to classify the many types of visualizations based on various criteria. For example, the "periodic table" of visualizations (http:// www.visual-literacy.org/periodic_table/periodic_table.html) includes a multifaceted but relatively traditional classification of visualization techniques. Tory and Moller (2004b) classified visualizations based on algorithms rather than data. Zhu and Chen (2005) argue that visualizations are typically categorized based on "application focus" such as information visualization, scientific visualization, and software visualization. Shneiderman, who conducted fundamental research in the field of human-computer interaction, has created one of the most highly regarded visualization classification schemes, which he based on data types (Shneiderman 1996).

14. One of the principal outcomes of the McCormick Report was the conclusion that an emerging discipline of scientific visualization, whose aim was to employ computational means to visualizing scientific problems, deserved significant federal support for provision visualization tools for the scientific and engineering community.

15. The concept of making visual data comprehensible and accessible to a broad public audience as a means of "education by the eye" was first investigated in the early 1920s by Otto Neurath, an Austrian philosopher and sociologist and one of the leading members of the Vienna Circle. Well known for his research in visual communication, Neurath believed that "the ordinary citizen ought to be able to get information freely about all subjects in which he is interested, just as he can get geographical knowledge from maps and atlases. There is no field where humanization of

knowledge through the eye would not be possible" (Neurath 1939, 3). As part of his research, Neurath along with his team developed an iconic language—the International System of Typographic Picture Education (Isotype)—that used simplified pictures and specific composition rules to represent information in terms of patterns, trends, and relationships.

16. Such applications as Virtual Globes (for example, Google Earth and NASA WorldWind) were originally designed for the general user, but eventually have become broadly adopted by the research community for produce massive, highly detailed geospatial data.

17. A heavy reliance on and extensive use of information Web-based technologies for research is particularly evident with regard to a younger generation of researchers— i.e., those researchers who were born between 1982 and 1991—who are often referred to as the "born-digital generation," "Generation Y," "Millennials," and the "Google generation" (Carpenter et al. 2010; Lippincott 2010).

18. Aghaei, Nematbakhsh, and Farsani (2012) provide a good overview of the four generations of the World Wide Web—from Web 1.0 to Web 4.0.

WORKS CITED

Abah, Joshua, and Francisca Ogwueleka. "Cloud Computing with Related Enabling Technologies." *International Journal of Cloud Computing and Services Science (IJ-CLOSER)* 2, no. 1 (2013): 40–49. doi:10.11591/closer.v2i1.1720.

Aghaei, Sareh, Mohammad Ali Nematbakhsh, and Hadi Khosravi Farsani. "Evolution of the World Wide Web: From Web 1.0 to Web 4.0." *International Journal of Web and Semantic Technology* 3, no. 1 (2012). http://airccse.org/journal/ijwest/papers/3112ijwest01.pdf (accessed February 25, 2014).

Anderson, Terry, and Heather Kanuka. *E-research: Methods, Strategies, and Issues.* Boston: Allyn and Bacon, 2003.

Androutsellis-Theotokis, Stephanos, and Diomidis Spinellis. "A Survey of Peer-to-Peer Content Distribution Technologies." *ACM Computing Surveys (CSUR)* 36, no. 4 (2004): 335–71. doi:10.1145/1041680.1041681.

Aymerich, Francesco Maria, Gianni Fenu, and Simone Surcis. "An Approach to a Cloud Computing Network." In *First International Conference on the Applications of Digital Information and Web Technologies, 2008 (ICADIWT 2008)*, 113–18. (2008). doi:10.1109/ICADIWT.2008.4664329.

Bederson, Benjamin B., and Ben Shneiderman, eds. *The Craft of Information Visualization: Readings and Reflections.* San Francisco: Morgan Kaufmann, 2003.

Bent, Moira, Pat Gannon-Leary, and Jo Webb. "Information Literacy in a Researcher's Learning Life: The Seven Ages of Research." *New Review of Information Networking* 13, no. 2 (2007): 81–99. doi:10.1080/13614570801899983.

Berners-Lee, Tim. "WWW: Past, Present, and Future." *Computer* 29, no. 10 (1996): 69–77. doi:10.1109/2.539724.

Berners-Lee, Tim, James Hendler, and Ora Lassila. "The Semantic Web. A New Form of Web Content That Is Meaningful to Computers Will Unleash a Revolution of New Possibilities." *Scientific American* 284, no. 5 (2001): 1–5.

Bote-Lorenzo, Miguel L., Yannis A. Dimitriadis, and Eduardo Gómez-Sánchez. "Grid Characteristics and Uses: A Grid Definition." In *Across Grids 2003*, edited by Fernandez Rivera et al., 291–98. New York: Springer Berlin Heidelberg, 2004.

Bulger, Monica E., Eric T. Meyer, Grace de la Flor, Melissa Terras, Sally Wyatt, Marina Jirotka, Katherine Eccles, and Christine McCarthy Madsen. "Reinventing Research? Information Practices in the Humanities." *Information Practices in the Humanities (March 2011): A Research Information Network Report.* 2011. http://papers.ssrn.com/sol3/papers.cfm?abstract_id=1859267 (accessed April 14, 2014).

Card, Stuart K., Jock D. Mackinlay, and Ben Shneiderman, eds. *Readings in Information Visualization: Using Vision to Think.* San Francisco: Morgan Kaufmann, 1999.

Carpenter, Julie, Louise Wetheridge, Nick Smith, Meg Goodman, and Oscar Struijvé. *Researchers of Tomorrow: A Three Year (BL/JISC) Study Tracking the Research Behaviour of "Generation Y" Doctoral Students: Annual Report 2009–2010.* 2010. http://www.jisc.ac.uk/publications/reports/2012/researchers-of-tomorrow (accessed February 25, 2014).

Chervenak, Ann, Ian Foster, Carl Kesselman, Charles Salisbury, and Steven Tuecke. "The Data Grid: Towards an Architecture for the Distributed Management and Analysis of Large Scientific Datasets." *Journal of Network and Computer Applications* 23, no. 3 (2000): 187–200. doi:10.1006/jnca.2000.0110.

Corrado, Edward M., and Heather Lea Moulaison, eds. *Getting Started with Cloud Computing: A LITA Guide.* New York: Neal-Schuman Publishers, 2011.

Data Center Quotes. "Define the Cloud." http://www.definethecloud.net/data-center -quotes/ (accessed February 23, 2014).

Fernandes, Alvaro A. "Middleware for Distributed Data Management." In *The SAGE Handbook of Online Research Methods*, edited by Nigel G. Fielding, Raymond M. Lee, and Grant Blank, 99–115. Beverly Hills, CA: Sage, 2008.

Foster, Ian, and Carl Kesselman, eds. *The Grid: Blueprint for a New Computing Infrastructure.* San Francisco: Morgan Kaufman, 1999.

Foster, Ian, Carl Kesselman, and Steven Tuecke. "The Anatomy of the Grid: Enabling Scalable Virtual Organizations." *International Journal of High Performance Computing Applications* 15, no. 3 (2001): 200–22. doi:10.1177/109434200 101500302.

Foster, Ian, Carl Kesselman, and Steven Tuecke. "What Is the Grid? A Three Point Checklist." *GRIDtoday* 1, no. 6 (2002).

Foster, Ian, Yong Zhao, Ioan Raicu, and Shiyong Lu. "Cloud Computing and Grid Computing 360-degree Compared." In *Grid Computing Environments Workshop, 2008 (GCE '08)*, 1–10. Piscataway, NJ: IEEE, 2008. doi:10.1109/GCE.2008.4738445.

Hamming, Richard. *Numerical Methods for Scientists and Engineers.* New York: Courier Dover Publications, 2012.

Henderson, Harry. *Encyclopedia of Computer Science and Technology.* New York: Infobase Publishing, 2009.

Hewson, Claire M., Dianna Laurent, and Carl M. Vogel. "Proper Methodologies for Psychological and Sociological Studies Conducted via the Internet." *Behavior Research Methods, Instruments, and Computers* 28, no. 2 (1996): 186–91. doi:10.3758/BF03204763.

Hey, Anthony, and Anne E. Trefethen. "The Data Deluge: An E-science Perspective." In *Grid Computing: Making the Global Infrastructure a Reality,* edited by F. Berman, A. Hey, and G. Fox, 809–24. Hoboken, NJ: Wiley, 2003.

Jankowski, Nicholas W., ed. *e-Research: Transformation in Scholarly Practice.* New York: Routledge, 2009.

Jennings, Roger. *Cloud Computing with the Windows Azure Platform.* New York: John Wiley & Sons, 2010.

Kambil, Ajit. "What Is Your Web 5.0 strategy?" *Journal of Business Strategy* 29, no. 6 (2008): 56–58. doi:10.1108/02756660810917255.

Keim, Daniel A. "Information Visualization and Visual Data Mining." *IEEE Transactions on Visualization and Computer Graphics* 8, no. 1 (2002): 1–8. doi:10.1109/2945.981847.

Kroll, Susan, and Rick Forsman. *A Slice of Research Life: Information Support for Research in the United States.* Dublin, OH: OCLC Online Computer Library Center, Inc., 2010. http://www.oclc.org/content/dam/research/publications/library/2010/2010-15.pdf (accessed February 25, 2014).

Kundra, Vivek. *Federal Cloud Computing Strategy.* Washington, DC: The White House, February 8, 2011. http://acmait.com/pdf/Federal-Cloud-Computing -Strategy.pdf (accessed July 14, 2014).

Lippincott, Joan K. "Information Commons: Meeting Millennials' Needs." *Journal of Library Administration* 50, no. 1 (2010). http://www.cni.org/staff/joanpubs/IC.jlibadmin.lippincott.preprint.pdf (accessed February 28, 2014).

Lougee, Carolyn C. "The Professional Implications of Electronic Information." *Leonardo* (1994): 143–54. http://www.jstor.org/stable/1575984 (accessed February 20, 2014).

Magoulès, Frédéric, ed. *Fundamentals of Grid Computing: Theory, Algorithms and Technologies.* Boca Raton, FL: CRC Press, 2009.

McCormick, Bruce Howard, Thomas A. DeFanti, and Maxine D. Brown. "Visualization in Scientific Computing." *IEEE Computer Graphics and Applications* 7, no. 10 (1987): 69–89.

Mell, Peter, and Timothy Grance. "The NIST Definition of Cloud Computing (Draft)." *NIST Special Publication* 800, no. 145 (2011): 7.

Menon, Goutham M., ed. *Using the Internet as a Research Tool for Social Work and Human Services.* New York: Haworth Press, 2002.

Muller, Nathan J. *Desktop Encyclopedia of the Internet.* Norwood, MA: Artech House, 1999.

Nayak, Smitha, and Ammar Yassir. "Cloud Computing as an Emerging Paradigm." *IJCSNS* 12, no. 1 (2012): 61. http://paper.ijcsns.org/07_book/201201/20120 109.pdf (accessed February 25, 2014).

Neurath, Otto. *International Picture Language; the First Rules of Isotype: With Isotype Pictures.* London: K. Paul, Trench, Trubner & Company, 1936.

Neurath, Otto. *Modern Man in the Making.* New York: A. A. Knopf, 1939.

Niemann, Paul. *Invention Mysteries: The Little-Known Stories behind Well-Known Inventions.* Quincy, IL: Horsefeathers Publishing Co., 2004.

O'Reilly T. "Call for a Blogger's Code of Conduct." *O'Reilly Radar,* March 31, 2007. http://radar.oreilly.com/2007/03/call-for-a-bloggers-code-of-co.html (accessed February 25, 2014).

O'Reilly, Tim. "Web 2.0 Compact Definition: Trying Again," *O'Reilly Radar,* December 10, 2006. http://radar.oreilly.com/2006/12/web-20-compact -definition-tryi.html (accessed February 23, 2014).

Plaszczak, Pawel, and Richard Wellner Jr. *Grid Computing: The Savvy Manager's Guide.* Amsterdam, Boston: Elsevier/Morgan Kaufmann, 2006.

Research.gov. "About the InCommon Integration at Research.gov." https://www.research.gov/research-portal/appmanager/base/desktop?_nfpb=true&_pageLabel=research_node_display&_nodePath=/researchGov/Generic/Common/InCommonURLS.html (accessed April 2, 2014).

Rosenthal, Arnon, Peter Mork, Maya Hao Li, Jean Stanford, David Koester, and Patti Reynolds. "Cloud Computing: A New Business Paradigm for Biomedical Information Sharing." *Journal of Biomedical Informatics* 43, no. 2 (2010): 342–53.

Rosling, Hans, Rönnlund A. Rosling, and Ola Rosling. "New Software Brings Statistics beyond the Eye." In *Statistics, Knowledge and Policy: Key Indicators to Inform Decision Making.* Paris: OECD Publishing (2005): 522–30.

Shneiderman, Ben. "The Eyes Have It: A Task by Data Type Taxonomy for Information Visualizations." In *Proceedings, IEEE Symposium on Visual Languages, 1996* (1996): 336–43. doi:10.1109/VL.1996.545307.

Spence, Robert. *Information Visualization: Design for Interaction.* 2nd ed. Harlow, UK: Pearson/Prentice Hall, 2007.

Stanoevska-Slabeva, Katarina, and Thomas Wozniak. "Grid Basics." In *Grid and Cloud Computing: A Business Perspective on Technology and Applications,* edited by Katarina Stanoevska-Slabeva, Thomas Wozniak, and Santi Ristol, 23–45. Heidelberg: Springer, 2010.

Stevens, Rick, Michael E. Papka, and Terry Disz. "Prototyping the Workspaces of the Future." *IEEE Internet Computing* 7, no. 4 (2003): 51–58. doi:10.1109/MIC.2003.1215660.

Subramanian, Ashok K., Andrew T. McAfee, and Jim P. Getzinger. "Use of the World Wide Web for Multisite Data Collection." *Academic Emergency Medicine* 4, no. 8 (1997): 811–17. doi:10.1111/j.1553-2712.1997.tb03792.x.

Tory, Melanie, and Torsten Moller. "Human Factors in Visualization Research." *IEEE Transactions on Visualization and Computer Graphics* 10, no. 1 (2004a): 72–84. doi:10.1109/TVCG.2004.1260759.

Tory, Melanie, and Torsten Moller. "Rethinking Visualization: A High-Level Taxonomy." In *IEEE Symposium on Information Visualization, 2004 (INFOVIS 2004), Proceedings,* edited by Matt Ward and Tamara Munzner, 151–58. Piscataway, NJ: Institute of Electrical and Electronics Engineers, 2004b. doi:10.1109/INFVIS.2004.59.

Vecchiola, Christian, Suraj Pandey, and Rajkumar Buyya. "High-Performance Cloud Computing: A View of Scientific Applications." In *2009 10th International Symposium on Pervasive Systems, Algorithms, and Networks (ISPAN),* 4–16. 2009.

Viégas, Fernanda B., Martin Wattenberg, Frank van Ham, Jesse Kriss, and Matt McKeon. "Many Eyes: A Site for Visualization at Internet Scale." *IEEE Transactions on Visualization and Computer Graphics* 13, no. 6 (2007): 1121–28. doi:10.1109/TVCG.2007.70577.

W3C. "W3C Mission." http://www.w3.org/Consortium/mission (accessed February 23, 2014).

Yang, Chaowei, Michael Goodchild, Qunying Huang, Doug Nebert, Robert Raskin, Yan Xu, Myra Bambacus, and Daniel Fay. "Spatial Cloud Computing: How Can the Geospatial Sciences Use and Help Shape Cloud Computing?"

International Journal of Digital Earth 4, no. 4 (2011): 305–29. doi:10.1080/ 17538947.2011.587547.

Zhu, Bin, and Hsinchun Chen. "Information Visualization." *Annual Review of Information Science and Technology* 39, no. 1 (2005): 139–77. doi:10.1002/ aris.1440390111.

SUGGESTED READINGS

Bederson, Benjamin B., and Ben Shneiderman, eds. *The Craft of Information Visualization: Readings and Reflections.* San Francisco, CA: Morgan Kaufmann, 2003.

Berners-Lee, Tim (with Mark Fischetti). *Weaving the Web: The Original Design and Ultimate Destiny of the World Wide Web by its Inventor.* San Francisco: HarperSanFrancisco, 1999.

Corrado, Edward M., and Heather Lea Moulaison, eds. *Getting Started with Cloud Computing: A LITA Guide.* New York: Neal-Schuman Publishers, 2011.

Foster, Ian, and Carl Kesselman, eds. *The Grid: Blueprint for a New Computing Infrastructure.* San Francisco: Morgan Kaufman, 1999.

Furht, Borko. "Cloud Computing Fundamentals." In *Handbook of Cloud Computing,* edited by Borko Furht and Armando Escalante, 3–19. New York: Springer, 2010.

Jacko, Julie, ed. *The Human-Computer Interaction Handbook: Fundamentals, Evolving Technologies, and Emerging Applications.* Boca Raton, FL: CRC Press, 2012.

Juan, Angel A., Thanasis Daradoumis, Meritxell Roca, Scott E. Grasman, and Javier Faulin, eds. *Collaborative and Distributed E-Research. Innovations in Technologies, Strategies and Applications.* Hershey, PA: IGI Global, 2012.

Magoulès, Frédéric, ed. *Fundamentals of Grid Computing: Theory, Algorithms and Technologies.* Boca Raton, FL: CRC Press, 2009.

4

Strength through Collaboration: Scholarly Communication in the Context of eResearch

Research teams are increasingly transdisciplinary, involving transient working relationships among individuals who are equals in power and authority. Participation in research teams has become, to some extent, democratized and globalized.

—Sandra Braman (2006, 4)

THE ROLE OF SCHOLARLY COMMUNICATION IN THE RESEARCH PROCESS

Research advancements build upon previous research and depend upon the availability of research findings. Therefore, an indispensable thread running through research in any discipline is scholarly communication—a social process, in which researchers share ideas, data, resources, methodologies, innovations, and discoveries with their peers and with the public. Not only do researchers want to disseminate the results of their work, but they also need to ensure that their research findings are original. The idea that a research life cycle is incomplete until research results are disseminated is one of the fundamental principles of research. Scholars, thus, are responsible for accomplishing a dual task—of doing research, and of communicating their research findings for the purpose of contributing to new knowledge (Jankowski 2009; Weller 2011).

Historically, dissemination of research results has been mediated by the formal and informal methods of scholarly communication. The formal methods of scholarly communication, which are still prominent across most disciplines, include publication of journal articles and monographs released by established scholarly publishers, submissions to conferences, and distribution of working papers.[1] In an academic environment, formal methods of scholarly communication, especially the proof of a strong publication record, continue to affect the institutional criteria for hiring and career advancement such as tenure and promotion (Harley et al. 2010; Weller 2011).

The informal methods of scholarly communication, sometimes referred to as "invisible colleges," consist of social networking activities among researchers (Carey 2011). In the past, these activities included informal manuscript reviews, such as marginal note-taking, as well as personal meetings of researchers (usually belonging to the same field of knowledge) who met regularly to witness experiments and discuss research topics (Crane 1972). Nowadays, "invisible college" activities have also integrated Web-enabled communication tools such as blogs, e-mail, discussion forums, social network sites, and professional and scholarly hubs. Even though informal scholarly communication practices are typically not considered as a measurement of research impact or criteria for career advancement, they make an important contribution to research by encouraging discussions and facilitating collaboration (Wouters et al. 2013).

THE SCHOLARLY COMMUNICATION LIFE CYCLE

The first and, to date, the most comprehensive scholarly communication lifecycle model was outlined by Bo-Christer Björk, professor at Hanken School of Economics, Finland (2007), and further extended by John Houghton, a professorial fellow at the Centre for Strategic Economic Studies, Victoria University, Melbourne, Australia (Houghton and Oppenheim 2010). According to Björk, who captured his model using the IDEF0 modeling technique, which is used in business process reengineering,[2] the scholarly communication life cycle consists of five top-level scholarly communication activities (which are broken down further into subactivities lower in the hierarchy):

1. Funding research and its communication
2. Performing research and communicating the results
3. Publishing research outputs
4. Facilitating dissemination, retrieval, and preservation
5. Studying publications and applying the knowledge derived (Björk 2007; Houghton and Oppenheim 2010).

Although Björk's model was intended to describe the scholarly communication lifecycle in the sciences and engineering, it can also be applicable to other disciplines (Swan 2010).

Another notable, even though less elaborated, model of the scholarly communication life cycle was proposed by Microsoft External Research (2008), an organization that is well known for its collaboration with prominent researchers in academia, industries, and governments around the world. According to Microsoft External Research, the scholarly communication life cycle can be divided into four major phases:

1. Data collection and analysis
2. Authoring
3. Publication and distribution
4. Archiving and preservation (Jankowski 2009).[3]

IMPACT OF DIGITAL TECHNOLOGIES ON SCHOLARLY COMMUNICATION PRACTICES

Even though the fundamental goal of scholarly communication—the generation and distribution of new knowledge—has remained intact for centuries, both formal and informal practices of scholarly communication have undergone significant technological transformations in the tools and processes of production, publishing, curation, and use of scholarship. Digital technologies, especially the Internet, have not only enabled the creation of new types of resources, services, and research environments that have not been possible before, but they have also simplified and expedited meeting the fundamental researchers' needs such as keeping abreast of current trends and developments within and outside their area of expertise, exchanging of research findings, news, and information in a timely manner, and finding and establishing research collaborations across geographical and temporal barriers.

ELECTRONIC PUBLISHING

One of the most significant transformations in scholarly communication practices enabled by the Internet is the increasing migration of scholarly publishing, especially journal publishing, from print to electronic formats. Journals have been the principal means of scholarly communication in many disciplines since the seventeenth century and are an essential part of the research process (Fjällbrant 1997). While the highlights of research discoveries are usually described in the mass media and later in books, the details and results of the most current research studies are largely reported through articles in peer-reviewed journals. Journals also provide quality control (through the peer reviewing or refereeing process), draw together research papers on particular subjects, and organize the distribution of research.

In the sciences, research is almost exclusively reported through articles in peer-reviewed journals (versus through monographs) for three reasons. The first reason is that scientific research results are often time-sensitive, especially in the biomedical fields, and the rapid accumulation of knowledge and data forces them to publish research findings as quickly as possible. Timely access to current research findings can be crucial, both for scientists, who discover new drugs and treatments for these diseases, and for clinicians, who care for patients suffering from these conditions. The second reason is that scientific research findings tend to go out of date more quickly than in other disciplines, largely because of the rapid changes in information technology and research methodology. Findings more than five years old are often considered to be out of date. Finally, peer-reviewed journals dominate scholarly communication in the sciences and other academic fields because the publication of peer-reviewed articles, especially in the journals with high-impact factors, is one of the most important criteria for promotion and tenure in academia (Harley et al. 2010).

Electronic journal publishing[4] has opened up new potentials for scholarly communication. Several studies, examining the current landscape of scholarly communication across a variety of disciplines, reported the benefits of electronic journal publishing for researchers in various fields of knowledge (Grefsheim and Rankin 2007; Haines et al. 2010; Harley et al. 2010; Hemminger et al. 2007). According to these studies, mainly using surveys and interviews, most researchers clearly prefer online access to full-text electronic journals versus print journals.[5]

One of the main benefits of electronic journals, [in the eyes of most respondents], is that [electronic] journals allow them to access full-text journal articles quickly [and conveniently] from office or home (or wherever they happen to be working). Furthermore, electronic journals are usually available on the Web weeks before they are available in print, which is particularly important in the biological sciences where currency of content and expediency of access are often crucial.[6] Other benefits of electronic journals include:

- Support for distance education courses
- [Easy] searchability
- Hyperlinks to other publications
- Simultaneous use by multiple persons
- Compatibility with adaptive technologies such as those for the visually impaired
- Personal/customized accounts

Some [researchers] are also finding that electronic journals can offer significant value beyond full-text access by incorporating novel multimedia and interactive features in their content, which can be important in the scholarship of many different fields as an enhanced means of communicating knowledge. For example, the *Journal of Visualized Experiments* (published by JoVE) incorporates video-based components ("video-articles") in its content. (Martin 2013, 276–77)

Another example is the open access multimodal journal *Vectors: Journal of Culture and Technology in a Dynamic Vernacular* (published by the Institute for Multimedia Literacy at the University of Southern California) that features images, animations, music, sound, and other digital multimedia effects. Though these innovations in some cases blur the lines between resource types and traditional publishing practices, they represent a shift to greater reliance on digital media among researchers.

Book publishing, on the other hand, has not undergone as fundamental a change as journal publishing. Beyond creating electronic versions of print books (or eBooks) that are often identical to their print counterparts, book publishing has remained essentially the same (Weller 2011; Wouters et al. 2013). This situation can be partly attributed to the fact that books are still one of the primary venues for scholarly communication in the humanities, where the nature and culture of scholarly communication differ from that in the sciences. Scientific research is mostly a "social, team-based enterprise" (Harley et al. 2010), in part because it takes place in laboratories and in teams organized around the use of expensive equipment and/or materials. While researchers in the social sciences and humanities may also work in teams or in collaboration with other researchers, the methods of academic recognition and reward for researchers in these fields put more emphasis on the individual scholar. In these fields, a book can be considered an author's crowning achievement.

OPEN ACCESS: REDEFINING SCHOLARLY IMPACT

The open access publishing model is akin in spirit to the open source code movement in the computer programming field. Open access means that full-text research papers are available online as soon as they are published, free of charge, and where most restrictions on access or use have been lifted. According to the Association of Research Libraries, open access "refers to works that are created with no expectation of direct monetary return and made available at no cost to the reader on the public internet for purposes of education and research" (Case and Matz 2003).

Under the prevailing subscription-based system, commercial publishers maintain a monopoly over the distribution of research results. They charge authors for the publication of their works, then charge the readers for subscription, advertising, and online access fees; in addition, they retain the copyright of the articles they publish. Consequently, though the vast majority of research is publicly financed by taxpayer dollars, access to research is not freely and publicly available: it is restricted to customers who can afford to pay for subscriptions.[7]

In the past two decades, the escalating cost of journals has forced many individuals and institutions to cancel their subscriptions, thus excluding large parts of the research community from scholarly interaction, especially in developing countries. While many publishers and researchers believed that there was no better way to disseminate research findings, a few initiatives began exploring the alternatives to traditional subscription-based standards, launching the idea of a new publishing model—open access.

The open access movement began in the late 1990s as a response to increasing journal costs, which priced many individual and institutional subscribers out of access to the latest research studies.[8] Because of an effective online system for submission, peer reviewing, and publication that makes research papers rapidly available for a worldwide audience, the open access publishing practice has primarily gained acceptance in the biomedical sciences, where speed to publication is crucial, due to a persistent concern among researchers about the time lags between authorship and publication as well as about the high cost of the scientific journals. The idea of open access is based on the view that research findings, particularly in the health sciences, should be freely and immediately available to the worldwide scientific community, clinicians, and the public.

Two publishers have been in the center of the open access movement: BioMed Central (BMC) and the Public Library of Science (PLoS). BMC, a UK-based publishing house, provides immediate and open access to full text of research articles published in its 258 online journals (at the time of this writing) covering all areas of biology and medicine. The BMC's commitment to open access, as stated on the BMC website, is based on the premise that "open access to research is central to rapid and efficient progress in science and that subscription-based access to research is hindering rather than helping scientific communication." Once published in BMC journals, all articles are indexed in PubMed, and, where appropriate, in BIOSIS, ISI, and other databases. The articles are also archived in PubMed Central, and deposited in CrossRef.

Following the lead of BMC in the open access movement, the Public Library of Science (PLoS), a California nonprofit group of bioscientists formed in 2000, has published two online peer-reviewed journals funded by a $9 million grant from the Gordon and Betty Moore Foundation. The founders of PloS—Michael Eisen, a biologist at Lawrence Berkeley National Laboratory, Harold Varmus, a Nobel laureate, and Patrick Brown, a biochemist at Stanford University—stated that their "intention is to do something that fundamentally changes the way scientific research is communicated" (Eisen 2003). If open access succeeds, they argued, "everyone with an internet connection will be a click away from a comprehensive online public library of scientific and medical knowledge" (ibid.). The first issue of *PLoS*

Biology, published on October 13, 2003, has been a success and received more than 500,000 hits throughout the world within a few hours after publication. As Eisen observed, "nothing else has ever argued so strongly for open-access publishing" (ibid.). In that first issue of *PLoS Biology*, Duke University researchers Miguel Nicoleis and Jose Carmena publicized their research findings about how they had trained monkeys with brain implants to move a robot arm with their thoughts, a discovery that might one day allow paraplegics to perform similar functions. In addition to publishing research material, *PLoS Biology* summarizes the main points of each article in order to make them more accessible for a nonspecialist reader.[9] Moreover, the Public Library of Science provides the ability for readers to rate and comment on, and to have discussion threads about, published articles.

More publishers are willing to experiment with the open access model. Oxford University Press (OUP) announced in June 2004 that the *Nucleic Acids Research (NAR)*, one of the most important OUP journals, would adopt an open access publishing model starting in January 2005. Springer, a publisher of 2,200 scientific journals, has taken a step toward open access by offering its authors the Springer Open Choice model. Authors who select the Springer Open Choice can now make their articles freely available online; however they must pay a considerable fee of US$3,000 per article. In addition to its established SpringerOpen journal portfolio, Springer expanded its open access program to include open access books across all areas of science, technology, and medicine (STM). Since 2005, Elsevier, a world-leading publisher of scientific, technical, and medical journals, allows authors to choose to publish open access in its 1,600+ traditional journals as well as 73 open access journals.[10] Starting January 1, 2014, Elsevier has flipped its seven traditional subscription-based journals to a gold open access model, meaning that articles in these journals, funded by an Article Processing Charge paid by the author, are available freely and without restriction on the publisher's website.[11] Among other organizations making the transition to open access is the Modern Language Association (MLA) that has adopted a new author agreement for its publications, including its flagship journal *PMLA: Publications of the Modern Language Association of America*. According to this agreement, MLA leaves copyright with authors, allowing them to deposit their work in open access repositories or on personal or institutional websites. These practices continue to foster the development of more equitable and transparent scholarly and educational processes and may produce a greater impact (in terms of readership) than non-open access.

While open access publications are intended to be free for readers, the open access publishing itself is not free and requires new cost-recovery models. Open access challenges the traditional subscription-based publishing model by offering an alternative—an article processing fee. Instead of charging subscribers, the open access publishers cover the cost of peer review and publication by charging authors, or research sponsors, for each article they publish.

This fee can be paid by authors or via their institute's membership. This is known as the gold (author pays) open access model.[12]

Contrary to commercial publishers, most (but not all) open access publishers require authors to abide by an open access Creative Commons Attribution (CC BY) license. This license allows authors to retain ownership of the copyright of their articles and, at the same time, permits any user to download, reuse, print out, archive, and distribute the article as long as appropriate credit is given to the authors and source of the work (Creative Commons 2014).

A strengthening belief in the value of open access as an important practice of scholarly communication has taken firm hold in many disciplines. There are many open access initiatives that work in the interests of the research enterprise and the society. Among the initiatives that deserve credit and special attention are:

- ACRL's Scholarly Communication Initiative
  http://www.ala.org/acrl/issues/scholcomm/scholcomminitiative
  Launched in 2002 by the Association of College and Research Libraries (ACRL), the initiative issued "Principles and Strategies for the Reform of Scholarly Communication" that articulated fair prices for scholarly publications, quality control in publishing through peer review, and preservation of knowledge for long-term use.

- Budapest Open Access Initiative
  http://www.budapestopenaccessinitiative.org/
  A set of principles for promoting and maintaining open access to research developed in January 2003 at a meeting of the Academies of Sciences in Budapest, Hungary.

- Create Change
  http://www.createchange.org/
  An educational initiative established by the Scholarly Publishing and Academic Resources Coalition (SPARC), the Association of College and Research Libraries (ACRL), and the Association of Research Libraries (ARL). Offers librarians, faculty members, educators, and administrators information materials for promoting and launching open access advocacy programs.

- Creative Commons
  http://creativecommons.org/
  A nonprofit organization founded in 2001 that provides free tools that allow creators in various disciplines to choose which authorship rights they want to reserve and which rights they want to waive. Science Commons (http://creativecommons.org/science) expands the use of the Creative Commons licenses to scientific research.

- Directory of Open Access Journals
  http://www.doaj.org/
  Founded in 2003 and maintained by the Lund University Libraries, Sweden, the directory aims to include all open access scholarly journals in all subjects and languages that use a quality control system.

- National Institutes of Health (NIH) Public Access Policy
  http://publicaccess.nih.gov/
  Implemented in 2008, the policy requires researchers "to submit final peer-reviewed journal manuscripts that arise from NIH funds to the digital archive PubMed Central *immediately upon acceptance for publication* [emphasis in original]" and make these published manuscripts "accessible to the public on PubMed Central no later than 12 months after publication" (National Institutes of Health Public Access 2014).

- PubMed Central
  http://www.ncbi.nlm.nih.gov/pmc/
  The National Library of Medicine's free full-text digital archive of life sciences journal literature and the repository of research papers that arise from the National Institutes of Health (NIH) funds.

- SPARC (Scholarly Publishing and Academic Resources Coalition)
  http://www.sparc.arl.org/
  Founded in 1998, under the sponsorship of the Association of Research Libraries (ARL), SPARC is a collaboration of nearly 300 institutions in North America, Europe, Asia, and Australia whose aim is to advance and promote the open access movement and offer advisory services to scholarly publishers.

Digital repositories and ePrint archives developed in the 1990s are additional open access mechanisms that support and enhance scholarly communication and research across the disciplines. They enable researchers to "self-archive" the digital versions of their manuscripts (ePrints) into publicly available institutional repositories or archives and thus ensure the long-term preservation of, and access to, research material.[13] For example, arXiv.org (http://www.arxiv.org), operated and funded by Cornell University, offers ePrints in the fields of physics, computer science, mathematics, and quantitative biology. DSpace (http://www.dspace.org/), a collaborative project of the Massachusetts Institute of Technology (MIT) Libraries and Hewlett-Packard Labs, serves as a digital repository for research and educational materials. The DSpace open source platform accepts all forms of digital materials and is customizable to the local needs of a research university or organization. PubMed Central (http://www.ncbi.nlm.nih.gov/pmc/) is the National Library of Medicine's free full-text digital archive of life sciences journal literature. It also serves as a repository for articles published by researchers funded by the National Institutes of Health.

While open access advocates consider the traditional commercial publishing system obsolete and believe that the future of scholarly publishing belongs to open access, skeptics still wonder whether open access journals will survive. Whether open access publishers will succeed largely depends on whether their journals can build prestige and encourage researchers to continue exploring the open access publishing model as well as other options for open scholarship.[14]

SCHOLARLY COMMUNICATION 2.0

The web is more a social creation than a technical one.

—Tim Berners-Lee

The Social Web, also known as Web 2.0, emphasizes user-generated online content and Web-based user interactions and aims to reach the broadest audience possible through a wide range of applications, including blogs, RSS, wikis, mashups, tags, folksonomy, and tag clouds. Among these various applications, the Social Network Sites (SNSs) and Read-Write Web applications gained more recognition within the research community than other Social Web technologies.

SOCIAL NETWORK SITES

Since the first major social network sites[15] (SNSs), such as SixDegreesCom, LiveJournal, and Black Planet, were launched at the end of the 1990s, SNSs have attracted a tremendous amount of attention and widespread adoption as a means of "technologised sociability" (Merchant 2012). Nicknamed "the wisdom of crowds" (Surowiecki 2005), hundreds of SNSs have been created to support social networking around various "social objects" (Engeström 2007) that included shared views and interests; a common language; professional, political, or religious affiliations; racial, ethnical, or sexual affinities; specific activities, e.g., online games; shared hardships, e.g., a disease or divorce; or a preferred type of communication, e.g., blogging or photo sharing.

Even though SNSs support the increasingly wide range of interests and preferences and attract more and more users from around the world, their three core characteristics have remained basically the same over the years. They all allow individual users or members (1) to create a public or semipublic profile on the site; (2) to compile a list of connections within the site ("friend lists"); and (3) to traverse both their friend lists and those made by others within the same site (Ellison 2007).

Despite the popularity and scale of adoption of SNSs, especially among the young,[16] for whom SNSs create a "sense of belonging" (Merchant 2012) and "a sense of place" in a social world (Spencer-Oatey 2007), the attitude toward their use varies. Within the research community, there is no agreement on the benefits or disadvantages of using SNSs to support professional communication and collaboration. Even though a majority of researchers use, at least occasionally, such academic sites as Academia.edu, Mendeley, ResearchID, and SciLink, as well as such general-purpose sites as Twitter, LinkedIn, and Facebook and find some potential value in them as a means of communication, these sites have not attained a high level of regard or adoption into research practice (Ellison 2007). In terms of sharing research findings, SNSs have even been considered dangerous, especially in the rapidly developing biomedical fields, where patents, promotion, and tenure often depend on who is the first to publish a new research finding, and where there is fear of the ideas being "stolen" or published by a competitor (Kroll and Forsman 2010; Waldrop 2008; Weller 2011).

Most researchers also emphasize the paramount importance of interpersonal versus online communication and generally prefer face-to-face interactions and personal introductions at meetings and conferences as a means to develop serious professional collaborations (Kroll and Forsman 2010; Weller 2011). Some researchers also believe that the use of Social Network Sites contradicts their scholarly values, negatively impacts their image, and creates tension between personal and professional boundaries and between casual socializing and scholarly communication (Veletsianos and Kimmons 2013).

The use of SNS as a research platform for the social sciences has been less controversial, especially for conducting behavioral and sociological studies. SNSs allow social scientists to collect research data on how different people interact, reason, and feel in different settings and enable them to reach specific populations and recruit potential participants for their studies as well as exploit and analyze user-generated information provided by the Social Web (Garaizar et al. 2012).

The old concept of "invisible colleges" that supported the organization of scientific activities has not disappeared. This concept originated in the seventeenth century in the Royal Society of London, whose members did not belong to any formal institution and referred to themselves as an invisible college (Carey 2011). "It served as an influential channel for information exchange among scholars and allowed them to monitor scientific progress in their field, usually by the means of marginalia. Today, these channels include social media such as e-mail, blogs, wikis, discussion lists, and society and professional hubs that have become widely accepted as [informal methods of] scholarly communication. [They] enable a wide range of interaction among [researchers], such as allowing scholars to connect to each other and to discover new ideas, provide daily updates in the field, and facilitate discussions on research findings" (Martin 2013, 274).

Unlike the "visible Web" (of social networks), the web of "invisible college" resources, the informal methods of scholarly communication such as blogs, e-mail, discussion forums, and professional and scholarly hubs, offer a richer vein for collaboration and are regarded more highly among the researchers as a means for publicizing their work, developing collaborations, or identifying who is conducting related research. Because eResearch is commonly a team-based enterprise, an informal communication network of scholars—"invisible colleges"—is still an important source of information for researchers.

THE READ-WRITE WEB

Another segment of the Social Web is the Read-Write Web. It enables users with little or no knowledge of HTML to collaboratively create and modify

Web-based content and engage in online conversations. These collaborative writing Web spaces, such as blogs and wikis, introduced over the last decade, provide users with a shared asynchronous environment for writing, editing, commenting, discussing, reflecting, and sharing information or advice.

A blog, an abbreviation of the term "weblog,"[17] is an ongoing set of postings, either on one topic or a range of topics, that is published chronologically, with the most current entries displayed first. Blogs often include embedded hypertext links and comments from readers who can also syndicate content from the blogs by using RSS (Really Simple Syndication) feeds that allow them to receive updates from blogs they are interested in. Most blogs are textual, while some include primarily images, such as photoblogs, or videos, such as videoblogs.

Even though the majority of blogs are personal or journalistic in nature, such as commentary, diary, or advice,[18] the research, or science, blogging has also grown significantly over the past few years and become popular within the scholarly community as a fast, less formal venue for discussion of scholarly information (Fausto et al. 2012; Shema, Bar-Ilan, and Thelwall 2012). Technorati (http://technorati.com/), a blog searching service and blog directory, reported in 2013 that among nearly 135 million blogs, approximately 16,000 were related to science. Research blogs are a useful source not only for scientists who are interested in cutting-edge research and first-hand comments from peers, but are also a useful source for the general reader as a medium for accessing scientific information provided by scientists and experts in their fields.

The Research Blogging (RB) platform (http://researchblogging.org/), created in 2007 by a science blogger, Dave Munger, acts as an important filter for scientific research. The purpose of the RB is to identify serious academic research and prevent the spread of pseudoscience content. To achieve this purpose, the RB aggregates research blog citations of peer-reviewed publications and enables bloggers to cite their sources in a scholarly manner (Fausto et al. 2012).

While blog entries are static and usually posted by a single author who may or may not welcome comments, wikis, a collection of hypertext documents that can be directly edited by anyone, are specifically designed for group writing and collaboration.[19] The "ownership" of a wiki is shared among all the contributors. Any user with an Internet connection and permission for access can contribute wiki content as well as edit and modify existing content. Wikis provide a more efficient and more effective mechanism for group writing and editing than Word documents with tracked changes forwarded via e-mail.

Wikipedia,[20] one of the most well-known wikis introduced in 2001 by the Wikimedia Foundation (http://wikimediafoundation.org/wiki/Home), is a free multilingual online encyclopedia whose content is generated by the thousands of contributors ("wikipedians") who, using the wiki software,[21] volunteer their time and knowledge to the Wikipedia's content for no monetary reward. Everyone with an Internet connection can directly edit articles written by "wikipedians." Every edit is recorded and can be traced by any user that allows a multitude of analyses and evaluations. In addition to Wikipedia, the Wikimedia Foundation is dedicated to designing a network of other free "knowledge projects," i.e., multilingual educational wiki sites available to the public free of charge, such as Wikispecies and Wikiversity, that enable users to create, edit, and share educational and research resources across multiple disciplines. Even though there is controversy regarding the accuracy of content published in Wikipedia and other Wikimedia sites, and there are increasing disputes among the contributors (especially with regard to articles with controversial content), the collaborative benefits of wikis is undeniable (Ba-Quy et al. 2008; West and West 2009).

Google Docs (http://docs.google.com/) is another application that supports collaborative research writing and does not require buying hardware or downloading software. Google Docs supports collaborative research writing by allowing registered users to access documents from any computer anywhere in the world and by sharing these documents with others as viewers or collaborators, or by publishing these documents on the Web. Similar to wiki sites, Google Docs further enables collaboration by allowing the editing of a document created by other scholars and by allowing them to suggest modifications through comment annotations, without editing the original document itself.

VIRTUAL RESEARCH ENVIRONMENTS: LABORATORIES WITHOUT WALLS

> Science is an inherently collaborative enterprise.
> —Thomas A. Finholt and Gary M. Olson (1997)

The idea of collaborative research environments, enabled by the Internet and sometimes characterized as "Science 2.0" (Waldrop 2008), was first explored in 1989 in a white paper by William Wulf, a computer scientist at the University of Virginia who was serving as assistant director of the National Science Foundation's Directorate for Computer and Information Science and Engineering. In his white paper *The National Collaboratory*, Wulf coined the term "collaboratory" (a combination of the words "collaboration" and "laboratory") and described it as "a center without walls, in which the nation's researchers can perform their research without regard to their physical location, interacting with colleagues, accessing instrumentation, sharing data and computational resources, and accessing information in digital libraries" (Wulf 1989, 9).

One of the earliest examples of a collaboratory was the Worm Community System (WCS). Started in 1990 as a small team project for a few biologists who were studying *c. elegans* (a sea worm), WCS gradually developed into a virtual collaborative organization that enabled communication and data sharing among biologists across geographically distributed sites.

The focus of collaboratories has gradually shifted from supporting research studies in a single discipline to supporting multidisciplinary research as the research challenges became more complex, often requiring researchers from different fields to work together on a problem that could not readily be solved by any one individual researcher (or research team), discipline, or organization. For example, large-scale studies such as cancer research or new drug design must draw on a wide range of scientific fields (e.g., biology, computer science, chemistry, medicine, information technology, and mathematics) in order to be successful, and will involve a great number of researchers from different domains. The nanoManipulator collaboratory was among the pioneer collaboratories to facilitate multidisciplinary research. Initiated in 1995, the nanoManipulator collaboratory supported the remote collaborative access to a specialized scientific instrument, called a nanoManipulator (nM), an interactive interface to atomic force microscopes, that enabled the team of chemists, physicists, and gene therapy researchers to synchronously conduct experiments, collecting and analyzing data from the nM and interact directly with physical samples—from DNA to single cells (Sonnenwald et al. 2001).

As research practices continued to become progressively cross-disciplinary, multi-institutional, and international in scope, requiring the integration of data from many disparate studies and disciplines, other variations of collaboratories have emerged, including Virtual Research Communities, Collaborative Work Environments, Virtual Research Environments, Social Virtual Research Environments, Virtual Research Organizations, and Virtual Collaborative Organizations. Even though these entities vary widely in size, scope, sociological and geographical structure, disciplinary context, and duration, they all pursue the common goal—to facilitate and enhance the researchers' output and productivity. To accomplish this goal, they provide individual researchers or research teams with a virtual workspace and the newest computing tools and resources that enable the researchers to work collaboratively on their joint research project (Dutton and Jeffreys 2010; Juan et al. 2012). For the sake of clarity, this book will use the term Virtual Research Environments (VREs) as synonymous to or subsuming the other terms.[22]

VREs support and facilitate research and scholarship of any type in any discipline by offering their members a set of online tools and services that have emerged around current communication and remote access technologies such as shared electronic whiteboards, video conferencing, instant messaging, virtual networked computing, project management tools, and shared access to research instruments, applications, and documents. These technologies facilitate core research activities, including project planning; the safe transfer and sharing of ideas, resources, and data; access to software and data repositories; authentication and rights management; and synchronous or asynchronous communication among the researchers working on a shared project. For example, AccessGrid.org (http://www.access grid.org/) supports the vision of highly distributed group-to-group collaborations in science, engineering, and education by providing high-quality real-time audio and video connections that enable a synchronous communication of research teams at multiple sites around the world. AccessGrid.org also shows the potential for integrating visualization tools that can support group analysis and interpretation of simulation through collaborative visualization (Childers et al. 2000; see also http://www.accessgrid.org).

More recently, VREs have experimented with adopting a Web 2.0 approach in creating a comfortable social infrastructure and providing researchers with familiar, more personalized interfaces. For example, the myExperiment project (http://www.myexperiment.org/) funded by the JISC Virtual Research Environments Programme and Microsoft Technical Computing Initiative and released in 2007, describes itself as a Web 2.0 Virtual Research Environment. By drawing upon the social software techniques, myExperiment created a user-friendly interface where researchers can discover, publish, and reuse bioinformatics workflows, work plans, and other research objects, such as data and documentation, that can be swapped, sorted, and searched like photos and videos via social networking tools (Newman et al. 2009).

VIVO (http://www.vivoweb.org/) is another project dedicated to fostering team work and scholarly communication across disciplinary and institutional boundaries. VIVO, an open source researcher networking and collaborative platform, enables the discovery of research and scholarship at a particular institution (and beyond) through detailed interlinked profiles of faculty and researchers, their scholarly activities, and other research-related information such as publications, research resources, events, funding, courses taught, awards, professional affiliations, and more. Originally designed at Cornell University in 2003, VIVO has further developed through a $12.2 million grant from the National Center for Research Resources (NCRR) of the National Institutes of Health (NIH) and now includes the seven partner institutions: the University of Florida, Cornell University, Indiana University, Ponce Medical College, the Scripps Research Institute, Washington University School of Medicine in St. Louis, and Weill Cornell Medical College (WCMC). Well established as an open source project with community participation from around the world, VIVO currently enables the international and interdisciplinary networking of researchers from over 20 countries and 50 organizations.

When researchers work across disciplinary and organizational boundaries, whether in a virtual or a non-virtual environment, they inevitably encounter a number of challenges ranging from different disciplinary cultures to different visions of project objectives that may lead to communication difficulties. For example, disciplines and organizations may have different notions of how to collect and document data, different attitudes toward technology, or different conceptions of the research outcome. Even though the VREs' technological innovations dramatically reduce the barriers to collaboration for geographically and organizationally distant researchers, the technology has not entirely conquered psychosocial issues such as personal compatibility, managing interpersonal relationships within the project, establishing trust and respect among the collaborators from different domains, and creating a sense of comfort and security among people who might have never met (Cummings and Kiesler 2005; Jankowski 2009; Kouzes, Myers, and Wulf 1996). Because these issues can become more prominent within the VREs due to the lack of frequent face-to-face communication, they require on the part of a VRE's developer the creation of clear guidelines regarding lines of authority, division of labor, ownership of data, and shared objectives.

Despite these challenges, VREs are recognized as a significant shift in conducting collaborative research made possible by the combination of technological enhancements and human "distributed intelligence." By "wiring" together geographically distributed and culturally diverse researchers (Zare 1997), VREs take advantage of their multiple perspectives, expertise, varying research methodologies, and different personalities and attitudes and thus increase the likelihood of discoveries and inventions (Cummings and Kiesler 2005; Weller 2011).

PEER REVIEW: WHAT HAS CHANGED? WHAT HAS REMAINED THE SAME?

Peer review, a practice in scholarly journal publishing (also called a prepublication peer review), has a long history. While scholars still debate the origin of prepublication peer review, most histories trace it back to the seventeenth century to the Royal Society of London and its journal called *Philosophical Transactions* (Holbrook 2010).[23]

Prepublication peer review has historically served as a "gatekeeping function" (ibid.). It is a process in which a group of external peers, who share disciplinary expertise, impose stringent criteria on acceptance of contributions for publication in an academic journal to determine whether the submitted manuscript is meritorious enough to warrant publication in that journal.[24] There are two traditional types of prepublication peer review: blind peer review and double-blind peer review. Blind peer review is a process in which the identity of the reviewers is concealed from the reviewee. Double-blind peer review is a process in which the identity of the reviewee is also concealed from the reviewers.

Peer review is "prospective" (rather than retrospective) in nature in that it "predicts the future" rather than evaluates the past, because it tries to determine whether a submitted manuscript will be well received or rejected by the discipline. From this viewpoint, peer review has been criticized for inhibiting innovation by being "inherently conservative" (Holbrook 2010), tending to favor conformity with already established research, thereby rejecting transformative or novel ideas. Other concerns among scholars about the ways, in which peer review is typically performed, include the following:

- Peer review slows up the publication or grant funding process because of the long time it takes to read manuscripts or grant proposals and to write and deliver peer review reports
- Peer review does not necessarily determine the true merit of the work or catch outdated or incorrect information in submitted manuscripts or falsified data in grant proposals
- Peer review may be biased against reviewees regardless of the merit of their work, which may not be fully appreciated by a conservative or more traditionally inclined reviewer
- Peer review allows for unethical behavior on the part of the reviewers such as using peer-review reports to promote their own work or using malicious and/ or incompetent comments (Rowland 2002; Hames 2007; Holbrook 2010)

While these are legitimate concerns, peer review does aim at serving an important purpose: to provide quality control of submitted manuscripts and proposals through the selection process and constructive criticism.

In the eResearch context, peer review is undergoing new developments as well as facing new challenges. Among them are:

- *More rapid peer review process of manuscripts submitted to electronic journals.* The peer review process takes less time because of an effective online system for peer review report submission and thus helps make research papers more rapidly available for a worldwide audience.
- *Open peer review.* Open peer review means that the reviewers' identities are disclosed, included on the peer review reports, and that these reports are (optionally) published alongside the article. Several publishers such as PLoS and BioMed Central are experimenting with the open peer review model. PLoS also encourages post-publication review in the form of comments and user ratings similar to commentary on a blog post. Like any emerging process, the practice of open peer review faces challenges to adoption and implementation. By taking the concept of openness to the next level, open peer review is questioning the traditional publisher's role and challenging the academic culture, and so far it has found little support among both researchers and publishers (Ford 2013; Kriegeskorte 2012; Ware 2013).
- *Post-publication peer review.* Some researchers argue that a published paper should not be the final step in the scholarly communication life cycle and that its post-publication critical evaluation, or post-publication peer review, should become part of the research process itself (Hunter 2012).

One of the most notable post-publication peer review services, Faculty of 1000 (http://f1000.com/), offers a rapid systematic review and rating of the most noteworthy primary research papers as judged by a panel of the world's leading researchers in the life sciences (called Faculty Members). Each Faculty Member is asked to recommend two to four published research papers a month from any source and in areas both within and outside their areas of expertise. For each paper they recommend, Faculty Members write a brief evaluative commentary and assign a rating ("recommended," "must read," or "exceptional"). They also categorize selected papers in at least one of the following areas: Novel Finding, Technical Advance, Important Confirmation, Interesting Hypothesis, and Controversial Findings. Each selected paper is assigned an F1000 Factor, which is derived from all the ratings the paper has received. Both the selected titles and the comments by Faculty Members are stored, archived, and available by subscription as a searchable database. The fact that Faculty of 1000 focuses exclusively on primary research literature (versus review articles) and identifies important papers published not only in major journals (such as *Science*, *Nature*, and *Cell*) but also in less prestigious journals makes it possible to compare scientific journals on the basis of their high-quality research articles rather than on the basis of the journals' impact factors. Faculty of 1000 offers an alternative to the way peers judge the significance of a scientific article, and subsequently scientists themselves, for they are acknowledged for their research merit and not for the journal in which they are published.

- *Peer review of data management plans.* In addition to other requirements, the National Science Foundation has mandated that data management plans will be subject to peer review and must be reviewed "as an integral part of the proposal, coming under Intellectual Merit or Broader Impacts or both, as appropriate for the scientific community of relevance" (National Science Foundation 2013).

- *Uncertainties around interdisciplinary peer review.* The process of evaluating interdisciplinary research (versus evaluating mono-disciplinary research) creates uncertainty and conflicting assumptions among reviewers (especially among those from "conceptually distant disciplines," i.e., the so-called "hard sciences" such as physics, astronomy, and mathematics, and "soft sciences" such as the social sciences and humanities) due to the lack of agreed-upon standards about the quality of research evaluation such as research goals, focus, norms, values, and expectations (Huutoniemi 2010). Overcoming this challenge requires on the part of a reviewer the commitment to new approaches such as learning new disciplinary concepts and adopting new terminology.

- *"Transdisciplinarization" of peer review.* The trend toward transdisciplinary research (discussed in Chapter 9) may extend peer review beyond the boundaries of academic disciplines and include other "peers" in the evaluation process (such as educators, policy makers, and artists), whose expertise may be particularly valuable in evaluating the extent of the societal impact of a specific research project, e.g., an educational, environmental, or aesthetic impact (Holbrook 2010).

NOTES

1. The term "working paper" is sometimes used synonymously as technical report and means the prepublication version of a journal article, book chapter, or review. Working papers are intended to encourage feedback, stimulate comments, or make research results more rapidly available to the peers and the public than it would otherwise be possible if done through a traditional publication process.

2. The IDEF0 (Integration Definition for Function Modeling) technique is based on the SADT (Structured Analysis and Design Technique) that was developed in the 1970s by Douglas T. Ross and SofTech, Inc. (Tah and Carr 2000).

3. In addition to designing the scholarly communication life cycle model, Microsoft External Research has developed a number of scholarly communication software, tools, and services that are specifically designed for researchers and educators in academia. Information about specific technologies developed by Microsoft External Research to support scholarly communication is available at: http://research .microsoft.com/en-us/collaboration/focus/education/scholarlycomm.aspx.

4. According to Lancaster (1995), Sondak and Schwarz were the first authors to come up with an idea of a scholarly journal published in electronic form that they envisioned as distribution of computer-readable "archival files" of journals to libraries and distribution of computer-output microfiche to individual subscribers (Sondak and Schwartz 1973).

5. Other terms used in literature are "eJournals," "e-journals," "electronic serials," "online journals," and "electronic periodicals." The distinction between these terms is not easily drawn. A loose definition of all these terms has been routinely used to describe any journal available electronically. A more rigid definition of "electronic journal" describes this as a journal created for the electronic medium and available only in this medium.

6. Electronic journal publishing and electronically assisted peer review help speed up the management of the peer review process. Some e-journals are also experimenting with "crowd-sourcing" the peer review process. Furthermore, authors can choose to publish articles as electronic "preprints," with or without reviewer comments attached, before a more final version is completed.

7. In June 2003, Martin Sabo, a Minnesota congressman, introduced a bill entitled the Public Access to Science Act (HR 2613). According to Sabo's bill, works resulting from scientific research substantially funded by the government would be excluded from copyright protection and become public domain. Since scientific research is largely funded by tax dollars, Sabo said, the results of research should be freely and immediately available to taxpayers who ultimately pay for conducting research. Sabo's bill poses a direct challenge to large commercial publishers. Under the established system, most scientific journals own the copyrights to research papers they publish. Authors traditionally assign copyright to the publisher, which means that they cannot freely distribute their works or allow open access to them. Under Sabo's bill, journals would not own the papers they publish.

8. A good and frequently updated overview and timeline of the open access movement is maintained by Peter Suber at Harvard University, who is considered one of the leaders of the worldwide open access movement. It can be accessed at: http:// legacy.earlham.edu/~peters/fos/overview.htm.

9. In December 2008, Harold Varmus, cofounder of the Public Library of Science and one of the most high-profile advocates of open access and the role of government in providing open access, was appointed by President-elect Barack Obama as a co-chair of the U.S. President's Council of Advisors on Science and Technology.

10. For more information about Elsevier's open access program, visit http://www.elsevier.com/openaccess.

11. In his book *Open Access* (2012), Peter Suber, who is considered one of the leaders in the OA movement and an expert on the subject, provides an overview of various open access models, including the green and gold open access models.

12. Jeffrey Beall, a University of Colorado librarian, cautions authors about deal-ing with what he calls "predatory open access publishers." According to Beall, these publishers exploit the open access publishing model for their own profit by using "deception to appear legitimate, entrapping researchers into submitting their work and then charging them to publish it" (Beall 2012). The 2014 Beall's List of predatory publishers is available at http://scholarlyoa.com/2014/01/02/list-of-predatory-publishers-2014/. The Open Access Scholarly Publishers Association (OASPA) main-tains the Code of Conduct that aims to ensure high ethical standards in OA publishing (http://oaspa.org/membership/code-of-conduct/).

13. SHERPA/RoMEO (http://www.sherpa.ac.uk/romeo) includes publishers' poli-cies on whether an author is permitted to self-archive, where, and under what conditions. It indexes policies for over 18,000 peer-reviewed journals and over 1,100 publishers.

14. There are several other models based on "open" paradigms—for example, the Open Archives Initiative aims to address concerns about the traditional journal pub-lishing model; the Open Knowledge Initiative allows educators to share learning tech-nologies; and the Open Law program enables collaboration among law professionals on creating legal arguments.

15. The terms "social network sites" and "social networking sites" are often used interchangeably in the literature and in public discourse.

16. According to Moran, Seaman, and Tinti-Kane (2011), who surveyed nearly 2,000 higher education faculty members, faculty have adopted SNS in growing num-bers also. The authors found that the majority of all surveyed were at the very least aware of the major SNS, over half of all surveyed visited Facebook in the previous month, and about 40 percent posted something to the SNS during that time period.

17. The term "weblog" is attributed to Jorn Barger, who, in 1997, called his website a "weblog." Two years later, Peter Merholz "playfully broke the word" into a pronoun and a verb, "we blog," thus giving a birth to a new noun, "blog" ("It's the Links, Stupid" 2006).

18. Arthur Caplan, a professor of bioethics at the University of Pennsylvania, com-pared blogs to an extended form of chatter that should not be treated as a trustworthy source of information (Berger 2007). In 2007, *A Blogger's Code of Conduct* (http://radar.oreilly.com/2007/03/call-for-a-bloggers-code-of-co.html) was proposed by Tim O'Reilly in response to violent threats made by a reader to blogger Kathy Sierra (O'Reilly 2008).

19. The first wiki, called WikiWikiWeb, was created by Ward Cunningham in 1995 by using the Hawaiian word "wiki" for "quick" and the allusion to the World Wide Web (Tapscott and Williams 2008).

20. The name Wikipedia, coined by a cofounder of Wikipedia, Larry Sanger, is the combination of the Hawaiian word "wiki" for "quick" and encyclopedia.

21. The wiki software was invented by Ward Cunningham in 1995 (Cunningham and Leuf 2001).

22. The term Virtual Research Environments originated in the United Kingdom in 2006 and was defined as "set of online tools, systems and processes interoperating to facilitate or enhance the research process within and without institutional boundaries" (Borda et al. 2006, 3).

23. Some authors claim that prepublication peer review did not become a common practice until 1959, when Xerox photocopiers became commercially available (Spier 2002).

24. Peer review is also used in the review of proposals for funding (grant proposal peer review) to determine whether the proposed activities deserve to receive funding. Grant proposal peer review began to be widely used around the middle of the twentieth century after the National Institutes of Health (and later the National Science Foundation) started incorporating peer review into their grant proposal evaluation practice (Spier 2002; Holbrook 2010) and in the review of applications for tenure and fellowship. Peer review may also be employed to conduct evaluation of the work of specific people, practices, or institutions, e.g., to evaluate the work performance of individual faculty members of the department relative to other faculty members of the same department or to assess strengths and weaknesses of a particular department on the institutional level.

WORKS CITED

Ba-Quy, Vuong, Ee-Peng Lim, Aixin Sun, Minh-Tam Le, Hady Wirawan Lauw, and Kuiyu Chang. "On Ranking Controversies in Wikipedia: Models and Evaluation." In *Proceedings of the 2008 International Conference on Web Search and Data Mining*, 171–82. New York: Association for Computer Machinery, 2008. doi:10.1145/1341531.1341556.

Beall, Jeffrey. "Predatory Publishing." *The Scientist*, August 1, 2012. http://www .the-scientist.com/?articles.view/articleNo/32426/title/Predatory-Publishing/ (accessed March 24, 2014).

Berger, Eric. "Emergency Medicine in the Blogosphere: The Irreverent Wit of the Specialty's Unofficial Voice." *Annals of Emergency Medicine* 49, no. 5 (2007): 612–14.

Björk, Bo-Christer. "A Model of Scientific Communication of a Global Distributed Information System." *Information Research* 12 (2007). http://InformationR .net/ir/12-2/paper307.html (accessed February 26, 2014).

Borda, Ann, Jason Careless, Maia Dimitrova, Michael Fraser, [. . .] et al. *Report of the Working Group on Virtual Research Communities for the Ost E-infrastructure Steering Group*. 2006. http://eprints.soton.ac.uk/id/eprint/42074 (accessed July 17, 2014).

Braman, Sandra. *What Do Researchers Need? Higher Education IT from the Researcher's Perspective*. Occasional Paper from the EDUCAUSE Center for Applied Research (ECAR), 2006. https://net.educause.edu/ir/library/pdf/ ECP0601.pdf (accessed February 26, 2014).

Carey, John. "Faculty of 1000 and VIVO: Invisible Colleges and Team Science." *Issues in Science and Technology Librarianship* 65 (Spring 2011). doi:10.5062/ F4F769GT.

Case, Mary M., and Judith Matz. "Framing the Issue: Open Access." *ARL: A Bimonthly Report on Research Library Issues and Actions from ARL, CNI, and SPARC* 226 (2003): 8–10.

Childers, Lisa, Terry Disz, Robert Olson, Michael E. Papka, Rick Stevens, and Tushar Udeshi. "Access Grid: Immersive Group-to-Group Collaborative Visualization." In *Proceedings, Fourth International Immersive Projection Technology Workshop* (2000). http://www.ipd.anl.gov/anlpubs/2000/07/36282.pdf (accessed February 26, 2014).

Crane, Diana. *Invisible Colleges: Diffusion of Knowledge in Scientific Communities.* Chicago: University of Chicago Press, 1972.

Creative Commons. "Attribution 3.0 United States—CC BY (3.0 US)." https://creativecommons.org/licenses/by/3.0/us/ (accessed July 17, 2014).

Cummings, Jonathon N., and Sara Kiesler. "Collaborative Research across Disciplinary and Organizational Boundaries." *Social Studies of Science* 35, no. 5 (2005): 703–22.

Cunningham, Ward, and Bo Leuf. *The Wiki Way: Quick Collaboration on the Web.* Boston: Addison-Wesley, 2001.

Dutton, William H., and Paul W. Jeffreys, eds. *World Wide Research: Reshaping the Sciences and Humanities.* Cambridge, MA: MIT Press, 2010.

Eisen, Michael. "Publish and Be Praised: Why It's High Time the Results of Scientific Research Were Freely Available to Everyone." *Guardian*, Science Pages (October 9, 2003): 6.

Ellison, Nicole B. "Social Network Sites: Definition, History, and Scholarship." *Journal of Computer-Mediated Communication* 13, no. 1 (2007): 210–30. doi:10.1111/j.1083-6101.2007.00393.x.

Engeström, Juri. "Microblogging: Tiny Social Objects: On the Future of Participatory Media, cited in K." Anderson (2008), blog entry 13 (2007). http://www.slideshare.net/jyri/microblogging-tiny-social-objects-on-the-future-of-participatory-media (accessed February 26, 2014).

Fausto, Sibele, Fabio A. Machado, Luiz Fernando J. Bento, Atila Iamarino, Tatiana R. Nahas, and David S. Munger. "Research Blogging: Indexing and Registering the Change in Science 2.0." *PloS One* 7, no. 12 (2012): e50109. doi:10.1371/journal.pone.0050109.

Finholt, Thomas A., and Gary M. Olson. "From Laboratories to Collaboratories: A New Organizational Form for Scientific Collaboration." *Psychological Science* 8, no. 1 (1997): 28–36.

Fjällbrant, Nancy. "Scholarly Communication—Historical Development and New Possibilities." *IATUL Proceedings* (1997). http://docs.lib.purdue.edu/cgi/viewcontent.cgi?article=1389&context=iatul (accessed February 26, 2014).

Ford, Emily. "Defining and Characterizing Open Peer Review: A Review of the Literature." *Journal of Scholarly Publishing* 44, no. 4 (2013): 311–26. doi:10.3138/jsp.44-4-001.

Garaizar, P., M. Vadillo, D. López-de-Ipina, and H. Matute. "The Web as a Platform for e-Research in the Social and Behavioral Sciences," In *Collaborative and Distributed E-Research: Innovations in Technologies, Strategies and Applications*, edited by Angel A. Juan et al., 34–61. Hershey, PA: IGI Global, 2012.

Grefsheim, Suzanne F., and Jocelyn A. Rankin. "Information Needs and Information Seeking in a Biomedical Research Setting: A Study of Scientists and Science

Administrators." *Journal of the Medical Library Association* 95, no. 4 (2007): 426–34. doi:10.3163/1536-5050.95.4.426.

Haines, Laura L., Jeanene Light, Donna O'Malley, and Frances A. Delwiche. "Information-Seeking Behavior of Basic Science Researchers: Implications for Library Services." *Journal of the Medical Library Association* 98, no. 1 (2010): 73–81. doi:10.3163/1536-5050.98.1.019.

Hames, Irene. *Peer Review and Manuscript Management in Scientific Journals: Guidelines for Good Practice*. Malden, MA: Blackwell Publishing, 2007.

Harley, Diane, Sophia Krzys Acord, Sarah Earl-Novell, Shannon Lawrence, and C. Judson King. *Assessing the Future Landscape of Scholarly Communication: An Exploration of Faculty Values and Needs in Seven Disciplines*. Berkeley, CA: Center for Studies in Higher Education, 2010. https://escholarship.org/uc/item/15x7385g (accessed February 26, 2014).

Hemminger, Bradley M., Dihui Lu, K. T. L. Vaughan, and Stephanie J. Adams. "Information Seeking Behavior of Academic Scientists." *Journal of the American Society for Information Science and Technology* 58, no. 14 (2007): 2205–25. doi:10.1002/asi.20686.

Holbrook, J. Britt. "Peer Review." In *The Oxford Handbook of Interdisciplinarity*, edited by Robert Frodeman et al., 321–32. Oxford: Oxford University Press, 2010.

Houghton, John W., and Charles Oppenheim. "The Economic Implications of Alternative Publishing Models." *Prometheus* 28, no. 1 (2010): 41–54. doi:10.1080/08109021003676359.

Hunter, Jane. "Post-Publication Peer Review: Opening up Scientific Conversation (Opinion Article)." *Frontiers in Computational Neuroscience* 6 (2012): 63. doi:10.3389/fncom.2012.00063.

Huutoniemi, Katri. "Evaluating Interdisciplinary Research." In *The Oxford Handbook of Interdisciplinarity*, edited by Robert Frodeman et al., 309–20. Oxford: Oxford University Press, 2010.

"It's the Links, Stupid." Special Report: New Media. *Economist*, April 20, 2006. http://www.economist.com/node/6794172 (accessed July 17, 2014).

Jankowski, Nicholas W., ed. *e-Research: Transformation in Scholarly Practice*. New York: Routledge, 2009.

Juan, Angel A., Thanasis Daradoumis, Meritxell Roca, Scott E. Grasman, and Javier Faulin, eds. *Collaborative and Distributed E-Research: Innovations in Technologies, Strategies and Applications*. Hershey, PA: IGI Global, 2012.

Kouzes, Richard T., James D. Myers, and William A. Wulf. "Collaboratories: Doing Science on the Internet." *Computer* 29, no. 8 (1996): 40–46. doi:10.1109/2.532044.

Kriegeskorte, Nikolaus. "Open Evaluation: A Vision for Entirely Transparent Post-Publication Peer Review and Rating for Science." *Frontiers in Computational Neuroscience* 6 (2012): 79. doi:10.3389/fncom.2012.00079.

Kroll, Susan, and Rick Forsman. *A Slice of Research Life: Information Support for Research in the United States*. Dublin, OH: OCLC Online Computer Library Center, Inc., 2010. http://www.oclc.org/content/dam/research/publications/library/2010/2010-15.pdf (accessed February 26, 2014).

Lancaster, Frederick. "The Evolution of Electronic Publishing." *Library Trends* 43, no. 4 (1995): 518–27.

Martin, Victoria. "Developing a Library Collection in Bioinformatics: Support for an Evolving Profession." In *Library Collection Development for Professional*

Programs: *Trends and* Best Practices, edited by Sara Holder, 269–89. Hershey, PA: IGI Global, Copyright © 2013. This material is used by permission of the publisher.

Merchant, Guy. "Unravelling the Social Network: Theory and Research." *Learning, Media and Technology* 37, no. 1 (2012): 4–19. doi:10.1080/17439884.2011 .5679922.

Moran, Mike, Jeff Seaman, and Hester Tinti-Kane. *Teaching, Learning, and Sharing: How Today's Higher Education Faculty Use Social Media*. Babson Park, MA: Babson Survey Research Group, 2011. http://files.eric.ed.gov/fulltext/ ED535130.pdf (accessed February 26, 2014).

National Institutes of Health Public Access. http://publicaccess.nih.gov/ (accessed March 29, 2014).

National Science Foundation. "Proposal Preparation Instructions." January 2013. http://www.nsf.gov/pubs/policydocs/pappguide/nsf13001/gpg_2.jsp (accessed February 23, 2014).

Newman, David, Sean Bechhofer, and David De Roure. "myExperiment: An Ontology for e-Research." In *Semantic Web Applications in Scientific Discourse*. Washington, DC, 2009. http://eprints.soton.ac.uk/id/eprint/267787 (accessed February 26, 2014).

O'Reilly T. (2008). "Call for a Blogger's Code of Conduct." *O'Reilly Radar*. http:// radar.oreilly.com/2007/03/call-for-a-bloggers-code-of-co.html (accessed July 17, 2014).

Rowland, Fytton. "The Peer-Review Process." *Learned Publishing* 15, no. 4 (2002): 247–58.

Shema, Hadas, Judit Bar-Ilan, and Mike Thelwall. "Research Blogs and the Discussion of Scholarly Information." *PloS One* 7, no. 5 (2012): e35869. doi:10.1371/ journal.pone.0035869.

Sondak, Norman E., and R. J. Schwartz. "Paperless Journal." *Chemical Engineering Progress* 69, no. 1 (1973): 82–83.

Sonnenwald, Diane H., Ronald E. Bergquist, Kelly L. Maglaughlin, Eileen Kupstas-Soo, and Mary C. Whitton. "Designing to Support Collaborative Scientific Research across Distances: The nanoManipulator Environment." In *Collaborative Virtual Environments*, 202–24. London: Springer, 2001.

Spencer-Oatey, Helen. "Theories of Identity and the Analysis of Face." *Journal of Pragmatics* 39, no. 4 (2007): 639–56. doi:10.1016/j.pragma.2006.12.004.

Spier, Ray. "The History of the Peer Review Process." *Trends in Biotechnology* 20, no. 8 (2002): 357–58. doi:10.1016/S0167-7799(02)01985-6.

Surowiecki, James. *The Wisdom of Crowds*. New York: Random House, 2005.

Swan, Alma. *Modelling Scholarly Communication Options: Costs and Benefits for Universities*. Joint Information Systems Committee, Bristol, London, 2010. http://ie-repository.jisc.ac.uk/442/ (accessed February 26, 2014).

Tapscott, Don, and Anthony D. Williams. *Wikinomics: How Mass Collaboration Changes Everything*. New York: Portfolio, 2008.

Veletsianos, George, and Royce Kimmons. "Scholars and Faculty Members' Lived Experiences in Online Social Networks." *Internet and Higher Education* 16 (2013): 43–50. doi:10.1016/j.iheduc.2012.01.004.

Waldrop, M. Mitchell. "Science 2.0: Great New Tool, or Great Risk? Wikis, Blogs and Other Collaborative Web Technologies Could Usher in a New Era of

Science. Or Not." *Scientific American* 298, no. 5 (2008): 68–73. doi:10.1038/scientificamerican0508-68.

Ware, Mark. "Current Peer Review Practice and Perceptions: The View from the Field." *Against the Grain* 21, no. 3 (2013): 7. http://docs.lib.purdue.edu/atg/vol21/iss3/7/ (accessed February 26, 2014).

Weller, Martin. *The Digital Scholar: How Technology Is Transforming Academic Practice*. London: A&C Black, 2011.

West, James A., and Margaret L. West. *Using Wikis for Online Collaboration: The Power of the Read-Write Web*. San Francisco, CA: Jossey-Bass, 2008.

Wouters, Paul, Anne Beaulieu, Andrea Scharnhorst, and Sally Wyatt, eds. *Virtual Knowledge: Experimenting in the Humanities and the Social Sciences*. Cambridge, MA: MIT Press, 2013.

Wulf, William A. "The National Collaboratory—a White Paper." Appendix A in *Toward a National Collaboratory*, unpublished report of a National Science Foundation invitational workshop held at Rockefeller University, 1989. Washington, DC: National Science Foundation, 1989.

Zare, Richard N. "Knowledge and Distributed Intelligence." *Science* 275, no. 5303 (1997): 1047. doi:10.1126/science.275.5303.1047.

SUGGESTED READINGS

Carusi, Annamaria, and Marina Jirotka. "Reshaping Research Collaborations: The Case of Virtual Research Environments." In *World Wide Research: Reshaping the Sciences and Humanities*. Cambridge, MA: MIT Press, 2010.

Crane, Diana. *Invisible Colleges: Diffusion of Knowledge in Scientific Communities*. Chicago: University of Chicago Press, 1972.

Finholt, Thomas A. (2002) "Collaboratories." *Annual Review of Information Science and Technology* 36, no. 1 (2005): 73–107.

Olson, Gary M., Ann Zimmerman, and Nathan Bos, eds. *Scientific Collaboration on the Internet*. Cambridge, MA: MIT Press, 2008.

Parker, John, N., Niki Vermeulen, and Bart Penders, eds. *Collaboration in the New Life Sciences*. Burlington, VT: Ashgate Publishing Company, 2010.

Sonnenwald, Dianne H. "Scientific Collaboration." *Annual Review of Information Science and Technology* 41, no. 1 (2007): 643–81.

Suber, Peter. *Open Access*. Cambridge, MA: MIT Press, 2012.

Tah, J. H. M., and V. Carr. "Information Modelling for a Construction Project Risk Management System." *Engineering Construction and Architectural Management* 7, no. 2 (2000): 107–19.

Voss, Alexander, and Rob Procter. "Virtual Research Environments in Scholarly Work and Communications." *Library Hi Tech Journal* 27, no 2 (2009): 174–90.

Willinsky, John. *The Access Principle: The Case for Open Access to Research and Scholarship*. Cambridge, MA: MIT Press, 2005.

5

eResearch across Disciplines

Here in the union of arts, humanities, and science, finally, we find the true
origin of all encompassing wisdom.
                                                        —Richard R. Ernst (2000, 127)

BIOLOGICAL SCIENCES: RESEARCHING
IN THE AGE OF "OMICS"

In the biological sciences,[1] multidisciplinary, data-driven research methods
are increasingly prevalent in the quest for new knowledge and often employ
the use of data generated in the laboratory setting, computationally imported
data, or a combination of the two. Laboratory research techniques are evolving rapidly as computational means for data collection, analysis, and simulation have become integral to traditional and novel experimentation methods.
Drawing on a wide range of disciplines, including such traditional fields as
biology and such emergent fields as bioinformatics, the rapidly growing biosciences research field also utilizes computational techniques borrowed from
other "nonbiological" fields such as computer science, artificial intelligence,
information technology, engineering, statistics, and mathematics.

> The combined strength of scientific collaboration across several disci-
> plines has brought [bioscientists] closer to an understanding of living
> systems across multiple levels of biological organization and has
> improved [the bioscientists' capacity] to understand the root causes of
> human, plant, and animal diseases and to find new cures for
> them. . . .
>   This confluence of technological and scientific advancements,
> coupled with the power of the Internet, has enabled researchers to com-
> municate with colleagues more quickly and efficiently and to share

biological data with other scientists in a collaborative [manner], while dramatically improving the productivity of [biosciences] research. It has taken research from a place where it was common to study a biological problem one gene at a time to today's standard, where it is possible to model multiple genes working together as they perform complex biological functions. It has enabled bioscientists, in just over a decade, to map the entire human genome. The Human Genome Project, started in 1990 and completed in 2002, mapped and sequenced the three billion nucleotide bases of DNA in human cells. The studies of DNA variation have continued in the International HapMap Project (completed in 2005 [and freely available on the Web]), which described the common patterns of human genetic variation.

Since the completion of these two projects [in accordance with the concept of "big science,"] a Genome-Wide Association Study (GWAS) was undertaken in 2005 with the purpose of uncovering the associations between genetic variants and human diseases and traits. These discoveries are making tremendous contributions to mankind, such as new drug design and development, diagnoses of hereditary diseases, and gene therapy and treatments. The impact of [biosciences research] is not . . . limited to the health care field. It has many practical applications in environmental science, biotechnology, and agriculture, [including] genetic engineering of drought-and-disease-resistant plants and microbial genome alterations for energy production, environmental cleanup, [industrial processing,] and waste reduction. (Martin 2013)

Financial support from the government has played a key role in the advancement of biosciences research, which has been supported through grants from the National Science Foundation (NSF), the National Institutes of Health (NIH), the Department of Energy (DOE), and other organizations. The establishment of specialized research institutes throughout the world, such as the National Center for Biotechnology Information (NCBI) in the United States and the European Bioinformatics Institute (EBI), located in Great Britain, has also been crucial to the growth of bioscience research.

PHYSICAL SCIENCES: EXPLORING THE PREVIOUSLY UNSEEN

The situation is similar in the physical sciences, where a single computer or a generic computing network is no longer sufficient to successfully process the data for complex physical science analyses and simulations, and where a collaboration of scientists from multiple disciplines must often be employed.[2] Physical scientists, who have traditionally aimed at discovering laws to explain observed physical phenomena, progressively rely on a highly distributed, advanced computing technology, model simulation, and visualization tools that can enable greater discoveries and explorations, both in outer space and in the macro- and micro- worlds.

One example of a major exploration of outer space is, undoubtedly, the Hubble Space Telescope project (http://hubble.nasa.gov/). It integrates advances from the physical and computational sciences that allow scientists to photograph the farthest stars, planets, and galaxies ever seen and that help them understand how these stars, planets, and galaxies form and evolve. What is more, the images obtained through the Hubble Space Telescope can be accessed freely through the Internet, regardless of location. This project, among others, serves as an example of how science supports and promotes the principle of openness in research.

Over the past few decades, Geographic Information Systems (GIS) have become an indispensable research tool in the study of the earth. GIS, a collection of geo-visualization software tools designed to manipulate geographic data, enables users to map spatial data, query and access map-related information, and perform predictive modeling in order to develop a greater understanding of the earth and its resources. Even though GIS tools have found the strongest application in geographic information science (GIScience),[3] they have also been widely used in other disciplines, including geology, archaeology, agriculture, environmental science, conservation biology, economics, political science, sociology, public health, history, and many others. Moreover, government and business organizations apply GIS tools to analyzing complex problems and decision making regarding land, resource, and facilities management; urban planning; and biodiversity preservation. In the public health setting, GIS tools have been applied to analyzing humanitarian emergencies such as hazard, vulnerability, and risk assessments, along with disease distribution and outbreak investigations. The wide use and rapid advancement of the GIS technology have also impacted higher education. Many colleges and universities around the world have either incorporated the study of GIS into their courses or created undergraduate, graduate, and postgraduate programs in GIS (Hasmadi and Imas 2010).

In recent years, spatial computing has become one of the core technologies for catalyzing advancements in the physical sciences, especially in the area of geoinformatics research. Spatial computing, which can be defined as a set of technologies that utilizes the concepts of space and time in computation, enables more effective analyses of geographical problems and physical phenomena. Large-scale projects, such as the Global Earth Observation System of Systems (GEOSS) (http://www.earthobservations.org/geoss.shtml), that aims to integrate a wide diversity of geographical observation data to address local- and global-scale issues, and the Spatial Data Infrastructure (SDI) (http://www.gsdi.org/SDILinks), that attempts to design infrastructure that would allow to share spatial data seamlessly, seek to address some of the world's fundamental problems—global climate change, ineffective emergency response (e.g., in forecasting tsunamis), and greater diffusion of contagious diseases, among others—that must be viewed in a multidimensional context in order to be effectively resolved.

At the atomic, molecular, and macromolecular levels, nanotechnologies have been found to be a radical source of innovation.[4] These technologies have a close relationship with precision engineering and enable researchers to observe and manipulate the previously unseen material—for example, individual molecules, atoms, and atomic bonds—that can lead to the formation of new structures that have never previously existed. In microscopy, multiple disciplines—biology, physics, and engineering—work together to enhance materials and services across various applications, including health care. For example, advanced telemicroscopy techniques allow users to control a microscope in one city from a laboratory in another by the use of high-speed, continent-spanning data networks and computer technology. These techniques assist in the diagnosis and treatment of patients with chronic conditions in their own homes.

eSOCIAL SCIENCE: WORKING WITH HUMAN DATA

Social scientists face a "data deluge" that is comparable to their colleagues in the other sciences.[5] Just as these other scientists apply computational technology tools to processing vast amounts of physical and biological data, so do researchers in the social sciences rely on the computer-aided manipulation of high volumes of human data that include information about nearly every facet of people's behavior and activity. Some of these data are obtained from the Social Web, as in posts on social networking sites, responses to online surveys, and product and service reviews; some from computer-mediated transactions and administrative records; and some from spatial and surveillance data such as GPS devices and mobile phone logs (Halfpenny and Procter 2010). Webometrics, a relatively new field of quantitative social science research, uses data from the World Wide Web such as hyperlinks between webpages in order to identify, among other factors, the visibility of websites. Human data from such large-scale sources as the Internet is at the heart of today's research in the social sciences. Furthermore, computational techniques, such as modeling and simulation, help address one of the core concerns of traditional social science research, which is "the inextricability of the subject of their research from its environment" (Brantingham et al. 2009, 13). The modeling and simulation software tools help social scientists overcome this limitation by creating scenarios inside a virtual environment and allow them to study human subjects and situations that would be difficult or impossible to study in real life (for example, in studying criminal activity) (Brantingham et al. 2009; Glässer and Vajihollahi 2008).

In 2005, a National Science Foundation (NSF) Workshop on Cyberinfrastructure and the Social Sciences concluded that cyberinfrastructure is "just as critical for the advancement of the social, behavioral, and economic (SBE) sciences as it is for engineering and the physical, natural, biological, and computer sciences," and that "the SBE sciences can also help assess the effects of cyberinfrastructure on science, engineering, technology, and society so that its potential can be realized and its benefits maximized" (Berman and Brady 2005, 4). The National Science Foundation (NSF) further identified four specific areas where data-intensive social science research seems to be particularly relevant: (1) population change; (2) source of disparities; (3) communication, language, and linguistics; and (4) technology, new media, and social networks (Gutmann and Friedlander 2011).

This vision led to the creation of a new research field—eSocial science (sometimes termed digital social research or computational social science). Existing at the intersection of computer science, statistics, and the social sciences, eSocial science is an emerging field that uses advanced information and computational technologies to generate and analyze human data. In eSocial science, researchers from disparate fields, including computer science and engineering, combine their expertise to investigate new ideas in a collaborative manner and, capitalizing on their multiple perspectives and expertise, use a wide variety of computational tools—from statistical analysis software to multidimensional visualizations—to analyze social trends and patterns and offer solutions for complex social problems. Around the world, eSocial science national initiatives, have been launched to provide insights on legal, ethical, policy, and other social issues. In Great Britain, this includes, for example, the National Centre for e-Social Science (NCeSS), now the Manchester eResearch Centre (MeRC), that was formed to stimulate the creation of computer-based tools and services for social sciences research. In the United States, the Institute for Computing in Humanities, Arts, and Social Science (I-CHASS) at the University of Illinois at Urbana-Champaign breaks new ground in computing in the social sciences, humanities, and arts.

DIGITAL HUMANITIES: TRANSFORMING THE STUDY OF HUMAN CULTURE

> [D]igital humanities stand not in opposition to the past, but on its shoulders.
> —Jeffrey Schnapp (2012)

The traditional goal of humanities research has been "to better understand ourselves, our history, and our cultural heritage" (Arthur 2012).[6] To achieve this goal, the humanities scholars collect and analyze research data from primary sources such as ancient manuscripts, excavated artifacts, original printed editions of classical works, and images of art and cultural objects (as well as the objects themselves). In this context, the humanities research is considered primarily qualitative rather than quantitative, acknowledging the subjective element and "hermeneutic and practice-led nature" of the research (Anderson, Blanke, and Dunn 2010).

Even though the traditional goal of humanities research has not changed, computational and information technologies are transforming, just as in other disciplines, the way humanities scholars conduct research, archive, and present their research findings to their peers and to a wider audience. As humanities research is being increasingly mediated through digital technology, a new mode of humanities scholarship—digital humanities—is gaining prominence as a recognized discipline within the field, with its own manifestos, scholarly associations, conferences, training and degree programs, journals, a growing body of experts, and encoding conventions for computer-readable texts.[7]

Digital humanities (originally called "computing in the humanities" or "humanities computing" and often abbreviated DH)[8] can be defined as "the application of information technology as an aid to fulfill the humanities basic tasks of preserving, reconstructing, transmitting, and interpreting the human record" (Frischer 2011, 28).[9] The field of digital humanities emerged in the late 1990s[10] when humanities projects became more technologically complex, involving advanced computational techniques to draw on and support the discipline's traditional core strengths such as "attention to complexity, medium specificity, historical context, analytical depth, critique and interpretation" (Schnapp and Presner 2009).[11]

For some time, the field of digital humanities has been considered a support service for "real" humanities scholars rather than as a creative endeavor in its own right (Berry 2012). This fact might explain, at least to some degree, why eResearch is still at an earlier stage of development in the humanities than in the sciences and social sciences. In addition, humanities scholars have been perceived in traditional terms as working largely on their own and being less dependent on technology than scholars in the sciences.

This perception of a humanities researcher as "a lone scholar" who prefers informal communication with his peers, works primarily with print-based materials, and in terms of technology requires only "general-purpose" computing resources such as a computer and the Internet to aid a research task at hand is changing with the rapid ascent and visibility of digital humanities in the scholarly community. Recent studies suggest that in addition to traditional printed and empirical research materials, humanities scholars utilize a wide variety of digital resources and formats for their research such as: text mining software of digitized resources; hypertextual scholarly archives; the Geographical Information Systems (GIS) for mapping historical trends and patterns; spatial technology to collect, store, analyze, and represent information in digital data sets; virtual reconstruction of fragile objects from antiquity; and three-dimensional scans of artifacts (Bulger et al. 2011; Meyer et al. 2009; Van Zundert et al. 2012).[12]

Humanities researchers are also increasingly engaging in large-scale collaborative projects, partly in response to funding opportunities but also in response to research possibilities opened up by text-mining, visualization, and advanced media tools. Examples of large-scale collaborative projects in the humanities include the Perseus Digital Library (PDL) project (http://www.perseus.tufts.edu/hopper/), a project that converts the corpus of classical Greco-Roman literature into digital form; and the Mapping the Republic of Letters Project (http://republicofletters.stanford.edu/), an initiative that uses digital technology to map and interpret correspondence among eighteenth-century American and European intellectuals.

Furthermore, humanities researchers have begun to engage in projects that require the expertise of researchers from multiple, often overlapping humanities fields. For example, the Ancient World Mapping Center (http://awmc.unc.edu/wordpress/), at the University of North Carolina at Chapel Hill, is an interdisciplinary collaborative project of historians, cartographers, and philologists that offers access to digitized maps, articles, images of artifacts, and bibliographies of the ancient world. Another example of such interdisciplinary transference includes the Archimedes Palimpsest project, a collaborative work between Walters Art Gallery, Rochester Institute of Technology, and the Stanford Linear Accelerator Center. The purpose of this project is to decipher the text in a tenth-century manuscript that includes seven treatises of Archimedes.

Web 2.0 tools, such as blogs and wikis, have proven to be useful for establishing new forums in the field and have promoted greater virtual collaboration among humanities scholars who are interested in sharing ideas, finding research peers, and identifying best practices in the field, among other possibilities. Examples of Web 2.0–based projects include the open access collaborative translation of Plato's *Protagoras* (http://openprotagoras.wikidot.com/), and the Digital Classicist wiki (http://wiki.digitalclassicist.org/) that serves as a hub for digital scholarship in classical studies.

Digital humanities scholars are taking their research one step further by establishing cross-disciplinary alliances with researchers and practitioners working in science, technology, and engineering fields. These alliances rely on the expertise (in addition to research and disciplinary skills) of various professionals, such as software programmers, graphic designers, interface engineers, and computer technologists, and blur the boundaries between scholarship and practice. Growing cross-disciplinary collaborations are demonstrated by such international networks as centerNet (http://digitalhumanities.org/centernet/) that includes more than 200 digital humanities centers. Moreover, their engagement with new technologies and other disciplines has led to the creation of new fields of study in the humanities, among which are cultural informatics, historical GIS, archaeological computing, and virtual heritage, which are positioned at the intersection of the humanities and computational sciences.[13]

While digital technology has made a profound impact on the humanities practices and research environment, the mere application of digital tools to humanities research (or simply the study of digital objects in place of physical objects) does not "qualify" as digital humanities (Schnapp 2012). The field of digital humanities is defined by the creative confluence of traditional and new research modes. Even though the methodology and practices of traditional and digital humanities may differ, they pursue a common goal—to analyze, interpret, and preserve what Panofsky (1955) called "the records left by man" and to address and reflect upon the human condition.

ARTISTS AS RESEARCHERS: INTEGRATING SCHOLARLY AND IMAGINATIVE INQUIRIES

> I never made a painting as a work of art, it's all research.
>   —Pablo Picasso

Art as research, or artistic research, is a relatively young concept that is still searching for an authoritative definition. Some scholars say that artistic research is a process that involves both the research process and the creation of artistic works, i.e., the research "in and through" the acts of creating and performing (Biggs and Karlsson 2010; Jefferies 2010; Wesseling 2011), while others argue that artistic investigations (i.e., creative endeavors undertaken by artists in studios, theaters, ateliers, or other places where artists work) are themselves a form of research grounded in practice, the form that simply follows a research path different from that in other fields (Sullivan 2010). In either case, art as research, in which the object (a work of art) is closely connected to the creator of that object (the artist), stands in contradistinction to the study of art such as in the disciplines of art history or art criticism, in which works of art simply serve as the object of study.[14] Thus, in artistic research, art and research are not two separate domains, but rather the two essential components of the research process. As Boomgaard (2011) stated, artists as researchers do not only "investigate an 'object,' but they also investigate with the aid of the 'object' " (70), which can be an image, a piece of music, or a performance. In these terms, the creative process and a work of art carry their own status as a form of new knowledge because of their capacity "to transform human understanding" (Sullivan 2010) and form "the pathway . . . through which new insights, understandings and products come into being" (Borgdorff 2010, 46). Nonetheless, the concept of artistic research, how it relates to academic research, whether the "new knowledge" it generates can be judged by the same terms as in other academic fields and how art-based research is to differentiate itself from fine art are still a matter of debate, even though the granting of doctoral degrees to artists (writers, composers, and painters) based on their artwork is a common practice in academia (Biggs and Karlsson 2010; Jefferies 2010; Sullivan 2010; Wesseling 2011).

Despite the differences of opinion that exist within the academic community about the place and role of the arts[15] in academic research, artists have been frequent collaborators on research projects in various academic fields.

Such disciplines as anthropology, ethnography, and sociology often rely on audio-visual authentication of data and have a tradition of using artistic practices—e.g., film, sound, drawing, and photography—that "can authenticate a research report in a way that words alone cannot" (Ball and Smith 1992, 9). Medical sciences have for centuries depended on art in the form of anatomical illustrations that is evident in the work of Leonardo da Vinci, Andreas Vesalius, and Henry Gray.

Although the adoption of advanced computational technologies, such as the Grid technologies, has been slower in the arts than in other research fields, the arts are increasingly utilizing digital techniques and tools to expand their traditional practices and methodologies.[16] Such tools as advanced text recognition, 3D visualization and imaging, and computer-mediated studios are becoming integral to certain digital art practices such as data visualization, visual digital art, and interactive graphic representation. The technical complexity of artistic research (that is particularly evident in digital art practices) consists of a wide array of technological inputs and outputs, including "pathways, nodes, links, networks, and connecting loops between visual, sonic, textual, and graphic elements" (Lovejoy 2004), and often requires artists to form alliances with experts with disparate skill sets such as computer scientists, engineers, and programmers who not only help them create instruments for making artworks, but also bring the best of their knowledge and experience together in innovative ways.

Furthermore, artists are making equal contributions to research by engaging in collaborative transdisciplinary projects with scientists, engineers, urban planners, and government officials on the projects that lead to transformations of economy and culture. As Wilson (1999) stated, "artists must work at the heart of the research process and not just as consumers of technological gadgets" (187). Examples of such collaborations include ecological art projects, in which works of art (sculpture, graphic design, and architecture) are used in combination with landscape and city design to enable a more empathic understanding of global environmental issues. Another example of how the arts and sciences work side by side is the advocacy of projects in epidemic disease, e.g., AIDS; or in stem cell research, on the projects in which visual artists present scientific concepts to the public in imaginative but convincing ways. Such collaborations between the arts and sciences (what Malina [2012] called "the third culture") enable scholars to view a research problem from different perspectives and thus have a more pronounced and more direct social and scholarly impact.

Within their disciplinary domain, artists have been particularly enthusiastic about the digitization of their resources that enables a new level of interaction with original artistic creations and dramatically increases the efficiency with which they can be discovered by other artists and the public. Examples include ARTStor (http://www.artstor.org/index.shtml), which holds hundreds of thousands of digital images contributed by museums, archaeological teams, and photo archive organizations; JSTOR (http://www.jstor.org/), a full-text digital archive of journal articles in many academic fields, including arts, literature, and humanities; and Europeana (http://www.europeana.eu/), a combination of digital library, museum, and archive that allows the users to search and browse through millions of digital images, texts, sounds, and videos held in museums and other cultural institutions across Europe. In musicology, the ASTRA (Ancient instruments Sound/Timbre Reconstruction Application) project (http://www.astraproject.org/index.html) brings together a team of scientists and musicians who aim to reconstruct the sound or timbre of ancient instruments, such as the epigonion, barbiton, syrinx, salpinx, and aulos, by using a technique called physical modeling synthesis to recreate these lost sounds. Once reconstructed, ASTRA's Lost Sounds Orchestra brings these instruments to life, giving performances using the reconstructed ancient instruments.

CONCLUDING REMARKS

Even though eResearch practices are no longer tied exclusively to the science disciplines, the degree to which these practices are adopted elsewhere is still discipline-dependent, and comparisons between the scholarly fields are inevitable (Appelbe and Bannon 2007; Collins, Bulger, and Meyer 2012). Scholars in various fields generate data and conduct research in diverse ways, and sensitivity to their traditional practices and epistemic methodologies is important. Disciplinary norms also affect the extent to which researchers incorporate digital technologies into their practice. Furthermore, research styles vary in different disciplines and are affected by disciplinary culture. The humanities and the arts, for example, have historically emphasized individual research and creative activities and outputs, such as a solo-authored book or a musical composition, rather than activities in and outputs from collaborative research teams (Berry 2012; Collins, Bulger, and Meyer 2012).

Although the comparison between disciplines is unavoidable, the core premise of eResearch across disciplines is the balance between respecting disciplinary differences and being open to change. Each scholarly field carries its unique set of disciplinary research methods and practices that is not easily amenable to change, but the possibilities opened up by computational and information technologies and research funding opportunities have had transformative consequences for all scholarly fields. Furthermore, dissolving of traditional disciplinary boundaries and engaging in scholarly activities that involve interdisciplinary interactions is becoming a common practice for most disciplines. This demonstrates that research practices and approaches evolve and change over time, not only by means of disciplinary differentiation, but also by disciplinary integration. In the eResearch environment, this integration of different knowledge domains is evidenced in the concrete manner in which disciplines interrelate and mutually enhance each other, and in how scholarship is moving toward a more global scale, even though, in contrast with already well-established research practices, this evolution is still ongoing.

NOTES

1. The biological sciences (also called the life sciences or biosciences) encompass all the disciplines that study living organisms—plants, animals, humans, and microorganisms, including biology, molecular biology, and microbiology, as well as many interdisciplinary fields such as biochemistry, biomedicine, biotechnology, bioinformatics, bioengineering, and so on.

2. The physical sciences, namely astronomy, chemistry, earth sciences, and physics, include the study of inanimate objects and the functions of matter and energy.

3. The term *geographic information science* (GIScience) was first defined in 1992 by Goodchild as "research on the generic issues that surround the use of GIS technology, impede its successful implementation, or emerge from an understanding of its potential capabilities" (Goodchild 1992, 31). Goodchild also noted that GIScience involved both research on GIS and research with GIS.

4. The online Merriam-Webster dictionary defines nanotechnology as the science of manipulating materials on an atomic or molecular scale especially to build microscopic devices (as robots) ("Nanotechnology," Merriam-Webster.com 2014).

5. The social sciences include anthropology, criminology, economics, education, law, political science, psychology, and sociology, among many other disciplines.

6. The humanities encompass such disciplines as archaeology, classical studies, history, linguistics, literature, and philosophy.

7. For an example of a digital humanities manifesto, see Schnapp and Presner (2009). Prominent scholarly organizations in the digital humanities include the Association for Literary and Linguistic Computing (ALLC), the Association for Computers and the Humanities (ACH), and the Alliance of Digital Humanities Organizations (ADHO). ADHO sponsors annual international conferences called "Digital Humanities." An example of a training program is the annual Digital Humanities Summer Institute (DHSI) at the University of Victoria, Canada, that provides training for scholars new to the field. Degree programs in the digital humanities are offered at such institutions as the University of California at Los Angeles (an undergraduate minor and a graduate certificate program), Kings College in London (MA and PhD programs), Loyola University in Chicago (MA program), and University of Alberta in Canada (MA program). The first specialized journal in the digital humanities— *Computers and the Humanities*—was published in 1966. Other prominent journals in the field include *Digital Humanities Quarterly* (DHQ) and *Literary and Linguistic Computing*. The Text Encoding Initiative (TEI), an international project seeking to develop encoding conventions for computer-readable texts, issued its Guidelines for Electronic Text Encoding and Interchange in 1994. These guidelines have achieved increasing importance not only in the humanities scholarship, but also across other disciplines and industries that use encoding conventions for electronic text types.

8. Hayles (2012) believes that the term "digital humanities" was coined by scholars at IATH (Institute for Advanced Technology in the Humanities) in the end of 1990s to replace the term "humanities computing," while Unsworth, who was at the time the director of the Institute for Advanced Technology in the Humanities at the University of Virginia, credits himself for suggesting the use of the term "digital humanities" for the book title *Companion to Digital Humanities* instead of *Companion to Digitized Humanities* "to shift the emphasis away from simple digitization" (Kirschenbaum 2012, 5).

9. Sengers (1999) introduced another term—"cultural informatics"—to describe the "confluence of computation and humanities."

10. Some authors argue that the beginning of digital humanities can be traced to 1949 when an Italian Jesuit priest, Roberto Busa, in collaboration with IBM, began working on creating an electronic text version of a concordance for the works of Thomas Aquinas. In 1980, Busa published *The Index Thomisticus*, first in print, then electronically. *The Index Thomisticus*, one of the major scholarly sources for philosophers, medievalists, Latin linguists, and theologians, is considered to be the first project in humanities computing (Gold 2012; Smith 2002; Schnapp 2012). For more information on this project, see Busa (1980) and Hockey (2004).

11. According to several authors (Berry 2012; Hayles 2012; Schnapp and Presner 2009), there have been at least three "waves" of development of digital humanities scholarship: (1) the first wave of digital humanities focused on digitization projects and building of the technological infrastructure; (2) the second wave of digital humanities (Digital Humanities 2.0) deals mostly with "born digital" materials such as Web-based literature and artifacts; and (3) the third wave of digital humanities (described as a "computational turn") focuses on the "computationality," i.e., on how information is transformed into knowledge through the use of computational techniques.

12. Digital humanities researchers often present their scholarship only in digital formats.

13. Unlike in the sciences, where the digitization of research was largely supported by academic or research organizations, libraries and museums have played a leading role in the advancement of the digital humanities. They were among the first organizations to establish digital repositories and digitization programs, to create and enhance online text and image collections, and to communicate the humanities research outputs to the public in widely accessible formats.

14. The humanities and social sciences may also make art practice their object of study.

15. The arts include literary arts (poetry and fiction), visual arts (painting, photography, sculpture, and architecture), and performing arts (drama, dance, and music).

16. The intersection of the arts and computer technology is not new: computer technology has been used in the arts since computers became available in the early 1960s. However, the use of digital technology in the field has increased significantly only since the early 1990s (Unsworth 2006). The field of artistic research has expanded since the turn of the century when a growing number of scholarly books was published on the topic and several academic journals were launched, among which are *Journal of Artistic Research*, *Leonardo*, and *Technoetic Arts: A Journal of Speculative Research*.

WORKS CITED

Anderson, Sheila, Tobias Blanke, and Stuart Dunn. "Methodological Commons: Arts and Humanities e-Science fundamentals." *Philosophical Transactions of the Royal Society A: Mathematical, Physical and Engineering Sciences* 368, no. 1925 (2010): 3779–96. doi:10.1098/rsta.2010.0156.

Appelbe, Bill, and David Bannon. "eResearch—Paradigm Shift or Propaganda?" *Journal of Research and Practice in Information Technology*, 39, no. 2 (2007): 83–90. http://ws.acs.org.au/jrpit/JRPITVolumes/JRPIT39/JRPIT39.2.83.pdf (accessed July 1, 2014).

Arthur, Paul. "Connecting and Enabling the Humanities: e-Research in the Border Zone." In *Collaborative and Distributed E-Research: Innovations in Technologies, Strategies and Applications*, edited by Angel A. Juan et al. Hershey, PA: IGI Global, 2012.

Ball, Michael, and Gregory Smith, eds. *Analyzing Visual Data*. Newbury Park, CA: Sage Publications, 1992.

Berman, Francine Denise, and Henry E. Brady. *Final Report: NSF SBE-CISE Workshop on Cyberinfrastructure and the Social Sciences*. Arlington, VA: National Science Foundation, 2005. http://ucdata.berkeley.edu/pubs/CyberInfrastructure_FINAL.pdf (accessed July 1, 2014).

Berry, David M., ed. *Understanding Digital Humanities*. New York: Palgrave Macmillan, 2012.

Biggs, Michael, and Henrik Karlsson, eds. *The Routledge Companion to Research in the Arts*. New York: Routledge, 2010.

Boomgaard, Jeroen. "The Chimera of Method." In *See It Again, Say It Again: The Artist as Researcher*, edited by Janneke Wesseling, 58–71. Amsterdam: Valiz, 2011.

Borgdorff, Henk. "The Production of Knowledge in Artistic Research." In *The Routledge Companion to Research in the Arts*, edited by Michael Biggs and Henrik Karlsson, 44–63. New York: Routledge, 2010.

Brantingham, Patricia, Uwe Glässer, Piper Jackson, and Mona Vajihollahi. "Modeling Criminal Activity in Urban Landscapes." In *Mathematical Methods in Counterterrorism*, edited by N. Memon, J. D. Farley, D. Hicks, and T. Rosenorn, 9–31. Vienna: Springer Vienna, 2009.

Bulger, Monica E., Eric T. Meyer, Grace De la Flor, Melissa Terras, Sally Wyatt, Marina Jirotka, Katherine Eccles, and Christine McCarthy Madsen. "Reinventing Research? Information Practices in the Humanities." *Information Practices in the Humanities (March 2011)*. A Research Information Network Report, April 2011. http://papers.ssrn.com/sol3/papers.cfm?abstract_id=1859267 (accessed April 14, 2014).

Busa, Roberto. "The Annals of Humanities Computing: The Index Thomisticus." *Computers and the Humanities* 14 (1980): 83–90.

Collins, Ellen, Monica E. Bulger, and Eric T. Meyer. "Discipline Matters: Technology Use in the Humanities." *Arts and Humanities in Higher Education* 11, no. 1–2 (2012): 76–92. doi:10.1177/1474022211427421.

Ernst, Richard. "Societal Responsibility of Universities, Wisdom and Foresight Leading to a Better World." In *Transdisciplinarity: ReCreating Integrated Knowledge*, edited by Margaret A. Sommerville and David J. Rapport, 121–36. Oxford: EOLSS Publishers Co., 2000.

Frischer, Bernard. "Art and Science in the Age of Digital Reproduction: From Mimetic Representation to Interactive Virtual Reality." *Virtual Archaeology Review* 2, no. 4 (2011): 19–32. http://varjournal.es/doc/varj02_004_06.pdf (accessed July 21, 2014).

Glässer, Uwe, and Mona Vajihollahi. "Computational Modeling of Criminal Activity." In *Intelligence and Security Informatics*, edited by H. Wang, C. Zeng, and M. Chang, 39–50. Berlin: Springer Berlin Heidelberg, 2008.

Goodchild, Michael F. "Geographical Information Science." *International Journal of Geographical Information Systems* 6, no. 1 (1992): 31–45.

Gutmann, Myron P., and Amy Friedlander. *Rebuilding the Mosaic: Fostering Research in the Social, Behavioral, and Economic Sciences at the National Science Foundation in the Next Decade*. Arlington, VA: National Science Foundation, 2011.

Halfpenny, Peter, and Rob Procter. "The e-Social Science Research Agenda." *Philosophical Transactions of the Royal Society A: Mathematical, Physical and Engineering Sciences* 368, no. 1925 (2010): 3761–78. doi:10.1098/rsta.2010.0154.

Hasmadi, Ismail Mohd, and Sukaesih Sitangang Imas. "Empowering GIS Education Program: Is GIS as a Science, Art or Tool?" *Journal of GIS Trends* 1, no. 1 (2010): 1–7. http://www.asciencejournal.net/asj/index.php/GIST/article/view/55/MOHD%20HASMADI (accessed July 1, 2014).

Hayles, N. Katherine. "How We Think: Transforming Power and Digital Technologies." In *Understanding Digital Humanities*, edited by David M. Berry, 42–67. New York: Palgrave Macmillan, 2012.

Hockey, Susan. "The History of Humanities Computing." In *A Companion to Digital Humanities*, edited by Susan Schreibman, Ray Siemens, and John Unsworth. Oxford: Blackwell, 2004.

Jefferies, Janis. "Artist as Researcher in a Computer Mediated Culture." In *Art Practice in a Digital Culture*, edited by Hazel Gardiner and Charlie Gere. Burlington, VT: Ashgate Publishing, 2010.

Kirschenbaum, Matthew. "What Is Digital Humanities and What's It Doing in English Departments?" In *Debates in the Digital Humanities*, edited by Matthew K. Gold. Minneapolis: University of Minnesota Press, 2012.

Lovejoy, Margot. *Digital Currents: Art in the Electronic Age*. New York: Routledge, 2004.

Malina, Roger F. "Third Culture? From the Arts to the Sciences and Back Again." *Technoetic Arts: A Journal of Speculative Research* 10, no. 2–3 (2012): 179–83.

Martin, Victoria. "Developing a Library Collection in Bioinformatics: Support for an Evolving Profession." In *Library Collection Development for Professional Programs: Trends and Best Practices*, edited by Sara Holder, 269–89. Hershey, PA: IGI Global, Copyright © 2013. This material is used by permission of the publisher.

Merriam-Webster.com. "Nanotechnology, n." http://www.merriam-webster.com/dictionary/nanotechnology (accessed July 21, 2014).

Meyer, Eric, Kathryn Eccles, Michael Thelwall, and Christine Madsen. *Final Report to JISC on the Usage and Impact Study of JISC Funded Phase 1 Digitisation Projects and the Toolkit for the Impact of Digitised Scholarly Resources (TIDSR)*. Oxford Internet Institute. University of Oxford, 2009.

http://microsites.oii.ox.ac.uk/tidsr/system/files/TIDSR_FinalReport_20July 2009.pdf (accessed April 14, 2014).

Panofsky, Erwin. *Meaning in the Visual Arts: Paper in and on Art History.* Ann Arbor, MI: University of Michigan Press, 1955.

Schnapp, Jeffrey. "The Short Guide to the Digital Humanities." In *Digital Humanities*, edited by Anne Burdick, Johanna Drucker, Peter Lunenfeld, Todd Presner, and Jeffrey Schnapp, 121–36. Cambridge, MA: MIT Press, 2012.

Schnapp, Jeffrey, and Todd Presner. *Digital Humanities Manifesto 2.0.* 2009. http://humanitiesblast.com/manifesto/Manifesto_V2.pdf (accessed April 14, 2014).

Sengers, Phoebe. "Practices for Machine Culture: A Case Study of Integrating Artificial Intelligence and Cultural Theory." *Surfaces* 8 (1999): 28.

Smith, Martha Nell. "Computing: What Has American Literary Study to Do with IT?" *American Literature* 74, no. 4 (2002): 833–57.

Sullivan, Graeme, ed. *Art Practice as Research: Inquiry in Visual Arts.* Thousand Oaks, CA: Sage Publications, 2010.

Unsworth, John. *Our Cultural Commonwealth: The Report of the American Council of Learned Societies Commission on Cyberinfrastructure for the Humanities and Social Sciences.* New York: ACLS, 2006. http://www.acls.org/uploaded-Files/Publications/Programs/Our_Cultural_Commonwealth.pdf (accessed July 21, 2014).

Unsworth, John. "Scholarly Primitives: What Methods Do Humanities Researchers Have in Common and How Might Our Tools Reflect This?" In *Humanities Computing, Formal Methods, Experimental Practice.* Symposium, Kings College, London, 5-00, 2000.

Van Zundert, Joris, Smiljana Antonijevic, Anne Beaulieu, Karina van Dalen-Oskam, Douwe Zeldenrust, and Tara L. Andrews. "Cultures of Formalization: Towards an Encounter between Humanities and Computing." In *Understanding Digital Humanities*, edited by David M. Berry. New York: Palgrave Macmillan, 2012.

Wesseling, Janneke, ed. *See It Again, Say It Again: The Artist as Researcher.* Amsterdam: Valiz, 2011.

Wilson, Stephen. "Reflections on PAIR." In *Art and Innovation: The Xerox PARC Artist-in-Residence Program*, edited by Craig Harris, 186–208. Cambridge, MA: MIT Press, 1999.

SUGGESTED READINGS

Berry, David M., ed. *Understanding Digital Humanities.* New York: Palgrave Macmillan, 2012.

Biggs, Michael, and Henrik Karlsson, eds. *The Routledge Companion to Research in the Arts.* New York: Routledge, 2010.

Cummings, Jonathon, N., and Sara Kiesler. "Collaborative Research across Disciplinary and Institutional Boundaries." *Social Studies of Science* 35 no. 5 (2005): 703–22.

Gold, Matthew K., ed. *Debates in the Digital Humanities.* Minneapolis: University of Minnesota Press, 2012.

Hirsch Hadorn, Gertrude, Holger Hoffmann-Riem, Susette Biber-Klemm, Walter
      Grossenbacher-Mansuy, Dominique Joye, Christian Pohl, Urs Wiesmann,
      and Elisabeth Zemp, eds. *Handbook of Transdisciplinary Research*. Berlin:
      Springer, 2008.
Juan, Angel A., Thanasis Daradoumis, Meritxell Roca, Scott E. Grasman, and Javier
      Faulin, eds. *Collaborative and Distributed E-Research: Innovations in
      Technologies, Strategies and Applications*. Hershey PA: IGI Global, 2012.

Part II

eResearch Librarianship

6

The Impact of eResearch
on Libraries

We need to spend as much time thinking about our future as we spend
remembering our past ... and ... work toward our vision of the future
using creative tension and living with emotional tension knowing our
results will be rooted in the values of our profession.
                                                    —Lee W. Hisle (2005)

CORE VALUES OF LIBRARIANSHIP

"Since the publication of *The Five Laws of Library Science* in 1931, the core
values of librarianship have remained fundamentally the same: (1) Books are
for use, (2) Every reader his or her book, (3) Every book its reader, (4) Save
the time of the reader, and (5) The library is a growing organism (Ranganathan 1931). Although in the [eResearch environment], the term 'book' can
be replaced with the term 'information resource' [or 'data'] and the term
'reader' with the term 'user' [or 'researcher,'] these core values continue to
motivate our emphasis on the user" (Martin 2013, 275). They also reinforce
the idea of a library as an evolving entity and stress the need for a continuous
readjustment, or, what Horava (2010) calls a "creative reimagining" of its
collections, services, and facilities. A library's commitment to continuous
"creative reimagining" is challenging, but essential if the library is to maintain its core values while translating its traditional strengths into the
networked research environment that is becoming increasingly digital, data-
driven, interdisciplinary, and collaborative. As the research environment
and, consequently, the information and technology needs of library users
change and grow, so should the library.

eRESEARCH AND LIBRARY MISSION

While mission statements of individual libraries vary and often depend on the library's type (i.e., academic, public, or special), the overarching mission of any library, regardless of its type, is to organize, preserve, and make the world's knowledge accessible to current and future scholars. Historically, libraries have supported this mission by organizing and providing access to library collections, offering reference and consulting services regarding the use of these collections, preserving special and rare materials, and creating physical spaces for learning and research. While this broad library mission has largely remained unchanged for centuries, transformations in scholarship and research practices are driving fundamental changes in how this library mission can be accomplished.

To achieve their mission in the eResearch environment, today's libraries are continually seeking opportunities to innovate and improve their services. These include providing seamless discovery of and access to digital scholarly and data resources; sharing expertise in locating, using, and managing these resources; engaging in long-term preservation efforts with an emphasis on digital content; and creating state-of-the art physical and virtual research spaces. As a result, the library strives to become a research collaborator within the scholarly community while retaining its distinct identity as a service and a place. To accomplish this goal, librarians are rethinking their roles and extending the full spectrum of their classic functions and professional strengths into the digital environment, while remaining focused on their core values.

Even though operating simultaneously in these two dimensions—the traditional and the new—is a challenging task and requires on the part of librarians the acquisition of additional, multidimensional skills, the future of any individual library, as well as the future of librarianship as a whole, may, to a significant degree, depend on the libraries' ability to understand and embrace change, redefine and articulate their new roles, and thus provide an added dimension of value to their mission. Thus, an ultimate success criterion for libraries will be in their ability to integrate the traditional library services with more innovative services in such a manner that they are stimulating and enhancing each other, rather than competing or replacing each other.[1]

RECONCEPTUALIZING ACADEMIC AND RESEARCH LIBRARIES

Even though all library types are challenged by the developments in information technology and by the exponential growth in knowledge production (Finnemann 2014), academic and research libraries, in particular, are at the forefront of the challenge of supporting digital scholarship.[2] Academic and research libraries have historically been essential for successfully achieving the mission of their host institutions, which can be defined as the pursuit of excellence in learning, teaching, and research, and thus have been closely connected to research activities conducted by the institution's faculty and students. Furthermore, academic and research librarians, who have traditionally been responsible for outreach in assigned academic and research programs and thus typically have good knowledge of research activities and initiatives within their departments, possess a unique opportunity for collaboration with faculty on their research projects. In these respects, academic and research libraries achieve a greater advantage, in comparison to other library types, in becoming potentially involved at every stage of new knowledge creation, dissemination, and use. This notion of a "diffuse library" (Lougee 2002, 2009) playing an active role in all stages of scholarship, rather than simply "archiving" knowledge, is one of the key forces that impact today's academic and research libraries.[3]

These opportunities also present academic and research libraries with a challenge of large scale and complexity. Today's researchers require access to a critical mass of digital tools and resources, including resource types that have not been traditionally collected by libraries (for example, data sets). To support this need, academic and research libraries are developing and aggregating discipline-based research tools and resources, building the digital infrastructure, and preserving their print and digital collections. This challenge is compounded by the sheer volume of available information resources and data, and the issues of documentation, copyright, and authentication, as well as by the constantly advancing (or becoming obsolete) digital technologies.

This transformation is both a profound change and a continuation of traditional practice of academic and research libraries. Academic and research librarians, who are already well qualified in the area of selection, evaluation, and organization of information resources in accordance with the highest values of scholarship, are further contributing to this process by facilitating enhanced access to digital scholarly and research content. They are also contributing to faculty research productivity in a number of other, less traditional ways, such as assisting faculty with their publication citation analysis expected for tenure and promotion, helping them with grant applications and data management plans, and consulting them about depositing their research outputs in institutional repositories (Lougee 2009; Oakleaf 2010; Smith 2008). To realize these opportunities, academic and research librarians must routinely refresh their pertinent skills, acquire new competencies, and even create new career paths by assuming new roles as information curators, data management assistants, and metadata experts that might, at times, better align with emerging needs and methodological shifts in research and scholarship.

SPECIAL LIBRARIES: PUTTING KNOWLEDGE TO WORK

The focus of special libraries is more enterprise-oriented than that of academic and research libraries.[4] "Putting knowledge to work" has been a guiding principle of special librarians adopted by the Special Libraries Association (SLA) soon after its founding in 1909 (Christianson 1976). The goal of special libraries, which are sponsored by private companies, government agencies, nonprofit or professional organizations, is to work actively for the advantage of their parent organization. Their goal is to support the organization's daily operations, help it meet its strategic goals, and assist its employees with professional and research activities. As a result, special libraries develop collections of a highly specialized blend of resources on one subject (or few related subjects) and employ librarians who possess expertise in the specific subject area of the organization, such as law, music, or health sciences. In the words of John C. Dana (1910), the first president of the Special Libraries Association (SLA), a special library is "managed by the experts who endeavor from day to day to gather together the latest things on the topic to which the library is devoted," and it is doing so for the benefit of the organization to which it belongs (Dana 1910, 5).

While the fundamental nature of services offered by today's special libraries does not differ substantially from that in the past, the nature of technological support of the organizational information and research needs has evolved just as dramatically in special libraries as it has in academic and research libraries (Semertzaki 2011). Although the degree of adoption of technology-based services is at an earlier stage in special libraries than it is in academic and research libraries, they increasingly integrate technological innovations into their daily practice, ranging from digital resource management to cloud solutions for data storage to virtual reference services that expand the libraries' availability to their clientele regardless of time and place.

Today's special libraries provide access to digital resources related to their subject coverage, offer specialized research consulting services, assist with managing research data sets to facilitate easier analysis, and serve as repositories of the work published by employees. They also deploy a variety of Web 2.0 and Web 3.0 tools in supporting scholarly communication practices among their employees and assist with organizing presentations and white papers produced by their organization. Although these services are performed at a smaller scale than in academic and research libraries, they nonetheless contribute to research activities at their organization. By impacting the employees' research productivity, special libraries impact the organizational success and, ultimately, contribute to the creation and distribution of new knowledge, which is the primary goal of research.

PUBLIC AND SCHOOL LIBRARIES: EDUCATING RESEARCHERS OF TOMORROW

The significance of the impact of eResearch practices on public and school libraries, as well as the degree of their contribution to eResearch as it has been defined in this book, is harder to determine.[5] Although public libraries have adopted a wide range of technology-enabled services such as computerized OPAC system, 24/7 online accessibility, and availability of numerous electronic information resources for their users, they have not expanded their roles beyond their traditional commitment to improving education of the general public, from children to elders (McCook 2011).

Throughout their history, public libraries were explicitly designed to serve an important social role—to enable their users to obtain purposeful information or pursue useful activity and thus serve the general public's education and leisure needs.[6] While public libraries are newer to providing eResearch support than academic and research libraries, the societal value of their contribution to people's education and thus of their potential impact on the advancement of scholarship at large should not be taken for granted or underestimated. By organizing and providing access to learning and information resources for people of all ages and across different cultural and socio-economic backgrounds, and by exposing these people to modern technology and expert assistance from information professionals, public libraries help broaden their educational and professional opportunities, promote lifelong learning, and empower their users to achieve a better quality of life.

In school libraries, librarians instruct students not only on finding books about a topic, but also on locating the underlying data. For example, biology classes can use data sets that record the growth of trees in a forest or the migration of birds. Furthermore, librarians teach students to find their own data in repositories of other libraries and national data centers, just as they instruct them on finding text-based reference materials. In this context, the school libraries' contribution to eResearch is more implicit than direct, since it is oriented toward educating "researchers of tomorrow" rather than toward serving "researchers of today."

NOTES

1. In *The World Is Flat* (Friedman, 2006), which reflects on the effects of technology and globalization on the world, Friedman predicted that the "flat world" will require "Versatilists" who can "apply depth of skill to a progressively widening scope of situations and experiences, gaining new competencies, building relationships, and assuming new roles" and who "are capable not only of constantly adapting but also

of constantly learning and growing" (Friedman 2006, 294). This notion is relevant to the world of libraries, which must constantly adapt and grow as scholarship changes and as new technologies emerge.

2. The *Dictionary for Library and Information Science* defines an academic library as a library that is "an integral part of a college, university, or other institution of postsecondary education, administered to meet the information needs of its students, faculty, and staff" (Reitz 2004, 4). There is no single definition of research libraries in reference resources and other publications. Most academic libraries are assumed to be performing the functions of research libraries. In the general article on libraries in the *Encyclopedia of Library and Information Science,* research libraries are not considered as a separate type and are merely included with other special libraries (Weil Arns 2009, 3283). More conservatively defined, research libraries are libraries at institutions classified as research universities by the Carnegie Classification of Institutions of Higher Education (http://classifications.carnegiefoundation.org/).

3. In her white paper for the Council on Library and Information Resources entitled *Diffuse Libraries*, Wendy Lougee described her vision of a diffuse library as follows: "In physics, 'diffusion' refers to the spreading out of elements, an intermingling (though not a combining) of molecules. Applying this analogy to libraries, we see the library becoming more deeply engaged in the fundamental mission of the academic institution—i.e., the creation and dissemination of knowledge—in ways that represent the library's contributions more broadly and that intertwine the library with the other stakeholders in these activities" (Lougee 2002, 4).

4. Special libraries include corporate libraries, law libraries, medical libraries, museum libraries, and libraries in research laboratories and consulting firms.

5. According to the National Center for Education Statistics, public libraries are supported in whole or in part with public funds and established to serve a community through providing: (1) an organized collection of print or other library materials; (2) library staff; (3) an established schedule of services; and (4) the facilities necessary to support such a collection, staff, and schedule (National Center for Education Statistics 2014, https://nces.ed.gov/).

6. In addition to their traditional goal of improving education of the general public, the public libraries' commitment to teaching their users basic "digital literacy skills" (that include information seeking and computer skills) has become one of the primary goals of today's public libraries (ALA Office for Research and Statistics 2011, http://www.ala.org/offices/ors).

WORKS CITED

Christianson, Elin B. "Special Libraries: Putting Knowledge to Work." *Library Trends* 25 (1976): 399–416.

Dana, John C. "The President's Opening Remarks." *Special Libraries* 1 (January 1909): 4–5.

Finnemann, Niels Ole. "Research Libraries and the Internet—on the Transformative Dynamic between Institutions and Digital Media." *Journal of Documentation* 70, no. 2 (2014): 202–20. doi:10.1108/JD-05-2013-0059.

Friedman, Thomas L. *The World Is Flat: A Brief History of the Twenty-first Century.* New York: Farrar, Straus and Giroux, 2006.

Hisle, W. Lee. "The Changing Role of the Library in the Academic Enterprise." *Information Services Staff Speeches and Presentations*, Paper 1, 2005. http://digitalcommons.conncoll.edu/isstaffsp/1/ (accessed February 27, 2014).

Horava, Tony. "Challenges and Possibilities for Collection Management in a Digital Age." *Library Resources and Technical Services* 54, no. 3 (2010): 142–52.

Lougee, Wendy. *Diffuse Libraries: Emergent Roles for the Research Library in the Digital Age*. Washington, DC: Council on Library and Information Resources, 2002. http://www.clir.org/pubs/reports/pub108/pub108.pdf (accessed July 2, 2014).

Lougee, Wendy. "The Diffuse Library Revisited: Aligning the Library as Strategic Asset." *Library Hi Tech* 27, no. 4 (2009): 610–23. doi:10.1108/07378830911007718.

Martin, Victoria. "Developing a Library Collection in Bioinformatics: Support for an Evolving Profession." In *Library Collection Development for Professional Programs: Trends and Best Practices*, edited by Sara Holder, 269–89. Hershey, PA: IGI Global, Copyright © 2013. This material is used by permission of the publisher.

McCook, Kathleen de la Peña. *Introduction to Public Librarianship*. New York: Neal-Schuman Publishers, 2011.

Oakleaf, Megan. *The Value of Academic Libraries: A Comprehensive Research Review and Report*. Chicago: Association of College and Research Libraries, 2010.

Ranganathan, Shiyali Ramamrita. *The Five Laws of Library Science*. London: Edward Goldston, 1931.

Reitz, Joan M. *Dictionary for Library and Information Science*. Westport, CT: Libraries Unlimited, 2004.

Semertzaki, Eva. *Special Libraries as Knowledge Management Centres*. Oxford: Chandos Publishing, 2011.

Smith, Abby. "The Research Library in the 21st Century: Collecting, Preserving, and Making Accessible Resources for Scholarship." In *No Brief Candle: Reconceiving Research Libraries for the 21st Century*, 13–20. Washington, DC: Council on Library and Information Resources, 2008. http://www.clir.org/pubs/reports/pub142/pub142.pdf (accessed February 27, 2014).

Weil Arns, J. "Libraries." In *Encyclopedia of Library and Information Sciences*, 3rd ed., 3281–86. New York: Taylor and Francis, 2009.

SUGGESTED READINGS

Bertot, John Carlo, Paul T. Jaeger, and Charles R. McClure, eds. *Public Libraries and the Internet: Roles, Perspectives, and Implications*." Santa Barbara, CA: Libraries Unlimited, 2011.

Lougee, Wendy. "The Diffuse Library Revisited: Aligning the Library as Strategic Asset." *Library Hi Tech* 27, no. 4 (2009): 610–23. doi:10.1108/0737883 0911007718.

Ranganathan, Shiyali Ramamrita. *The Five Laws of Library Science*. London: Edward Goldston; and Madras: Madras Library Association, 1931.

Semertzaki, Eva. *Special Libraries as Knowledge Management Centres*. Oxford: Chandos Publishing, 2011.

7

Expanding Traditional Library Services into the eResearch Environment: Classic Roles in a New Context

> As we develop a framework for new roles, we must be aware that even our more traditional roles are undergoing significant changes.
> —Karen Williams (2009, 5)

TRADITION AND INNOVATION: THE LIBRARIES' TWOFOLD CHALLENGE

A stronger dependency and reliance on digital resources and technologies has given rise to new research methodologies, encouraged global multidisciplinary collaboration, and resulted in a more porous flow of scholarly communication processes. These transformations, which have seen exponential growth during the last two decades (what Hess and Ostrom [2007] called a "*hyperchange*"), have fundamentally altered the ways researchers seek information and interact with each other, what tools and services they employ, and how they document and disseminate their research results. By extension, this has affected how, when, and for what purpose they use library resources and services (Harley et al. 2010; Hemminger et al. 2007; Lougee 2009).

To adapt to researchers' changing information-seeking behavior, libraries are continually "diffusing" their traditional services toward supporting digital scholarship and research and trying to discover more effective methods to facilitate researchers' needs and preferences in how they find and use information. The challenge that libraries face today is thus twofold—to both preserve and innovate—and is a natural element of the service continuum rooted in a library's core values. As Maceviciute (2014) argued, "digital scholarship as a new domain is deeply rooted in old ideas" (285). This notion can be applied to eResearch librarianship.

The fuzzy boundaries between the traditional and the innovative are affecting both the practices of librarians and the research processes they are supporting. The libraries have already experienced pervasive technological developments (e.g., the use of cloud computing and the Social Web) and different means of conducting library research on and through the Internet, as well as significant innovation of library functions—from automation to virtualization (Dutton and Jeffreys 2010). Despite the resilience of research libraries and their ability to change within a short period of time (ibid.), the transition to "all digital" scholarship is still underway and is based upon the gradual extension of libraries' traditional services into the realm where, as some authors predict, "the shelves in one library can be replaced with a server in any given location ... and the large buildings ... can be replaced by internet and broadband access" (Finnemann 2014, 213). According to Lewis, the libraries are still at an early stage of the transition to the "electronic" library that began in the 1990s with the development of full-text databases, the Internet, and the World Wide Web, and this transition is "likely to run another decade or two" (Lewis 2004, 70).

While all libraries, regardless of their type, face this twofold challenge to some degree, this challenge impacts academic and research libraries in a more dramatic way than other libraries. The immediate environment of academic and research libraries consists of institutions that are conducting research and disseminating the outcomes of their research. Because of their central position in supporting research activities at their institutions, and thus their more active involvement in the creation and dissemination of new knowledge, academic and research libraries must promptly accommodate the technologically and methodologically innovative ways of the scholarship they support.

FROM COLLECTION TO CONNECTION

For centuries, libraries have largely been defined by the size of their collections, that is, the number of books and journals they owned. As Horava (2010) observed, the metaphor of a warehouse was typical in describing this collection development approach. The libraries have also been defined by what Spiro and Henry (2010) call the "good collection stewardship" practices, which include the libraries' ability to select and acquire materials appropriate for a particular community, organize and make these materials available to their target community, and preserve their collections for future use. At present, these practices have expanded to include collecting and managing digital information resources with restricted proprietary rights as well as open access resources.

Even though most libraries are making the transition from print-only to print and digital, evolving into digital-only (or digital-mostly) collections, their classic collection development role—to collect, organize, share, and preserve—remains largely intact. The practices of "good collection steward-ship" outlined above can also, to a great extent, be translated into the digital realm. The principles that guide good collection stewardship of print materials can also be applied to the management of digital collections through securing ownership of digital content (usually through a license), storing the content on library servers and making it accessible to the library users via the Internet, and ensuring the longevity of access to this content for future use (given that the license conditions permit this) through digital preservation practices.

As access to collections gradually overtakes the ownership of collections, which is a model for many academic and research libraries today, it is becom-ing more difficult to define the actual borders of a library collection that is "everywhere and nowhere—it is a cloud of distributed resources in a variety of places around the globe that are made centrally available via the library" (Horava 2010, 151). It is critical to assimilate this knowledge into collection-building practices while maintaining collection development core values—determining which resources best meet researchers' needs and add-ing the most suitable resources to the collection—whether these resources are physically located in a particular building or are made accessible by some other means.

EVALUATING THE ROLE OF BOOKS FOR eRESEARCH

The importance of books for eResearch varies among (and within) disciplines and in accordance with the task at hand. In most scientific and engineering fields, books are not the primary means for communicating research findings and thus typically play a minor or complementary role (for example, for class preparation or as a reference source) (Grefsheim and Rankin 2007; Haglund and Olsson 2008; Harley et al. 2010; Hemminger et al. 2007). Other fields of study rely more heavily on books for research—for example, the humanities where books continue to play an important role in conducting and communi-cating research (ibid.). Furthermore, teaching and studying in all disciplines often requires textbooks, thus further sustaining the book (and eBook) market.

In the sciences, research findings more than five years old are often consid-ered to be out of date. Thus, the demand for science books drops off sharply after they are published, while in the humanities, the demand for books declines slowly and sometimes even grows (ibid.). A regularly updated collec-tion development policy, which guides book selection for various disciplines, a carefully crafted and coherent approval plan, and a subject profile policy can assist a librarian with book selection decisions to ensure that acquired titles take into the account the disciplinary differences.

In any research fields, older materials should be purchased if they are requested by faculty. The above-mentioned studies revealed that researchers find these two types of historical book material useful: (1) the "classics" (for example, Darwin's *On the Origins of Species* or Freud's *Civilization and Its Discontents*); and (2) the naturalistic descriptions of particular animal or ecological systems, which can provide a then-and-now comparison. For some emerging fields such as neuroinformatics or ecological humanities, where the body of knowledge is still in its infancy and the quantity of publications is still limited, it may be necessary to collect all available material (if it otherwise meets the selection criteria). Utilizing hard copies of print catalogs for book selection has its advantages. They allow a librarian to mark or highlight selected titles as well as the catalog pages in place of book order forms. However, publishers often provide more information about their publications on their websites than they do in their print catalogs, including book reviews, tables of contents, text excerpts, and links to new and forthcoming titles within the same subject area or topic. Established scholarly publishers such as Elsevier, CRC Press, Wiley, Cold Spring Harbor Laboratory Press, and Springer publish high-quality scholarly books and provide online catalogs on their websites as well as other helpful resources for librarians.

ELECTRONIC BOOKS: CURRENT PERCEPTIONS AND PREDICTIONS FOR THE FUTURE

Even though some authors speculate that "books and printed materials can now be replaced by electronic texts" (Finnemann 2014) and that electronic books (eBooks)[1] will likely play a significant role in research in the near future, eBooks have not yet gained a wide acceptance within most disciplinary research groups (Henry and Smith 2010; Zhang and Beckman 2011). According to a 2009 survey by Stanford University's HighWire Press, constraints imposed by some Digital Rights Management (DRM), such as eBook text usage restrictions, were identified as the most significant factor that hinders eBook use by researchers (Newman and Bui 2010). Among other concerns expressed by eBook users are "difficulties in reading from the computer screen, problems related to locating eBooks, and navigation issues" (Martin 2013, 280). Furthermore, not every book is well suited for an electronic format. For example, art books work better in physical formats.

For some readers, one of the strongest arguments in favor of an "old-fashioned" print book is its physical "feel" including the texture of its paper, the quality of its printing, and even its special "musty" smell that attracts some readers as opposed to "odorless" eBooks (Darnton 2008). The researchers interviewed by the Renaissance English Knowledgebase/Professional Reading Environment (REKn/PReE) project noted, "the electronic is mostly used for information seeking and writing up of results, but pure reading is still handled in print" (Spiro and Henry 2010, 16).

As supporting technologies, such as eBook readers, continue to develop or the alternatives to eBook readers become available, such as notebooks and smartphones, eBooks might gain a wider adoption among researchers.

> The value-added features of eBooks are obvious: 24/7 desktop availability, concurrent access for multiple users, searching and saving features of eBooks, downloadable graphics, and capability to print and download sections or chapters, as well as the ability to bookmark, highlight, and annotate text [and thus allowing readers to interact with the text in the ways that would be destructive and/or prohibited in print library books. As Bierman, Ortega, and Rupp-Serrano (2010) observed,] "just as e-journals have found acceptance, e-books are likely to become more commonplace in the near future. The convenience factor alone will be a significant driver" (85). (Martin 2013, 280)

PEER-REVIEWED JOURNALS: FROM PRINT COLLECTIONS TO DIGITAL ARCHIVES

As discussed in Chapter 4 (Scholarly Communication in the eResearch Context), research articles published in peer-reviewed journals are the principal means of scholarly communication across many disciplines and are an essential part of the research process. In scientific and engineering fields of study, peer-reviewed journals make up the bulk of scholarly publications. In some fields—for example, the biological and biomedical sciences, where the currency and expediency of access to latest research findings is crucial—research is almost exclusively communicated through articles in peer-reviewed journals.

In an academic setting, researchers consider the provision of current subscriptions to full-text electronic journals (eJournals) as one of the library's most valuable contributions to their teaching and research (Harley et al. 2010). eJournal articles account for the majority of researchers' readings, and many scholars, who appreciate the eJournals' greater speed of access compared to their print editions, use eJournals daily or weekly (Tenopir, Birch, and Allard 2012). Many researchers are also finding that eJournals offer significant value beyond full-text access through such features as nonlinearity (the presence of internal links within articles), multimedia (the presence of video or audio clips, simulations, and other downloadable materials within articles), and interactivity (the ability to directly communicate with the author[s] of the article through comments, e-mail, or forums).

"For libraries, some of the long-term benefits of electronic journals include reduction in shelving, processing, and binding costs, and, in some cases, savings on print subscription costs when a library is willing to cancel print subscriptions in favor of electronic access. Another benefit is increased availability and accuracy of usage statistics that helps with collection development decisions" (Martin 2013, 277).

While library journal collections are rapidly evolving into digitized archives—and, as a consequence, libraries are seeing a marked decrease in the use of their print journal collections— print journals continue to play an important role in research. "First, not all journals are yet available electronically. For example, some specialty areas may lag behind others in providing electronic access. Second, some researchers still rely on print journals as a convenient means for browsing current issues of relevant journals in hard copy, or when computers are down. Just as some readers prefer a print book over an electronic book, some still desire access to traditional print journals" (ibid). Even though most scholarly journals have produced an electronic version in addition to their print versions and many are moving toward producing "paperless journals," or the combination of the two, there is a general consensus within the library community that electronic journals will not replace but continue to "coexist" with print journals (Grefsheim and Rankin 2007; Haines et al. 2010; Harley et al. 2010; Hemminger et al. 2007).

> In some cases, maintaining flagship journal titles in both print and electronic formats is justified. . . . The availability of these flagship publications in their print version provides important benefits when [power is out or Internet access is down]. When both formats are not affordable, acquiring electronic journal titles is more critical [because of the currency and expediency of access considerations]." (Martin 2013, 277)
>
> Journal ranking [known as journal impact factors, provided] by the Journal Citation Reports (JCR), currently available through Thomson Reuters (http://thomsonreuters.com/journal-citation-reports/), plays an important evaluative role in identifying the journals that have been cited the most. [In the research community,] journal impact factors are well known and considered important in author decisions about where to submit work as well as in the tenure review process. [Even though] some researchers, as well as some librarians, consider JCR's ranked list of journals for a specific discipline to represent the core journal list for that discipline, the evaluative importance of citation count data is "predicated on the assumption that citation is evidence of contribution to scholarly communications and presumably an indicator of quality" (Nisonger 2007, 57). Some suggest that the importance of journal impact factors is overrated (Monastersky 2005a, 2005b) [because] high-quality research papers also appear in journals with low impact factors as well as in journals with small circulation. (Martin 2013, 278)

Other resources for identifying core journals in specific disciplines include journal lists maintained by professional organizations—for example, Core Journals in Psychology compiled by the Association of College and Research Libraries—and librarian collection development guides—for example,

Magazines for Libraries. Faculty of 1000 (discussed in Chapter 4) is another resource that may help librarians with journal selection decisions. Unlike journal impact factors, which capture only the number of published citations to a journal, the Faculty of 1000 (F1000) factor, a numerical ranking derived from all the ratings the paper has received in Faculty of 1000, is calculated from "a value judgment given by identified experts, and the reason for their value judgment can be traced" (Monastersky 2005a). A key benefit of Faculty of 1000 for librarians is in that it can help them identify the journals that publish the highest number of most important papers within the specific disciplines.

OPEN ACCESS JOURNALS: FREE TO READ, FREE TO COLLECT

For libraries that play a critical role in fostering scholarly communication, the support of open access publishing is "a logical consequence of library philosophy that embraces the idea of information for everyone regardless of their wealth, status, and opportunities" (Maceviciute 2014). Libraries can contribute to this process by keeping researchers well informed about publishing alternatives such as publishing in open access journals, and by incorporating open access journals into their collections.[2] They can "collect" open access journals by making them available through various venues that are familiar to researchers and that are more likely to be used, for example, through electronic journal lists (Collins and Walters 2010). "This will ensure that researchers know how to access open access journals in their field quickly and conveniently. In turn, open access journals will show greater use 'due to greater web visibility and ease of discovery (and, of course, less cost)' (Mullen 2010, 129)" (Martin 2013, 278). Adding open access journals to their collections can position libraries for leadership in such an important scholarly communication initiative and maximize the value of their collections.

FROM PRINT INDEXES TO COMPUTER DATABASES

While most researchers have a high regard for journal literature as one of the primary sources of information and a means for scholarly communication, they seldom utilize the library's bibliographic databases to find information (PubMed's Medline and Web of Science being the exception) (Grefsheim and Rankin 2007; Haglund and Olsson 2008; Harley et al. 2010; Hemminger et al. 2007; Hightower and Caldwell 2010).[3] Many researchers are either unaware of the library's bibliographic databases or consult these databases infrequently due to lack of time or search skills. They prefer to locate relevant journal articles through tracing references (what is sometimes called "citation chaining"), word of mouth or personal reference, or a Google (or Google

Scholar) search rather than through other, more "library correct," search methods (ibid.).

Because of the interdisciplinary nature of eResearch, a decision to subscribe to a bibliographic database for an eResearch community may often involve several subject librarians, whose primary goal is evaluation of the quality of a database's content and its appropriateness for the researchers. Such a collaborative approach to the selection and evaluation of a database is crucial. Each subject librarian can bring to the selection decisions his or her knowledge of the specialized needs of researchers within a specific discipline. "This knowledge may lead to preferring one database [over the other or one database platform] over the other, given a choice" (Martin 2013, 280).

> The content of a database is evaluated by using the same criteria that govern the evaluation of other types of electronic library materials: relevance, authority, scope, coverage, and frequency of updates. A traditional database evaluation checklist is useful when evaluating the content of a database for eResearch. The following questions should be asked in order to make the best choices for the institution and users.

- Is a database's publisher/vendor reputable?
- What are the dates of coverage?
- How often is the content updated?
- How unique is this database to the library's current collection? Does it fill current gaps in the collection? Does it duplicate resources already provided by the library?
- If a database is available on more than one vendor platform, which platform will allow the user to locate information more quickly and efficiently?
- If the database is later canceled, will the library still have access to the licensed content?
- Does the database have a user-friendly search interface—[i.e., has a clear, uncluttered display and includes ADA-compliant features]?

> Preference is given to full-text databases that provide access to the most current scholarly content, including, when possible, access to preprints, conference proceedings, and those databases that enable such features as citation count, links to referenced publications, image representation, and convenient article printing options (such as a PDF file). (Martin 2013, 280)

In addition to bibliographic databases, databases that contain multimedia resources (such as audio, video, 3D visualizations, or a combination of the above) provide an added value to an eResearch library collection. By pairing scholarly content with the latest technology, these databases enhance learning, teaching, and research in virtually every discipline. Examples of multimedia databases include Alexander Street Press (http://alexander street.com/), Anatomy.TV (https://www.anatomy.tv/default.aspx/), PsycVIDEO (http://www.apa.org/pubs/psycvideo-psycextra.aspx/), and Naxos Music Library (http://www.naxosmusiclibrary.com/).

CHARACTERISTICS OF A LIBRARY COLLECTION WITHIN THE eRESEARCH ENVIRONMENT

The value of a library collection that aspires to support eResearch activities within their institution should be measured in new ways. No single approach will suffice because each library should address the diverse research needs of its library users. The specific subject focus of a collection and its scope are dependent on particular research areas within an individual institution.

The general goals of a library collection whose purpose is to support eResearch are similar to the goals of most collections at higher education institutions. According to Martin (2013), these goals are:

- To support teaching, learning, and research of the faculty and students in their institution
- To collect materials suitable for a particular discipline and audience
- To give preference to high-quality research materials, including books produced by established scholarly publishers and journals with a high-impact factor

The uniqueness of such a collection lies in four characteristics:

1. Its highly interdisciplinary and multidisciplinary nature, evolving at the interfaces among various disciplines and subdisciplines
2. Its currency, with an emphasis on facilitating expedited access to the most current research—for example, via providing access to electronic journals rather than via subscribing to print versions
3. Its diversity, consolidating resources in various formats and from diverse sources, which might not always be considered as part of a traditional library collection but are essential in the field of eResearch (for example, data sets or data mining tools)
4. Its openness, supporting the open scholarly communication model and promoting access to open access and "invisible college" resources

EXTENDING USER SERVICES BEYOND THE REFERENCE DESK

> Technology was formerly a backbone of libraries, and now it's become the front door of public service.
>
> —ALA Office for Research (2011, 6)

In addition to developing library collections that support faculty teaching and research, one of the primary contributions of academic and research libraries to faculty research is through reference and consultation services. These user services[4] have traditionally focused on collections support such as assisting researchers (usually at the reference desk or via the phone) with locating library resources and helping them use these resources more effectively. As the online resources are becoming 24/7-accessible, and resource discovery tools from Google Scholar to PubMed are continually being enhanced to enable researchers to locate information without a librarian's assistance, the reference and consultation services have become less crucial.

Several studies, mostly using surveys, have reported overall declining in-library attendance among researchers and declining use of in-library services such as reference and consulting (Rutner and Schonfeld 2012; Schonfeld and Housewright 2010; Shaffer 2013; Williams and Rowlands 2008). In an attempt to understand what services libraries should provide to researchers, these surveys asked whether researchers were aware of the resources and services in the library and whether they considered the library as an important source of information. The studies revealed that most researchers, especially those in scientific and engineering disciplines, rarely utilized the libraries as a primary source of information. Even when researchers cannot locate resources they need, they might bypass library document delivery services, which they may perceive as "expensive and cumbersome," and instead contact their peers for help (ibid.). The majority of respondents have also reported having learned about information sources, such as journal literature databases, in their laboratories or at the conferences, from mentors and peers, rather than in libraries from librarians. Knowledge about these resources and how to use them was often passed on by word of mouth to novice researchers by more experienced peers.

The scholars' lesser reliance on libraries as their primary source of information, their lack of awareness of the valuable resources libraries have to offer, or their insufficient skills in using these resources might hinder their effective use of information resources that, in the long term, might impact the quality of their research and, by extension, undermine the academic and research libraries' mission—to support learning and research through the provision of access to the world's knowledge.

While a wide availability of online scholarly resources diminish incentive for researchers to physically visit the library to use the library's collections on site, new needs have also emerged within the research community with regard to library services. Key among these needs are:

- Expert assistance with finding and navigating information resources
- Data storage and preservation that enable knowledge reuse
- Data management support
- Assistance with designing data management plans
- Copyright and authorship consulting

As today's researchers often begin, and end, their quest for information "on the greater network" rather than in libraries, the libraries are driven to develop more flexible, integrated user services that support virtual inquiry and make services available at the point of demand rather than via more traditional means such as at the reference desk. Digital reference services, also known as virtual reference services, are becoming widely available in most libraries around the world. These services provide assistance to remote users through different formats ranging from e-mail reference and "Ask-a" (Instant Message) chat services, to more technologically advanced reference interactions through technologies that "capture" the user's workstation in order to "co-browse" networked resources. These digital reference functions can be incorporated as "visible and discrete services" into the research environments, such as collaboratories or research portals, and enable researchers to seek reference assistance when it is needed (Lougee 2009). The application of the Web 2.0 concepts and technologies to the library services and collections is often termed as "Library 2.0."[5]

A growing number of libraries are also offering text reference services that allow users to seek information assistance from librarians via texting (Luo 2014; Luo and Bell 2010). For example, My Info Quest, a collaborative text reference service initiated by the Alliance Library System (ALS), provides users with a phone number to which they can text their questions.

Collaborative virtual reference services, in particular, can bring benefits to both researchers and librarians. A collaborative virtual reference service, a consortium-based service offered by several libraries, allows the member libraries to provide reference service to the users from their distributed reference desks through chat or e-mail. For example, the QuestionPoint Reference Service (http://www.QuestionPoint.org/) coordinated by OCLC and staffed by a collaborative network of reference librarians, provides member libraries with the tools to interact with users worldwide. By using collaborative virtual reference services, researchers have an opportunity to ask subject librarians for specialized information without being restricted by time and location. For librarians, the benefits of participating in the collaborative virtual reference services include resource sharing, shared staffing responsibilities, and opportunities for interdisciplinary multi-institutional collaborations that are in accordance with the spirit of eResearch they support.

CONCLUDING REMARKS

While the nature of classic library roles is changing, the concept of library as a research and educational center remains important in the eResearch context. Despite the researchers' greater reliance on technology and their perceived self-sufficiency as information seekers, they may benefit from the libraries' expertise as knowledge managers who can help them navigate and facilitate access to information *"resourceome"* (Cannata, Merelli, and Altman 2005). In this context, collaboration between researchers and librarians is mutually beneficial. In this collaboration, both professionals—a researcher and an information specialist—can bring to their partnership their unique skills and competencies. Researchers can rely on the expertise of librarians to guide them through information resources and services; librarians can seek the advice of researchers in the subject matter (for example, for collection development purposes) and benefit from the opportunity to secure the library's future as a significant partner in knowledge creation (Case 2008).

NOTES

1. Electronic book (also called e-book, eBook, e-Book, ebook, digital book, and online book) is a full-length book publication in a digital format that can be read via a computer or via handheld devices called eBook readers (for example, Kindle, Nook, or iBook).

2. Open access journals and free journals are not synonymous. Open access journals typically use the Creative Commons Attribution license, according to which the material can be freely shared and adapted for any use as long as you "give appropriate credit, provide a link to the license, and indicate if changes were made" (http://creativecommons.org/licenses/by/3.0/us/).

3. A bibliographic database is an organized, searchable (and often "browseable") online collection of citations, abstracts, and often full text of published literature such as journal and newspaper articles, conference proceedings, books, and other publications.

4. In this book, user services refer to reference and consulting services.

5. The term Library 2.0 was coined by Michael Casey in 2006 on his blog *Library Crunch* to refer to social and technological changes that facilitate library-patron interactions, focus on user needs, and are responsive to user needs.

WORKS CITED

ALA Office for Research, ed. *The Transforming Public Library Technology Infrastructure.* Vol. 47, no. 6. Chicago: American Library Association, 2011.

Bierman, James, Lina Ortega, and Karen Rupp-Serrano. "E-book Usage in Pure and Applied Sciences." *Science and Technology Libraries* 29, no. 1–2 (2010): 69–91. doi:10.1080/01942620903579393.

Cannata, Nicola, Emanuela Merelli, and Russ B. Altman. "Time to Organize the Bioinformatics Resourceome." *PLoS Computational Biology* 1, no. 7 (2005): e76. doi:10.1371/journal.pcbi.0010076.

Case, Mary M. "Partners in Knowledge Creation: An Expanded Role for Research Libraries in the Digital Future." *Journal of Library Administration* 48, no. 2 (2008): 141–56. doi:10.1080/01930820802231336.

Collins, Cheryl S., and William H. Walters. "Open Access Journals in College Library Collections." *Serials Librarian* 59, no. 2 (2010): 194–214. doi:10.1080/03615261003623187.

Darnton, Robert. "The Research Library in the Digital Age." *Bulletin of the American Academy of Arts and Sciences* 61 (2008): 9–15.

Dutton, William H., and Paul W. Jeffreys, eds. *World Wide Research: Reshaping the Sciences and Humanities.* Cambridge, MA: MIT Press, 2010.

Finnemann, Niels Ole. "Research Libraries and the Internet—on the Transformative Dynamic between Institutions and Digital Media." *Journal of Documentation* 70, no. 2 (2014): 202–20. doi:10.1108/JD-05-2013-0059.

Grefsheim, Suzanne F., and Jocelyn A. Rankin. "Information Needs and Information Seeking in a Biomedical Research Setting: A Study of Scientists and Science Administrators." *Journal of the Medical Library Association* 95, no. 4 (2007): 426–34. doi:10.3163/1536-5050.95.4.426.

Haglund, Lotta, and Per Olsson. "The Impact on University Libraries of Changes in Information Behavior among Academic Researchers: A Multiple Case Study." *Journal of Academic Librarianship* 34, no. 1 (2008): 52–59. doi:10.1016/j.acalib.2007.11.010.

Haines, Laura L., Jeanene Light, Donna O'Malley, and Frances A. Delwiche. "Information-Seeking Behavior of Basic Science Researchers: Implications for Library Services." *Journal of the Medical Library Association* 98, no. 1 (2010): 73–81. doi:10.3163/1536-5050.98.1.019.

Harley, Diane, Sophia Krzys Acord, Sarah Earl-Novell, Shannon Lawrence, and C. Judson King. *Assessing the Future Landscape of Scholarly Communication: An Exploration of Faculty Values and Needs in Seven Disciplines.* Berkeley, CA: Center for Studies in Higher Education, 2010. https://escholarship.org/uc/item/15x7385g (accessed February 26, 2014).

Hemminger, Bradley M., Dihui Lu, K. T. L. Vaughan, and Stephanie J. Adams. "Information Seeking Behavior of Academic Scientists." *Journal of the American Society for Information Science and Technology* 58, no. 14 (2007): 2205–25. doi:10.1002/asi.20686.

Henry, Charles, and Kathlin Smith. "Ghostlier Demarcations: Large-Scale Text Digitization Projects and Their Utility for Contemporary Humanities Scholarship. In *The Idea of Order: Transforming Research Collections for 21st Century Scholarship,* 106–15. Washington, DC: Council on Library and Information Resources, 2010. http://www.clir.org/pubs/reports/pub147/pub147.pdf#page=112 (accessed February 27, 2014).

Hess, Charlotte, and Elinor Ostrom, eds. *Understanding Knowledge as a Commons: From Theory to Practice.* Cambridge, MA: MIT Press, 2007.

Hightower, Christy, and Christy Caldwell. "Shifting Sands: Science Researchers on Google Scholar, Web of Science, and PubMed, with implications for Library Collections Budgets." *Issues in Science and Technology Librarianship* 63, no. 4 (2010).

Horava, Tony. "Challenges and Possibilities for Collection Management in a Digital Age." *Library Resources and Technical Services* 54, no. 3 (2010): 142–52.

Lewis, David W. "The Innovator's Dilemma: Disruptive Change and Academic Libraries." *Library Administration and Management* 18, no. 2 (2004): 68–74.

Luo, Lili. "Text a Librarian: A Look from the User Perspective." *Reference Services Review* 42, no. 1 (2014): 4–15.

Luo, Lili, and Lori Bell. "Text 4 Answers: A Collaborative Service Model." *Reference Services Review* 38, no. 2 (2010): 274–83.

Lougee, Wendy. "The Diffuse Library Revisited: Aligning the Library as Strategic Asset." *Library Hi Tech* 27, no. 4 (2009): 610–23. doi:10.1108/073788309 11007718.

Maceviciute, Elena. "Research Libraries in Modern Environment." *Journal of Documentation* 70, no. 2 (2014): 282–302. doi:10.1108/JD-04-2013-0044.

Martin, Victoria. "Developing a Library Collection in Bioinformatics: Support for an Evolving Profession." In *Library Collection Development for Professional Programs: Trends and Best Practices*, edited by Sara Holder, 269–89. Hershey, PA: IGI Global, Copyright © 2013. This material is used by permission of the publisher.

Monastersky, Richard. "Impact Factors Run Into Competition: Researchers Look for Other Ways to Evaluate a Paper's Importance." *Chronicle of Higher Education*, October 14, 2005a.

Monastersky, Richard. "The Number That's Devouring Science." *Chronicle of Higher Education* 52, no. 8 (2005b): A12.

Mullen, Laura Bowering. *Open Access and Its Practical Impact on the Work of Academic Librarians: Collection Development, Public Services, and the Library and Information Science Literature.* Oxford: Chandos Publishing, 2010.

Newman, Michael, and Anh Bui. *HighWire Press 2009 Librarian eBook Survey.* Palo Alto, CA: HighWire Press, Stanford University, 2010. http://highwire.stanford .edu/PR/HighWireEBookSurvey2010.pdf (accessed February 27, 2014).

Nisonger, Thomas E. "Journals in the Core Collection: Definition, Identification, and Applications." *Serials Librarian* 51, no. 3–4 (2007): 51–73. doi:10.1300/ J123v51n03_05.

Rutner, Jennifer, and Roger C. Schonfeld. *Supporting the Changing Research Practices of Historians.* Final Report from ITHAKA S+R, 2012. http://www.sr .ithaka.org/sites/default/files/reports/supporting-the-changing-research-practices -of-historians.pdf (accessed February 27, 2014).

Schonfeld, Roger C., and Ross Housewright. *Faculty Survey 2009: Key Strategic Insights for Libraries, Publishers, and Societies.* Ithaka S+R, 2010. http:// cyber.law.harvard.edu/communia2010/sites/communia2010/images/Faculty _Study_2009.pdf (accessed February 27, 2014).

Shaffer, Christopher J. "The Role of the Library in the Research Enterprise." *Journal of eScience Librarianship* 2, no. 1 (2013): doi:10.7191/jeslib.2013.1043.

Spiro, Lisa, and Geneva Henry. "Can a New Research Library Be All-Digital?" In *The Idea of Order: Transforming Research Collections for 21st Century Scholarship*, 5–80. Washington, DC: Council on Library and Information Resources, 2010. http://www.clir.org/pubs/reports/pub147/pub147.pdf# page=11 (accessed February 27, 2014).

Tenopir, Carol, Ben Birch, and Suzie Allard. *Academic Libraries and Research Data Services.* Chicago: Association of College and Research Libraries, 2012. http:// www.ala.org/acrl/sites/ala.org.acrl/files/content/publications/whitepapers/ Tenopir_Birch_Allard.pdf (accessed February 27, 2014).

Williams, Karen. "A Framework for Articulating New Library Roles." *Research Library Issues: A Bimonthly Report from ARL, CNI, and SPARC* 265 (2009): 3–8. http://old.arl.org/bm~doc/rli-265-williams.pdf (accessed February 27, 2014).

Williams, Peter, and Ian Rowlands. *Information Behavior of the Researcher of the Future. A Study Commissioned by the British Library and JISC.* 2008. http:// jdrulv01.jisc.ulcc.ac.uk/media/documents/programmes/reppres/ggworkpackageii .pdf (accessed February 27, 2014).

Zhang, Yuening, and Roger Beckman. "E-book Usage among Chemists, Biochemists and Biologists: Findings of a Survey and Interviews." *Issues in Science and Technology Librarianship* 65 (Spring 2011). doi:10.5062/F49G5JR3.

SUGGESTED READINGS

Dewey, Barbara, ed. *Transforming Research Libraries for the Global Knowledge Society.* Oxford: Chandos Publishing, 2010.
Foo, Schubert, Dion Goh, and Jin-Cheon Na. *Handbook of Research on Digital Libraries: Design, Development, and Impact.* Hershey, PA: Information Science Reference, 2009.

8

In an Uncharted Territory: Libraries' New and Emerging Services for eResearch

> The future is now, not ten years away, and ... libraries have no option but to understand and design systems around the actual behavior of today's virtual scholar.
> —Peter Williams and Ian Rowlands (2008)

Traditional library functions, discussed in the previous chapter, are only a fraction of what today's librarians do. Librarians are not only extending their classic services into the eResearch environment, but also creating new services that support evolving research practices. As research practices are being rethought and rearticulated, so are the library services that facilitate them. Some of these innovative services are a natural extension of established library functions, while other services reflect a significant break from traditional library roles and require additional investments and new skills. These new roles/services are the result of broadening the scope of what libraries do to support the evolving nature of academic research and scholarly communication.

As the scholarly and research environment is becoming increasingly Web based, online knowledge management is becoming an essential activity for most librarians whose work includes supporting research in their libraries.[1] In addition to traditional areas of expertise, such as gathering credible content, developing taxonomies, and providing guidance with regard to copyright issues, librarians are assuming the roles as open access publishers, digital library and portal designers, data curators, and metadata experts.

These new library roles have their genesis in the research community they serve and, to a great degree, correspond to and co-evolve with researchers' changing patterns of work. For example, the movement toward open access scholarship has offered a new entrée for libraries into open access publishing and enabled them to better connect and share innovations both with their peers and researchers they support. Further, librarians, like researchers, are challenged to work together in teams and collaborate on various projects across multiple institutional domains as well as across multiple professions and areas of expertise. For example, the E-Science Institute, designed to help librarians develop a strategic agenda for eResearch support at their institutions, involves intensive multi-institutional team work in which each team includes at least one person external to the library, such as an administrator or a faculty researcher.

In 2009, the four leading associations serving research universities—the Association of American Universities, Association of Research Libraries, Coalition for Networked Information, and the National Association of State Universities and Land Grant Colleges—"issued a call to action urging libraries to expand the dissemination of the full range of products of the university community's research and scholarship" (Hahn et al. 2009). Even though there is, as yet, no consensus on what products should be considered essential for libraries to provide in order to ensure eResearch support at their institutions, libraries responded to this call by taking on new roles that fall beyond the scope of their established practices and competencies. Among these new roles are data management and curation, establishment of digital repositories, electronic publishing, digitization of library materials, creation of digital libraries and research portals, and redesign of physical library spaces in order to integrate virtual collections and services.

DATA MANAGEMENT AND DATA CURATION

> Scientists are not necessarily good data managers and can more fruitfully spend their time doing science.
>
> —Clifford Lynch (2008, 28)

While the term *data* is broad and open to several interpretations, in the context of data management and data curation this term typically refers to "any information in binary digital form" (Digital Curation Centre 2008) that can be either born-digital or digitized.[2] Data management comprises of all aspects and processes related to the storage, use, access, and preservation of digital data produced from a given research project. Data curation is a broader concept and can be defined as ongoing management of data throughout its life cycle, from creation to the time when it is archived for future research purposes or later reuse.

Recently, data curation has been identified as one of the most important trends in academic libraries (Tenopir, Birch, and Allard 2012). This trend, to a great degree, is the libraries' response to the National Science Foundation's (NSF) mandate for managing federally funded research data, issued in 2011. NSF as well as other major research funders, among which are the Wellcome Trust, the UK Research Councils, the National Institutes of Health (NIH), and the National Endowment for the Humanities (NEH), are now requiring that grant applications include a data management plan (DMP) that outlines an applicant's strategy for how data will be produced in the course of a research project, where these data will be stored, how they will be preserved, and how they will be shared for the life of the research project and beyond.

In response to these requirements, libraries have taken an active role in managing and curating research data within their home institutions and in assisting researchers with designing data management plans. These services can be seen as a natural outgrowth of the library's core functions—to collect, to preserve, and to consult. Where data management and data curation services differ from traditional library functions is the need for librarians to establish and foster closer collaborations with researchers in order to become valuable and competent partners in the research process. To accomplish this goal, librarians are striving to broaden their awareness of data management needs and eResearch activities at their institutions to get a clear understanding of the role they can play in these activities and to identify new skills and competencies required for effective data management and data curation (Pryor 2009; Shaffer 2013).[3]

DATA CURATION STAGES

The five organizational stages for data curation developed by Kenney and McGovern (2003) may provide librarians with a tool with which they can assess their current status, performance, and future impact in the area of data curation. These stages are:

- Stage 1: Acknowledge (recognize a local issue/need to be addressed)
- Stage 2: Act (initiate relevant projects outside mainstream library functions)
- Stage 3: Consolidate (shift from relevant projects to long-term programs)
- Stage 4: Institutionalize (incorporate long-term programs into the broader institutional environment)
- Stage 5: Externalize (develop inter-institutional collaborations)

When fully realized, this five-stage "maturity model" for data curation can help address data management needs at the particular institution as well as gain prominence and cultivate partnerships with external organizations.

DATA CURATION INITIATIVES IN SELECTED LIBRARIES

Digital information lasts forever or five years, whichever comes first.
—Jeff Rothenberg (1997)

Tenopir, Birch, and Allard (2012) found that up to a third of all academic libraries are planning to offer data management and data curation services in the next few years, mostly in the realm of providing guides on how to locate and cite data sets and in assisting with data management plans. The libraries at Purdue, Cornell, Johns Hopkins, Massachusetts Institute of Technology (MIT), University of Virginia, George Mason University, University of Minnesota, and other institutions are already actively engaged in data curation activities at the university level. The Purdue University Libraries, for example, created the Distributed Data Curation Center (D2C2) (http://d2c2.lib.purdue.edu/) as a mechanism to bring researchers together to investigate different ways to manage data sets at Purdue. One of the most notable projects of D2C2 was an award-winning data curation profile toolkit (http://datacurationprofiles.org/) that provides "a flexible and interactive framework for libraries to become involved in the data management needs of their campuses" so that librarians and other information professionals can "begin meaningful conversations with faculty and administrators about the preservation of data, while building a community around data management" (Kinson 2013). The publicly available data curation profile toolkit developed at Purdue captures requirements for specific data sets generated by researchers as described by the researchers themselves and articulates an individual researcher's needs for managing that data set. In 2013, the D2C2 at Purdue Libraries received the Association of College and Research Libraries' Innovation in Science and Technology Librarianship Award for their work on the data curation toolkit.

At Cornell University, Albert R. Mann Library hosts DataStaR, an experimental *Data Sta*ging Repository (http://datastar.mannlib.cornell.edu/) that provides an environment for researchers to share data with peers, create metadata, and publish data sets to external repositories. At DataStaR, researchers can also obtain assistance from librarians at any stage of the research process (Steinhart 2010). In 2013, the DataStaR project has changed its focus to that of data registry. In partnership with Washington University in St. Louis, this project aims to "analyze researchers' needs and preferences to share and discover datasets and to enhance the DataStaR semantic platform for this use" (https://sites.google.com/site/datastarsite/). In addition, the Cornell University Libraries (CUL) manages two other digital data projects, the Cornell University Geospatial Information Repository (CUGIR) (http://cugir.mannlib.cornell.edu/) and the USDA Economics, Statistics and Marketing Information System (USDA-ESMIS) (http://usda.mannlib.cornell.edu/), as well as various digital collections. CUL also runs the Data Discussion Group (DDG—formerly Data Working Group

[DaWG]) (https://confluence.cornell.edu/display/culddg/Home) that hosts discussions and presentations by DDG members and Cornell faculty and staff to exchange information about data curation developments and activities in general as well as those taking place at CUL (Steinhart et al. 2008).

To address a growing need among faculty and students for data management and data curation skills, several academic libraries have developed "data curation literacy" programs at their universities to provide training in data management, including data planning, storage and backup, metadata, sharing and reuse, ethics, and preservation (Carlson et al. 2011). For example, the Data Literacy Project (http://wiki.lib.purdue.edu/display/ste/Home), funded by the grant from the Institute of Museum and Library Services (IMLS) and led by the Purdue University Libraries (in partnership with the libraries of the University of Minnesota, the University of Oregon, and Cornell University), is tasked to design and implement data information literacy (DIL) instruction programs for graduate students. Many of these DIL instruction programs are based on the suite of core DIL competencies proposed by Carlson et al. (2011), who stated that DIL "involves understanding what data mean, including how to read graphs and charts appropriately, draw correct conclusions from data, and recognize when data are being used in misleading or inappropriate ways" (633).

At Johns Hopkins University (JHU), Data Management Services (DMS) Group (http://dmp.data.jhu.edu/about-us/history-and-the-team/) consults JHU principal investigators (PIs) preparing National Science Foundation proposals on writing data management plans and makes available data management and archiving services using systems developed by the Data Conservancy (http://dataconservancy.org/). The MIT Libraries runs a series of the Digital Preservation Management Workshops (http://www.dpworkshop.org/work shops/fiveday.html) that explores core issues of digital preservation management and provides practical guidance for developing digital preservation programs to managers of digital content at various kinds of organizations. The University of Virginia Library has developed the Data Management Consulting Group (DMConsult) (http://dmconsult.library.virginia.edu/), in which librarians and data managers act as advisors for researchers.[4] The University of Minnesota Libraries offers the workshop titled "Creating a Data Management Plan for Your Grant Application" that satisfies the requirement for the continuing education component to maintain a PI's eligibility. George Mason University Libraries, in collaboration with University of Virginia, Virginia Tech, James Madison University, and Old Dominion University, has recently offered a two-and-a-half day Data Management Boot Camp designed for graduate students interested in learning more about data management issues and best practices. This collaborative training event featured data experts from across the state of Virginia and was offered via the 4VA telepresence system across five sites, thus providing an opportunity for hands-on practical experience. Other examples include a five-day course on Research Data Management (RDM) for graduate students in all disciplines at the University of Wisconsin–Madison and a data information literacy course for science and engineering students offered by Purdue University.

Another role that libraries are well positioned to play is that of providing researchers with skilled assistance during grant proposal writing. As Lynch (2003) observed, "faculty are typically best at creating new knowledge, not maintaining the record of this process of creation" (330). Stepping beyond traditional research consultation practices, librarians are assisting researchers with crafting data management plans, advising them on the use of the Data Management Plan Tool (DMPTool), drafting templates for data management plans to use in grant applications, and developing data management plan guides that can be used as templates. These activities provide librarians with an opportunity to extend their information management and consulting skills that fall within the scope of previous library practice into data curation services. This more advanced level of services is an important direction for library support of eResearch that can position the library as a vital service point for data curation needs.

DIGITAL REPOSITORIES

> Researchers ... struggle unsuccessfully with storage and management of a burgeoning volume of documents and data sets that they need and that result from their work ... and flounder in a disorganized and rising accumulation of useful findings that may be lost or unavailable when conducting future research.
> —Susan Kroll and Rick Forsman (2010)

The creation and maintenance of digital repositories is another key role that librarians have assumed in supporting eResearch. As research papers are increasingly being stored as a file, the new role of capturing scholarly records in digital media (some of which have never been published by traditional means), making them accessible, and preserving them over time offers librarians yet another opportunity to expand access to knowledge and thus further contribute to the scholarly communication system.

DIGITAL REPOSITORIES: AN OVERVIEW

A digital repository, in simplest terms, is a database for archiving digital content in the form of "digital objects."[5] While archiving is a typical function of libraries, the archiving of materials that can exist in a wide variety of digital formats (e.g., ASCII, HTML, JPEG, or PDF) is a challenge for librarians and requires collaboration with other professionals, including information technologists, archivists, administrators, and policy makers.

There are several types of digital repositories, the most common of which are research (or disciplinary) repositories, institutional repositories, e-print repositories, learning object repositories, and data repositories. While the mission and features of these digital repositories overlap, what distinguishes them from one another is the type of materials they collect, preserve, and make accessible.

Research, or disciplinary, repositories are usually sponsored by research funding or an organization and typically include scholarly works in either one specific discipline or a few associated disciplines. An example of a research (disciplinary) repository is PubMed Central (http://www.ncbi.nlm.nih.gov/pmc/), a repository of research papers in the life sciences maintained by the U.S. National Institutes of Health's National Library of Medicine.

Institutional repositories (IR) are a set of services for the management and dissemination of the intellectual output of a single or multi-institutional community. A typical institutional repository contains and facilitates access to "traditional" scholarly works (in a digital form) such as journal articles, book chapters, and thesis and dissertations authored by the institution's faculty, students, and staff. It can also include "supplementary" documentation of the intellectual life of the universities such as symposia, presentations, technical reports, working papers, learning and teaching materials and other types of documentation that libraries identify "as worth collecting" (Lynch 2003). SMARTech (https://smartech.gatech.edu/) at the Georgia Institute of Technology and D-Scholarship@Pitt (http://d-scholarship.pitt.edu/) at the University of Pittsburgh are the examples of institutional repositories.

ePrint repositories (also called ePrint archives) contain electronic copies of research papers, including preprints and postprints.[6] One of the first ePrint repositories was arXiv (http://www.arxiv.org/), created in 1991, a repository of research papers in particle, high-energy physics, and related fields. Originally based at the Los Alamos National Laboratory, arXiv has gradually expanded its coverage to include other scientific disciplines such as mathematics, computer science, astronomy, and quantitative biology and is currently funded and operated by Cornell University.

Learning object repositories store, manage, and share educational content ("learning objects") for reuse by educators and researchers. Learning objects can include modules, quizzes, presentations, images, videos, or other kinds of material or files that can assist with learning or can be used to create course content. The examples of learning object repositories are the Health Education Assets Library (HEAL) from the University of Utah (http://library.med.utah.edu/heal/), and the Texas Learning Object Repository (TxLOR) (http://www.txlor.org/) managed by the University of Texas at San Antonio.

Data repositories are designated for data storage and intended for making the data underlying scholarly publications discoverable, accessible, and reusable for researchers. There are presently hundreds of data repositories around the world where researchers can deposit and share their data. DataDryad.org (http://datadryad.org/), one of the well-established, reputable nonprofit international data repositories, stores data underlying the scientific and medical literature. Other examples include Data-PASS (http://www.data-pass.org/), a data repository for social science research, and ArtSTOR (http://www.artstor.org/index.shtml/), a repository of images in the arts, the humanities, and the sciences.[7]

The main components in the construction of a digital repository are information technologies and metadata. A set of information technologies, commercial or open source, provides mechanisms for importing, exporting, identifying, storing, and retrieving digital assets. Two of the largest providers of open source software for managing digital repositories are DSpace and Fedora. DSpace repository software (http://www.dspace.org/), created by the Massachusetts Institute of Technology in collaboration with the Hewlett Packard Corporation and released in 2002, provides access to the digital work of the whole organization through one interface. As the needs of these organizations might differ, DSpace allows customization of the workflow and other aspects of the system to make it fit the intended use of each organization. Fedora (Flexible Extensible Digital Object Repository Architecture) (http://fedora-commons.org/), originally developed at Cornell University and the University of Virginia Library in 1997, provides a general-purpose architecture for digital objects. DSpace and Fedora are presently managed by DuraSpace (http://www.duraspace.org/), a nonprofit organization that provides open source and cloud-based technologies for institutional repositories, digital libraries, digital archives, and virtual research environments. One of the newest services developed by DuraSpace is DuraCloud (http://www.duracloud.org/), launched in 2011, an open source technology for managing digital content in the cloud. Other major repository software tools used by libraries include EPrints (http://www.eprints.org/software/) and OPUS (Online Publications at University of Stuttgart) (http://elib.uni-stuttgart.de/opus/doku/about.php?la=en).

REDCap (Research Electronic Data Capture) (http://project-redcap.org/), developed by Vanderbilt University, is a newer open source electronic data capture tool targeted toward investigators working on clinical translational research. Researchers can input their experimental data directly into the system and then analyze, track, manipulate, and share their data with others.

The compilation of information technologies used for the construction and maintenance of a digital repository, however, is not "a fixed set of software and hardware" (Lynch 2003), but an evolving entity. One of the primary responsibilities of a digital repository is to provide a *continuous* access to its content even when the technologies that create and sustain it change or evolve. In order to function properly and achieve their mission—to capture and preserve the scholarly output "across time and new technologies" (ibid.)—digital repositories must ensure the longevity of the digital objects they collect. This mission can be accomplished only by an ongoing digital curation activities and management of technological changes—from backup procedures at regular intervals and maintenance of multiple copies of digital objects to the migration of digital content from one set of information technologies to the next.

Metadata are used to organize and control a wide range of different types of documents in a digital repository so that they can be discoverable, identifiable, and accessible. This is usually accomplished by assigning persistent identifiers to digital objects and describing them in well-supported standard formats.[8] The basic Dublin Core metadata schema, discussed in Chapter 2, is still widely used by digital repositories. Other, more complex metadata schemas used to describe digital objects are METS (Metadata Encoding and Transmission Standard), MODS (Metadata Object Description Schema), and PREMIS (Preservation Metadata: Implementation Strategies), among which METS, developed by OCLC and the Library of Congress, is presently the frontrunner for institutional repositories. For learning objects, the IEEE's Learning Object Metadata (LOM) standard is often used as the metadata schema.

INSTITUTIONAL REPOSITORIES

> Most individual faculty lack the time, resources, or expertise to ensure preservation of their own scholarly work even in the short term, and clearly can't do it in the long term that extends beyond their careers; the long term can *only* be addressed by an organizationally based strategy.
> —Clifford Lynch (2003, 330)

According to Clifford Lynch, executive director of the Coalition for Networked Information (CNI), an institutional repository (IR) is "a set of services that a university offers to the members of its community for the management and dissemination of digital materials created by the institution and its community members" and "a framework for organized stewardship and accessibility of these materials" (Lynch 2003, 328, 331).[9] What distinguishes institutional repositories from other types of repositories, and what makes them particularly valuable for researchers, is a greater degree of their commitment to long-term preservation and sustainability. In the words of Charles W. Bailey (2005), "Funding agencies may decide to stop supporting disciplinary archives with generous grants, or the individuals or organizations that offer them may lose interest. Once established as part of the institutional mission, IRs will persist" (265).

One of the important missions of IRs is the management of theses and dissertations by students in their universities. Although these materials are neither monographs nor serials, they often present original research findings of publishable quality that can result in a significant contribution to new knowledge.

While the major portion of an institutional repository's content is still concentrated on research publications authored by the institution's faculty, students, and staff, institutional repositories are now also collecting and maintaining access to other types of materials such as websites, learning objects, media, and 3D topographical representations. Some institutional repositories also include and maintain research data and data sets. What is being included into an institutional repository, how long the included materials are to be kept, and whether any of them might need to be disposed or transferred elsewhere are less an issue of the IR's software capacity and more a policy decision made by each institution. Even though, as Lynch has emphasized, solving these issues might be more challenging to solve on the policy front than on the technical side, such a selection policy can help improve the quality of digital repositories while reducing the quantity of maintained digital objects.

There is still a low level of awareness of institutional repositories among researchers and their value in generating greater exposure of research and potentially a larger number of citations and thus a higher research impact (Connaway and Dickey 2010). In addition, researchers lack confidence in such complex legal areas as intellectual property rights, copyright, and plagiarism (ibid.). Institutional repositories offer academic librarians an opportunity to become more deeply embedded as a core element in an institution's research enterprise by offering much-needed expertise in information management. They also enable academic librarians to develop new partnerships upon their preexisting relationships with academic units and research departments.

While much responsibility for the operational, technological, and administrative management of an institutional repository is situated in different units of the institution, librarians have taken on proactive roles in planning, establishing, and supporting institutional repositories. These roles include:

- Defining collecting priorities
- Managing digital collections
- Assisting in designing user-friendly institutional repository's interfaces
- Advocating and promoting use of institutional repositories, seeking out contributors, and serving as spokespersons to publicize the repositories' benefits and uses
- Providing user support and training
- Working collaboratively with information technologists and cataloguers on metadata schemes appropriate for a specific repository's digital collection
- Drafting policies and procedures and providing feedback about how they work in practice

Because institutional repositories rely on copyright agreements with publishers that allow or prohibit researchers to use their own texts in certain ways, libraries can also act as consultants for researchers on copyright issues, Creative Commons licensing options, and publisher ePrint policies.

LIBRARIES' NEW ROLES IN THE SCHOLARLY COMMUNICATION PROCESS

The scholarly communication process is a complex interdependent partnership among a number of key players: researchers, peer reviewers, editors, publishers, scholarly associations, academic institutions, and libraries. Until recently, libraries have primarily contributed to this partnership by providing access to scholarly collections and thus promoted a more efficient dissemination of knowledge—the main goal of scholarly communication. As the nature and context of scholarly communication are changing in that the scholarship becomes increasingly open, collaborative, and Web-based, so are the libraries' roles as partners in this process. For librarians, who are already making substantial investments in relatively unfamiliar (to them) areas of data management and digital repository services (among other things), these changes suggest additional new roles, among which are digital publishing and open access advocacy.

LIBRARY AS PARTNER IN PUBLISHING

Publishing represents an important part of the scholarly communication process (see Chapter 4). One way today's libraries are contributing to this process is by partnering with university presses and other scholarly publishers in order to enhance access to scholarly content through new publishing platforms.

Libraries have become more directly involved in the scholarly publishing process since 1993, when the Association of American University Presses (AAUP) and the Coalition for Networked Information (CNI) proposed a joint initiative forging nontraditional publishing alliances among university presses, university libraries, and university computer centers ("Coalition for Networked Information" 2010). Twenty-three universities were selected to participate in this joint initiative. Johns Hopkins University was the first to collaborate with its campus library and computer center to make the established scholarly journals published by the Johns Hopkins University Press (JHUP) available electronically. The result of this collaboration was Project MUSE.

Project MUSE (http://muse.jhu.edu/), a partnership between JHUP, Johns Hopkins's Milton S. Eisenhower Library, and Homewood Academic Computing, provides online access to electronic versions of print journals, primarily in the humanities and social sciences, published by JHUP, the oldest university press in the United States. In addition to its journal collection, Project MUSE in 2012 began offering access to peer-reviewed digital books from major university presses and scholarly publishers through the UPCC Book Collections, which are fully integrated with Project MUSE's journal content.[10]

HighWire Press (http://highwire.stanford.edu/), one of the leading ePublishing platforms in the sciences, is another notable example of the library-publisher partnership. Established in 1995 by Stanford University Libraries to address a growing concern about the dominant print-and-paper publishing model, HighWire Press aimed to assist scientific societies, scientific associations, and university presses with the publication of scholarly journals, accessible without subscription. HighWire Press's first project was the digital publication of the highly cited *Journal of Biological Chemistry* (*JBC Online*). Since then, HireWire Press has consistently maintained a cutting-edge design, functionality, and content capabilities and produced electronic editions of hundreds of scholarly high-impact journals, with an emphasis on the scientific, technical, and medical (STM) titles. Recently, both HighWire Press's scope and type of published material has expanded to include books, proceedings, and reference resources, including the *Oxford English Dictionary* (*OED*) online.[11]

Other libraries have also seized an opportunity to collaborate with publishers on new publishing models. For example, the University of California Press and the California Digital Library Publishing Group jointly produce print and eJournals, technical papers, print and eBooks, and conference proceedings as well as maintain the joint repository service eScholarship (http://www.cdlib.org/services/access_publishing/publishing/escholarship.html). Another example is the e-Pubs Journal Publishing Services (http://docs.lib.purdue.edu/), a collaboration of the Purdue University Libraries and Purdue University Press. The e-Pubs Journal Publishing Services offer free online access to Purdue-affiliated publications. In addition, they provide online publishing support for original publications, most of which are open access journals affiliated with schools or departments at Purdue.

In addition to complying with funders' mandates, researchers, both as authors and publishers, also need to comply with a number of other legal requirements related to intellectual property rights, copyright, and plagiarism, the complex areas in which they lack confidence (Connaway and Dickey 2010).

LIBRARY AS PUBLISHER

> With libraries moving toward digital publishing as a central or peripheral role, librarians have had to envision the library as not just a place to hold collections but as a possible creator of scholarly publications.
> —Laura Mullen (2010)

While the trend toward deeper integration between libraries and publishers accelerates, even though with varying degrees of success at different institutions, libraries are venturing one step further by taking on an actual publisher role themselves (Maughan Perry et al., 2011). Digital publishing technologies, combined with librarians' expertise in information management, access, and dissemination, enable librarians to play a more active role in the distribution of scholarly knowledge beyond simple archiving and mediation for published works.

The advent of open source–customizable publishing applications, such as Open Journal Systems (OJS) (http://pkp.sfu.ca/ojs/), has made the publishing process easier for librarians who might not have had enough experience in this area. OJS, developed by the Public Knowledge Project (PKP) (http://pkp.sfu.ca/) and released in 2001, supports author submissions, peer review, and indexing, making it an optimal choice for publishing scholarly journals. Other prevalent publishing platforms used by libraries are DSpace (http://www.dspace.org/), created by the Massachusetts Institute of Technology and managed by DuraSpace (http://www.duraspace.org/); CONTENTdm (http://www.contentdm.org/), currently managed by OCLC; and Digital Commons (http://digitalcommons.bepress.com/repository-software/books/), a commercial software produced by Bepress and is optimized for serials publishing (Mullins et al. 2012).

Over the past decade, many libraries have developed the capacity to publish scholarly literature in a digital environment. Mullins et al. (2012) found that around 75 percent of the 43 responding ARL (Association of Research Libraries) libraries published between one and six journals, most of which included open access journals. For libraries, who are already promoting open access publishing options to faculty, this trend presents an opportunity to align themselves more closely with the open access movement.

The recently established Library Publishing Coalition (LPC) (http://www.librarypublishing.org/) includes over 50 academic libraries whose mission is to support and promote library publishing initiatives, create a forum for sharing resources and best practices, and provide centralized leadership in such areas as training, networking, and professional development across institutions.

OPEN ACCESS INITIATIVES

The libraries' motivation to support open access (OA) publishing is due to at least three reasons: (1) the increasing journal costs and thus a potential for libraries to save in collection development costs and in serials management; (2) the emergence of public policies mandating open access to publications arising from government-funded research that position the library as a vital service point for supporting OA initiatives (i.e., establishing OA institutional memberships and OA publishing funds); and (3) the libraries' commitment to maintain one of their core values—the support and promotion of new models of scholarship.

OPEN ACCESS INSTITUTIONAL MEMBERSHIPS

Libraries can be among those academic units that support the open access publishing model through OA institutional memberships. These memberships subsidize author publication fees for affiliated faculty and thus encourage researchers to submit their work to OA journals. For example, prominent institutions around the world have joined in the BioMed Central (BMC) membership program (http://www.biomedcentral.com/libraries/membership) that, at the time of this writing, included over 500 members. The BMC's Institutional Membership waives the article processing charge (APC), which varies from journal to journal, and covers the entire cost of the article's publication process, including peer reviewing, editing, publishing, maintaining, and archiving.

The Public Library of Science (PLoS) launched the Institutional Accounts Program (http://www.plos.org/institutional-membership-program/), which allows institutions to make arrangements with PLoS to pay the APCs on behalf of their researchers. As of October 2013, the Institutional Accounts Program replaced PLoS's initial Institutional Membership Program, according to which institutional members were entitled to reduced charges for publication in all PLoS journals.

OPEN ACCESS PUBLISHING FUNDS

In addition to promoting open access authorship through OA institutional membership programs, a growing number of academic and research libraries are also establishing funds to support open access publishing (Open Access Directory 2014). According to SPARC (2014), an open access publishing fund (also called "a campus-based open access author fund" or "a campus open access fund") is "a pool of money set aside by an institution specifically to reimburse article processing or membership fees for articles published by members of the institution in open-access journals." Depending on the institution's financial capacity, an institutional open access publishing fund can cover either fully or partially the article processing charges, required by some open access publishers, such as PLoS, BioMedCentral, Frontiers, and Hindawi Publishing Corporation, and thus make it easier for researchers to publish in open access journals.[12]

OPEN ARCHIVES INITIATIVE (OAI)

Closely related to the mission of the open access movement, i.e., to facilitate free online access to research, is that of the Open Archives Initiative (OAI) (also referred to as the Open Archives Initiatives-for Metadata Harvesting [OAI-PMH]) (http://www.openarchives.org/). Developed by a team of researchers and librarians, OAI was launched at the Santa Fe Convention in 1999 as a means to provide interoperability among multiple information sources in order to enhance access to scholarly content. Sponsored by the Andrew W. Mellon Foundation, the Coalition for Network Information (CNI), Digital Library Federation (DLF), and the National Science Foundation (NSF),[13] the OAI is based on the hypertext transport protocol (HTTP) and extensible markup language (XML) open standards, and provides a mechanism for facilitating the collection, discovery, and sharing of distributed digital resources. This mechanism allows digital objects within repositories to be accessed by a greater number of external users. Even though the OAI's original purpose was to disseminate digital content from research archives, it is now also being used for other types of digital content and is becoming an important part of the digital library infrastructure. For example, Virginia Tech has applied the OAI to its Networked Digital Library of Theses and Dissertations (NDLTD).

ONLINE CONTENT MANAGEMENT

> Knowledge management is becoming an essential dimension of what we do.
> —Tony Horava (2010, 146)

Convenience of access to information has become a crucial factor in researchers' information-seeking. Researchers expect library support that is driven by their needs, "integrated into their workflows, available at the point of need, is good enough and is discipline specific" (Auckland 2012). To address this expectation, many libraries use traditional content management means, such as creation of online guides, to help researchers navigate information resources, while other libraries provide more targeted services tailored to specific needs and disciplines.

Given the volume and diversity of information resources, libraries have recognized the need to identify, organize, annotate, and better facilitate access to reliable scholarly resources through a single entry point. To address this need, library portals emerged "as a preferred enabling tool to connect users with electronic information resources" (Jackson 2005). This task provides librarians with an opportunity to apply their selection, evaluation, and resource organization skills to library portal development and thus provide a valuable service for researchers who face time-consuming tasks.

PORTAL DEFINITION

No consensus has emerged in library literature on a single definition of the term *portal*. This lack of consistency in how libraries define a portal is due to the diversity of concepts under the umbrella name "portal." Publications on library portals can be found under such subject headings as "web portals," "educational technology," "information management," and "federated searching applications." Several examples illustrate the diversity of definitions of the term portal:

- "[A] doorway that can be customized by individual users to automatically filter information from the web" (Zhou 2003, 120)

- "[A] customized learning and transactional Web environment, designed purposefully to enable an individual end-user to 'personalize' the content and look of the website for his/her own individual preference" (Lakos 2004, 9)
- "[A] portal is a user-centric customized, personalized, adaptive desktop" (Strauss, 2003, 29)

The term has also been used loosely by some libraries to describe home pages, aggregations of subject-specific links, or enhanced but static websites (Strauss 2003; Van Brakel 2003). Miller described this as "portalisation" and argued that the loose use of the term portal "diluted" its meaning (Miller 2003).

THE HISTORY OF PORTALS

Zhou traced the history of library portals to the 1960s, when the National Library of Medicine had digitized the *Index Medicus*, a bibliographic index of scientific journal articles focusing on medical science fields (Zhou 2003). However, the term *portal* did not appear in the library world until 1998, when the North Carolina State University Libraries launched the first library portal, called *MyLibrary@NCState*, conceived in 1998 and released in 2000. This portal, which allowed individual users to customize webpages that contained their most frequently consulted library resources and services by category and thus claimed to help them reduce "information overload," introduced the "My" concept of personalization to academic libraries (Ketchell 2000).

In the late 1990s, the rise of corporate portals, with their main purpose being to provide easy access to enterprise digital information, had prompted the growth of portals in academic libraries. These portals helped, or claimed to help, the user to "wade" through an overwhelming volume of Web-based information and to provide the user with an alternative way of retrieving dependable information beyond the capacity of Google and other " information.coms" (Jackson 2003). However, library portals did not proliferate much further after the robust initial phase. By the end of 2002, only one-half of 1 percent of libraries had implemented portals (Boss 2002).

PORTAL FEATURES

Various components and features of a library portal were discussed by different authors who largely agreed that the purpose of a library portal was to provide a single point of access to an organized collection of relevant resources in multiple formats and to provide the user with personalization and customization tools. Mary Jackson, project manager for the Scholars Portal project at the Association of Research Libraries (ARL) and one of the most prolific authors on the topic, described portals as "super discovery tools" through which users could identify "library-vetted" content as well as to cross-search databases and to access supporting services and tools such as interlibrary loan and online reference services (Jackson 2002, 2003, 2005). Campbell (2001) suggested that a portal should:

- Include high-quality content
- Be based on standards
- Search across multiple and disparate databases
- Offer many supporting tools
- Offer enhanced support services
- Integrate electronic thesauri

Some authors disputed the concept of library portals as "one-stop shops" for library services and suggested that in order to function effectively, they should not be isolated from the rest of the university learning experience and should be integrated with other college and university portals and systems where their visibility would be most prominent. Dempsey (2003) argued that a library portal should be embedded in course content management systems "where it makes most sense" (108). Strauss (2003) stated that libraries should not have their own portals but should instead have a series of portal pages aimed at different user groups, all contained within "one and only one" portal that would cover the needs of the entire university community.

NOTABLE PORTAL PROJECTS

Several library portal projects deserve special attention. Among them are:

- *The Scholars Portal project.* Launched in 2000 by seven member libraries of the Association of Research Libraries (ARL), The Scholars Portal Project aimed at creating a "single search," or cross-platform search tool, targeted at the higher education community.
- *MyGateway portal.* Designed as the personalized component of the University of Washington Libraries information gateway, MyGateway portal allowed users to create and maintain selected lists of resources.
- *MyLibrary portal.* Developed at Cornell University Library, MyLibrary portal is a collection of electronic resources and services that can be personalized and accessed at any time from any computer on the Internet.
- *The Wissensportal, or Knowledge Portal.* Designed by ETH-Bibliothek at the Swiss Federal Institute of Technology in Zurich, Switzerland, Knowledge Portal provides a single access point to all digital collections at the ETH-Bibliothek, including databases, eJournals, and audiovisual materials.

RESEARCH PORTALS

Few libraries, however, have well-developed research portals that act as information gateways to selected, organized, and annotated scholarly resources in a particular discipline or research field. While a research portal incorporates many elements of a typical library portal, its principal purpose is to create a virtual research space designed with the needs of the particular research community in mind and with special emphasis on discipline-specific information. Among the libraries that designed research portals at their institutions are the Health Sciences Library System (HSLS) at the University of Pittsburgh, which developed the Online Bioinformatics Resources Collection (OBRC) (http://www.hsls.pitt.edu/obrc/); and the University Libraries of George Mason University, which have created a large number of subject-specific research portals for the university's graduate programs (http://library.gmu.edu/portals.html/). These research portals, which combine the features of a blog, a resource database, a search engine, a collection of useful links, and RSS feeds for the tables of contents from the latest issues of selected discipline-specific journals, and which integrate library-owned materials with free Internet resources, provide access to both subscribed and free content in one convenient place. The research portal initiative at George Mason University is still evolving, but it has already received national recognition. In August 2009, the research portal initiative won a national Technology Innovator award from the *Campus Technology* magazine (http://campustechnology.com/articles/2009/07/22/campus-technology -innovators-awards-2009-portals.aspx).

Research portals, combining internal and external resources, can be viewed as a natural extension of the library's collection as well as an expansion of roles for librarians looking for new ways to contribute to research activities at their institutions. Other opportunities include a greater ability to increase the library's presence within the institution, to reach more users, and to better market library resources to the university community and thus encourage more effective use of library collections.

Staying on top of this dynamic trend is challenging but essential and may require a new set of skills and competencies. The following set of skills and competencies will equip a librarian to meet the challenge of developing a library research portal in a specific subject discipline.

- Ability to adapt to changing technological environments
- Good knowledge of current trends, discoveries, and resources within the discipline
- Knowledge of intellectual property management
- Knowledge of Web design and the ability to produce blogs, wikis, websites, and other electronic methods of communication
- Time management skills

Such key personality traits as flexibility, open-mindedness, ability to embrace change, and commitment to continual learning are also essential.

Furthermore, research portal development provides an opportunity for librarians to enhance their technical and communication skills by working collaboratively with colleagues from different library units who can bring to the partnership their unique expertise, competencies, and knowledge. It can also motivate librarians to stay current in their subject field and to further contribute to scholarship by keeping researchers well informed—through the portal's blog entries—about information resources in their subject area and alternative models for scholarly communication such as open access.

DIGITIZATION: MAKING THE PAST ACCESSIBLE

Digitization of books and other materials is now part of the work of many libraries around the world. Library digitization is the process of converting original library resources into digital format by utilizing scanners, optical character recognition (OCR) software, and other technologies. The ultimate purpose of library digitization is to ensure preservation while providing greater access to collections.

Digitization offers significant benefits both for researchers and for libraries. For researchers, the benefit of digitization manifests itself in the convenience of access to scholarly materials and the ability to search across and within works. For libraries, digitization provides a solution to the problem of preservation. Hughes and Green (2004) stated that "developing a digital surrogate [via digitization] of a rare or fragile original object can provide access to users while preventing the original from being damaged by handling or display" (327). In the United States and some other countries, preservation of historical, rare, and cultural heritage materials is one of the primary goals of digitization projects (Liu 2004; Henry and Smith 2010).

There are two kinds of digitization projects: mass digitization that aims to digitize a massive amount of printed materials, regardless of their content or value; and non-mass digitization that involves a careful selection of materials to be digitized. Examples of mass digitization projects are the Internet Archive (https://archive.org/), a free collection of digitized books, films, music records, and other materials; and the Open Content Alliance (OCA) (http://www.opencontentalliance.org/), which aims to digitize and provide open access to works in the public domain. Examples of non-mass digitization projects include the Nuremberg Trials Project from the Harvard Law School Library (http://nuremberg.law.harvard.edu/php/docs_swi.php?DI=1&text=overview), which digitized documents from the Nuremberg war crimes trials; and the Octavo Editions (http://octavo.com/editions/), which reproduces rare books in digital formats.

Project Gutenberg (http://www.gutenberg.org/), founded in 1971 by Michael Hart, who pioneered downloading eBook texts across what would become the Internet, is one of the oldest digitization projects and an early example of crowd-sourcing. Based on the efforts of volunteers who converted and submitted the books (Hart typed in the early postings himself), Project Gutenberg is developing a free library of public-domain eBooks. At the time of this writing, Project Gutenberg claimed to offer over 42,000 free digitized books available online.

In the library domain, the Library of Congress in the United States was one of the first national libraries to undertake a major library digitization project— the National Digital Library Program (NDLP) (http://memory.loc.gov/ammem/ dli2/html/lcndlp.html), launched in 1995. The purpose of the NDLP was to digitize the Library of Congress's selected collections that chronicled "the nation's rich cultural heritage," including books, pamphlets, motion pictures, manuscripts, and sound recordings. Since then, the Library of Congress has completed other major digitization projects and is currently one of the largest providers of noncommercial digitized content on the Internet. Among the more recent digitization projects initiated by the Library of Congress are American Memory (http://memory.loc.gov/ammem/index.html), a digitized collection of "written and spoken words, sound recordings, still and moving images, prints, maps, and sheet music"; and Historic Newspapers (http://chronicling america.loc.gov/), which offers access to digitized copies of newspapers from 1836 to 1922.

In Europe, the British Library and the Bibliothèque Nationale de France were among the pioneers of library digitization. One of the first projects sponsored by the British Library was The International Dunhuang Project (IDP) (http://idp.bl.uk/). Established by the British Library in 1994 and cur-rently being maintained in partnership with 22 libraries, museums, and research institutes from 12 countries, IDP provides access to thousands of digitized copies of artifacts from Dunhuang and archaeological sites of the Eastern Silk Road, such as manuscripts, paintings, and textiles. The Biblio-thèque Nationale de France's digital library Gallica (http://gallica.bnf.fr/? lang=EN), founded in 1997, offers online access to over 2.5 million digitized documents, including books, maps, manuscripts, sound recordings, and images. More recently, the Bibliothèque Nationale de France has been coordinating the international Europeana (http://www.europeana.eu/) and Europeana Regia (http://www.europeanaregia.eu/) digitization projects. Together, Europeana's and Europeana Regia's collections contain millions of digital versions of manuscripts representative of the European historical and cultural heritage.

Examples of journal digitization projects include JSTOR (http://www .jstor.org/) and e-depot (http://www.kb.nl/en/). JSTOR, a not-for-profit digi-tal library, has digitized the back files of nearly 2000 journals, reaching back into the mid-nineteenth century for some titles, and over two million primary sources. In addition, it currently provides access to over 19,000 books. E-depot at the Koninklijke Bibliotheek (The National Library of the

Netherlands) is one of the world's first digital archiving systems for academic publications. Launched in 2003, it now contains millions of journal articles and serves as the digital archive of the Dutch academic institutional repositories and of all research papers published by a UK-based open access publisher, BioMed Central. E-depot also archives online journals published by Elsevier, Springer, and other scientific publishers.

Many other libraries around the world are initiating digitization projects also as they convert their resources to digital formats and offer access to these resources through electronic means. The items selected for digitization are mainly those primary materials that are susceptible to physical damage or loss, such as old manuscripts, photographs, and noncommercial live-audio recordings. For example, the Valley of the Shadow (http://valley.lib.virginia.edu/) archives the primary resources that document the lives of people in Augusta County, Virginia, and Franklin County, Pennsylvania, during the American Civil War. Created by the University of Virginia, the Valley of the Shadow's materials are collected by the University Library and disseminated digitally through the University Library's managed content (LMC) environment. This process, which Smith (2008) described as "making the past accessible," is especially beneficial for scholars in the humanities, who rely heavily on historical documents as primary sources for their research (Rutner and Schonfeld 2012).

Another noteworthy project is the Tufts University's Perseus Digital Library project in that it integrates text material with images and archaeological data. A pioneer in applying HTML for textual analysis, Perseus Digital Library combines what it calls "human readable information," "machine actionable knowledge," and "machine generated knowledge" (Perseus Digital Library 2014).

Public and school libraries are undertaking digitization projects also, even though they are performed on a smaller, more local scale. Many of these projects aspire to preserve counties' and towns' history and culture through the digitization of local newspaper articles, photographs, postcards, and letters (Scally 1999). These libraries can also play an important, although indirect, role in supporting and contributing to community research projects such as Shaping San Francisco Digital Archive (http://www.shapingsf.org/), a creator of the interactive website FoundSF (http://foundsf.org/) that provides users with access to the city's history through images, stories, and videos.

DIGITAL LIBRARIES: A COLLECTION AND A SERVICE

The creation of digital libraries is another step toward improving online access to scholarly information resources. The concept of digital libraries is different from that of library digitization. Library digitization is a process of converting library resources from a physical medium, for example paper or photograph, into a digital format, while a digital library is an organized collection of library digitized resources available via the Internet. Digital libraries offer services to researchers that include bibliographic and full-text searching, results management, metadata, and text and image display.

Even though digital libraries take many forms, they all share a common goal. The goal of a digital library is threefold: to provide a long-term preservation of digitized content, to improve access to this content, and to emulate and extend library services. Digital libraries also share a common infrastructure: they are built upon collections of born-digital or digitized materials and rely on the Internet for accessing and sharing these collections.

The advantages of digital libraries for eResearch are obvious. By providing a convenient mechanism for locating, searching, and browsing the organized annotated scholarly resources, digital libraries reduce information overload and enable researchers to target specific types of documents they need for their research. Digital libraries also add value to their collections through services that enable researchers to explore and interact with information resources, for example, through integrated audio and video components, as well as connect to resources in other collections. Moreover, digital libraries act as curators of research materials, preserving them for future use.

An example of a digital library that provides support for eResearch, especially for research in the humanities, is the HathiTrust Digital Library (http://www.hathitrust.org/). Established in 2008 by 13 universities of the Committee on Institutional Cooperation (CIC) and the University of California, HathiTrust is an open digital library of primary sources scanned from the collections of nearly 80 academic and research libraries across North America and Europe.[14] The recently established HathiTrust Research Center (HTRC) (http://www.hathitrust.org/htrc), launched jointly with Indiana University and the University of Illinois at Urbana-Champaign, has been designed to make the technology serve the researcher. It develops software tools and a cyberinfrastructure to support research by enabling researchers to customize their environment, combine their own data with those of the HTRC, and allowing them to contribute their own tools.

In addition to collecting, organizing, and making available scholarly resources, digital libraries also collect and provide access to data. For example, Digital Morphology (http://www.digimorph.org/), a National Science Foundation digital library at the University of Texas at Austin, provides access to collections of X-ray-computed tomography of biological specimens. Other examples of data digital libraries are the Land Treatment Digital Library (https://ltdl.wr.usgs.gov/), created by the U.S. Geological Survey to provide access to land treatment data in text, tabular, spatial, and image formats; and the NSO Digital Library (http://diglib.nso.edu/), an online archive of major astronomical data sets from the National Solar Observatory.

A growing need to manage large amounts of data and information resources presents a challenge for digital libraries that have been exploring cloud computing as an economical infrastructure that would allow the provision of information technology resources on demand, and thus lower management complexity and cost involved in managing the information technology infrastructure themselves (Yang and Wanjun 2010; Han and Wang 2011).[15] By bridging the gap between digital libraries and information technology, cloud computing may help digital libraries find more appropriate solutions that meet the demands of researchers who need rapid and reliable access to a growing body of digitized knowledge.

LIBRARY AS PLACE: ADJUSTING TO A DIGITAL RESEARCH ENVIRONMENT

> The philosophy of warehousing large book collections, "just-in-case-they-are-needed," is rapidly becoming redundant as users turn their backs on the library as a physical space.
> —Peter Williams and Ian Rowlands (2008)

Ultimately, what matters most to researchers is whether they can work effectively. With regard to library services and collections, this means speed, flexibility, and ease of online access to scholarly resources, delivered most particularly to their desktops. Even though the methods of discovering information resources vary among researchers, the common theme among all these methods is the expectation that scholarly resources should be only a few keystrokes away and available without too much intermediated assistance and too much time spent going from one website to another. According to Prabha et al. (2007), researchers seek information by "satisficing," i.e., accepting an adequate solution over an optimal one. Williams and Rowlands (2008) described this information-seeking behavior pattern as horizontal, bouncing, checking, flicking, and viewing in nature. The unavailability of convenient access to a particular library resource may even reflect researchers' belief in the nonexistence of the resource itself (Connaway and Dickey 2010; Lippincott 2010).

The importance of meeting these needs to enhance the productivity of researchers—and, ultimately, to the advancement of scholarship in general—cannot be overestimated. While numerous factors affect how each individual library fulfills these needs and addresses the pressures of declining library budgets and increasing eJournal prices, the researchers' needs for access to scholarly resources is key in any library where support of research activities is a critical service.

Given their user-oriented mission, libraries will make any effort to not only provide access to resources required by their research communities, but also take into account the researchers' "wayfinding" preferences with regard to locating and accessing resources, which typically means accessing resources remotely via the World Wide Web. These efforts result in enabling researchers in academia to access bibliographic databases, journals, and books without leaving their offices or homes. Outside the institutional system of libraries, scholars can have individual access to digital libraries and a vast array of open access resources from all over the world.

As the use of digital and computational technology for conducting research grows, libraries find that they must expand beyond traditional conceptions of the library as space and shift an emphasis from the housing of print collections and servicing users at reference desks to accommodating researchers' preferences for accessing collections and services remotely via the Web. In addition, the increased use of mobile technology and social networking is also encouraging further reexamination of the design of a library as a space in which physical and virtual spaces can coexist. This may include providing self-service research inquiry points, for example, via virtual reference service, as well as providing more traditional service points for research assistance, for example, at reference desks (Khan 2009). In this sense, a virtual library is a complement and a supplement, rather than a substitute, for a physical library. This complementary and interconnected nature of the physical and the virtual libraries can optimize the productivity of researchers with regard to access to scholarly resources by allowing them to "make the most of each seamlessly" (Cribb and Schmidt 2011).

Contrary to common belief, a future library might not become "all-digital," meaning that it will provide *only* online access to its collections and services (Finnemann 2014). While pressures for libraries to "re-imagine" their services and collections continue, the concept of library as place remains important in both physical and virtual environments. According to the New York University's (NYU) 21st Century Library Project study, three main themes have emerged with regard to the role of library as place: "1) unfettered, seamless, and comprehensive access to library collections and other research materials; 2) the importance of physical and virtual spaces for both contemplation and research; and 3) the role of the library as a gateway to the world's resources" (New York University 2007).

While some libraries see strategic advantages in transitioning to "all-digital" collections and services, no single approach to library design will suffice. Each approach is important for addressing the specific library community's diverse information and research needs. The role of "physical" library as a common ground for formal and informal communication that connects researchers, librarians, technology, and resources has continued value. In recent years, it has gained particular popularity as a "social" space or group study space. At the same time, the physicality of library as space is being challenged as it is progressively incorporating the notion of library as "a virtual space."

Virtual Research Environments (VREs), discussed in detail in Chapter 4, are being increasingly integrated into the library's "virtual space" as Virtual Learning Environments (VLEs) are at the present time.[16] Libraries, especially those in the higher education institutions, are actively facilitating the research process by setting up VREs that provide a wide range of Web-based administrative and management tools, as well as research tools, to support individual and team research projects at their institutions. The libraries' role as a knowledge manager and research facilitator is crucial for the successful development of VREs, even though this role would require the acquisition of new skills. As Kranich (2007) observed, "with research resources diffused throughout the campus and beyond, their broad scope requires stewardship well beyond the boundaries of the edifices or structures that defined them in the past" (106).

NOTES

1. Davenport and Prusak (1998) defined *knowledge management* as the process of capturing, distributing, and effectively using knowledge. From the library's perspective, knowledge management means an efficient management of online information resources.

2. Harvey (2010) defines "born-digital" materials as "materials created using a computer" and "digitized" materials as materials that are "the result of a process of digitizing analog materials" (46). These materials are not limited to scientific data and also include data in the humanities, social sciences, and other disciplines.

3. Although there is no evidence in published literature that librarians are involved in the process of generating research data, they do engage in advising researchers on how to locate and identify preexisting research data (Auckland 2012).

4. Initially named the Scientific Data Consulting Group (SciDaC), the group was renamed the Data Management Consulting Group to reflect its broader mission of working with researchers in various disciplines.

5. In their highly regarded article *A Framework for Distributed Digital Object Services,* Kahn and Wilensky (2006) defined a digital object as "a data structure whose principal components are digital material, or data, plus a unique identifier for this material, called a handle" (116).

6. A preprint is an electronic draft of a research paper before it has been peer-reviewed and published. A postprint is an electronic draft of a research paper that has been peer-reviewed but not yet published. Both preprints and postprints are called ePrints.

7. Databib (http://databib.org/), a searchable bibliography of data repositories, simplifies the task of navigating data repositories by offering access to a registry of more than 500 data repositories worldwide.

8. According to Harvey (2010), persistent identifiers are "labels for digital objects that remain the same regardless of where the object is located ... even when it moves to another server or to other repositories or archives" (72). Examples of persistent identifiers include a URL (Uniform Resource Locator), URN (Uniform Resource Name), PURL (Persistent Uniform Resource Locator), and DOI (digital object identifier).

9. Institutional repositories originated in universities but have spread into other types of educational organizations such as colleges and research institutes.

10. The University Press Content Consortium (UPCC) was launched in 2012 to offer readers a new way to locate and browse eBooks. More information about the UPCC can be found at http://muse.jhu.edu/about/UPCC.html.

11. In 1999, Oxford University Press (OUP) selected HighWire Press as a supplier to construct and host the *Oxford English Dictionary (OED)* online.

12. A complete guide to setting up an Open Access Publishing Fund and detailed information regarding the operation of existing funds is available at http://sparc.arl.org/resources/funds.

13. Other institutions involved in OAI include Harvard University, Cornell University, OCLC, The Library of Congress, the Joint Information Systems Committee of the UK, and many others.

14. HathiTrust takes its name from the Hindi word "*huthi*" for "*elephant*," an animal celebrated for its long memory and thus symbolizing the digital library's commitment to preservation.

15. The libraries' use of a cloud-based SaaS (Software as a Service) delivery model reaches back into early 2000 with the establishment of companies like SerialsSolutions (http://serialssolutions.com) and LibGuides (http://www.libguides.com).

16. The concept of VREs is similar to and in common with the older notion of VLEs such as open source products Sakai and uPortal, as well as commercial products such as Blackboard, that have become commonplace across university campuses.

WORKS CITED

Auckland, Mary. *Re-skilling for Research: An Investigation into the Role and Skills of Subject and Liaison Librarians Required to Effectively Support the Evolving Information Needs of Researchers*. Research Libraries UK (RLUK), 2012. http://hdl.voced.edu.au/10707/204093 (accessed February 9, 2014).

Bailey, Charles W., Jr. "The Role of Reference Librarians in Institutional Repositories." *Reference Services Review* 33, no. 3 (2005): 259–67. doi:10.1108/00907320510611294.

Boss, Richard. "How to Plan and Implement a Library Portal." *Library Technology Reports* 5 (2002).

Campbell, Jerry Dean. "The Case for Creating a Scholars Portal to the Web: A White Paper." *portal: Libraries and the Academy* 1, no. 1 (2001): 15–21. doi:10.1353/pla.2001.0002.

Carlson, Jacob, Michael Fosmire, C. C. Miller, and Megan Sapp Nelson. "Determining Data Information Literacy Needs: A Study of Students and Research Faculty." *portal: Libraries and the Academy* 11, no. 2 (2011): 629–57. doi:10.1353/pla.2011.0022.

"Coalition for Networked Information (CNI)." In *Encyclopedia of Library and Information Science*, 3rd ed., edited by Marcia J. Bates and Mary Niles Maack. Boca Raton, FL: CRC Press, 2010.

Connaway, Lynn S., and Timothy J. Dickey. *The Digital Information Seeker: Findings from Selected OCLC, RIN and JISC User Behaviour Projects*. 2010. http://www.jisc.ac.uk/publications/reports/2010/digitalinformationseekers.aspx (accessed February 27, 2014).

Cribb, Gülçin, and Janine Schmidt. "Online Space Displacing Physical Space in Libraries: The Impact of Online Use on the Transformation of Library Design." 2011. http://hdl.handle.net/10679/154 (accessed February 28, 2014).

Davenport, Thomas H., and Laurence Prusak. Working Knowledge: How Organizations Manage What They Know. Boston: Harvard Business School Press, 1998.

Dempsey, Lorcan. "The Recombinant Library: Portals and People." *Journal of Library Administration* 39, no. 4 (2003): 103–36. doi:10.1300/J111v39n04_10.

Digital Curation Centre. "DCC Charter and Statement of Principles." Edinburgh: Digital Curation Centre, 2008. http://www.dcc.ac.uk/docs/publications/DCCLifecycle.pdf (accessed February 27, 2014).

Finnemann, Niels Ole. "Research Libraries and the Internet—on the Transformative Dynamic between Institutions and Digital Media." *Journal of Documentation* 70, no. 2 (2014): 202–20. doi:10.1108/JD-05-2013-0059.

Hahn, Karla, Charles Lowry, Clifford Lynch, David Shulenberger, and John Vaughn. "The University's Role in the Dissemination of Research and Scholarship—a Call to Action." Washington, DC: Association of American Universities, 2009. http://www.aau.edu/WorkArea/DownloadAsset.aspx?id=8924 (accessed February 27, 2014).

Han, Lingling, and Lijie Wang. "Research on Digital Library Platform Based on Cloud Computing." In *Advances in Computer Science, Environment, Ecoinformatics, and Education*, 176–80. Berlin: Springer Berlin Heidelberg, 2011.

Harvey, Douglas Ross. *Digital Curation: A How-to-Do-It Manual*. Chicago: Neal-Schuman Publishers, 2010.

Henry, Charles, and Kathlin Smith. "Ghostlier Demarcations: Large-Scale Text Digitization Projects and Their Utility for Contemporary Humanities Scholarship." In *The Idea of Order: Transforming Research Collections for 21st Century Scholarship*, 106–15. Washington, DC: Council on Library and Information Resources, 2010. http://www.clir.org/pubs/reports/pub147/pub147.pdf#page=112 (accessed February 27, 2014).

Horava, Tony. "Challenges and Possibilities for Collection Management in a Digital Age." *Library Resources and Technical Services* 54, no. 3 (2010): 142–52.

Hughes, Lorna M., and David Green. *Digitizing Collections: Strategic Issues for the Information Manager*. London: Facet Publishing, 2004.

Jackson, Mary E. "The Advent of Portals." *The entity from which ERIC acquires the content, including journal, organization, and conference names, or by means of online submission from the author.Library Journal* 127, no. 15 (2002): 36–39.

Jackson, Mary E. "Looking Ahead: The Future of Portals." *Journal of Library Administration* 43, no. 1–2 (2005): 205–20. doi:10.1300/J111v43n01_13.

Jackson, Mary E. "Portals, Access, and Research Libraries." *Journal of Library Administration* 39, no. 4 (2003): 57–63. doi:10.1300/J111v39n04_06.

Kahn, Robert, and Robert Wilensky. "A Framework for Distributed Digital Object Services." *International Journal on Digital Libraries* 6, no. 2 (2006): 115–23. doi:10.1007/s00799-005-0128-x.

Kenney, Anne R., and Nancy Y. McGovern. "The Five Organizational Stages of Digital Preservation." In *Digital Libraries: A Vision for the 21st Century: A Festschrift in Honor of Wendy Lougee on the Occasion of her Departure from the University of Michigan*, edited by P. Hodges, M. Bonn, M. Sandler, and J. P. Wilkin. Ann Arbor: University of Michigan Library, Scholarly Publishing Office, 2003.

Ketchell, Debra S. "Too Many Channels: Making Sense out of Portals and Personalization." *Information Technology and Libraries* 19, no. 4 (2000): 175–79.

Khan, Ayub. *Better by Design: An Introduction to Planning and Designing a New Library Building*. London: Facet Publishing, 2009.

Kinson, Casey. "ACRL Honors the 2013 Award Winners, Part 2: A Recognition of Professional Development." *College and Research Libraries News* 74, no. 5 (2013): 230–37. http://crlnews.highwire.org/content/74/5/230.full (accessed February 27, 2014).

Kranich, Nancy. "Countering Enclosure: Reclaiming the Knowledge Commons." In *Understanding Knowledge as a Commons: From Theory to Practice*, edited by C. Hess and E. Ostrom, 85–122. Cambridge, MA: MIT Press, 2007.

Kroll, Susan, and Rick Forsman. *A Slice of Research Life: Information Support for Research in the United States*. Dublin, OH: OCLC Online Computer Library Center, Inc., 2010, http://www.oclc.org/content/dam/research/publications/library/2010/2010-15.pdf (accessed February 27, 2014).

Lakos, Amos A. "Portals in Libraries. Portal Vision." *Bulletin of the American Society for Information Science and Technology* 31, no. 8–9 (2004). doi:10.1002/bult.1720310105.

Liu, Yan Quan. "Best Practices, Standards and Techniques for Digitizing Library Materials: A Snapshot of Library Digitization Practices in the USA." *Online Information Review* 28, no. 5 (2004): 338–45. doi:10.1108/14684520410564262.

Lippincott, Joan K. "Information Commons: Meeting Millennials' Needs." *Journal of Library Administration* 50, no. 1 (2010). http://www.cni.org/staff/joanpubs/IC.jlibadmin.lippincott.preprint.pdf (accessed February 28, 2014).

Lynch, Clifford A. "Big Data: How Do Your Data Grow?" *Nature* 455, no. 7209 (2008): 28–29. doi:10.1038/455028a.

Lynch, Clifford A. "Institutional Repositories: Essential Infrastructure for Scholarship in the Digital Age." *portal: Libraries and the Academy* 3, no. 2 (2003): 327–36. doi:10.1353/pla.2003.0039.

Maughan Perry, Anali, Carol Ann Borchert, Timothy S. Deliyannides, Andrea Kosavic, Rebecca Kennison, and Sharon Dyas-Correia. "Libraries as Journal Publishers." *Serials Review* 37, no. 3 (2011): 196–204. doi:10.1016/j.serrev.2011.06.006.

Miller, Paul. "Towards a Typology for Portals." *Ariadne* 37 (October 2003). http://www.ariadne.ac.uk/issue37/miller (accessed February 27, 2014).

Mullen, Laura Bowering. *Open Access and Its Practical Impact on the Work of Academic Librarians: Collection Development, Public Services, and the Library and Information Science Literature*. Oxford: Chandos Publishing, 2010.

Mullins, J. L., C. Murray-Rust, J. L. Ogburn, R. Crow, O. Ivins, A. Mower, D. Nesdill, M. P. Newton, J. Speer, and C. Watkinson. Library Publishing Services: Strategies for Success: Final Research Report. Washington, DC: SPARC, 2012. http://docs.lib.purdue.edu/purduepress_ebooks/24/ (accessed February 27, 2014).

New York University. *NYU 21st Century Library Project: Designing a Research Library of the Future for New York University Report of a Study of Faculty and Graduate Student Needs for Research and Teaching*. January 2007. http://library.nyu.edu/about/KPLReport.pdf (accessed February 28, 2014).

Open Access Directory. "OA Journal Funds." http://oad.simmons.edu/oadwiki/OA_journal_funds (accessed February 1, 2014).

Perseus Digital Library. "Research." http://www.perseus.tufts.edu/hopper/research (accessed April 21, 2014).

Prabha, Chandra, Lynn Silipigni Connaway, Lawrence Olszewski, and Lillie R. Jenkins. "What Is Enough? Satisficing Information Needs." *Journal of Documentation* 63, no. 1 (2007): 74–89. doi:10.1108/00220410710723894.

Pryor, Graham, and Martin Donnelly. "Skilling Up to Do Data: Whose Role, Whose Responsibility, Whose Career?" *International Journal of Digital Curation* 4, no. 2 (2009): 158–70. doi:10.2218/ijdc.v4i2.105.

Rothenberg, Jeff. "Digital Information Lasts Forever—or Five Years, Whichever Comes First." *RAND Video* 79 (1997).

Rutner, Jennifer, and Roger C. Schonfeld. "Supporting the Changing Research Practices of Historians." *Final Report from ITHAKA S+R*. December 2012. http://www.sr.ithaka.org/sites/default/files/reports/supporting-the-changing-research -practices-of-historians.pdf (accessed February 27, 2014).

Scally, Patricia H. "Digital Technology Projects Already Thriving in Public Libraries." *Public Libraries* 38, no. 1 (1999): 48–50. http://www.editlib.org/p/86314 (accessed February 28, 2014).

Shaffer, Christopher J. "The Role of the Library in the Research Enterprise." *Journal of eScience Librarianship* 2, no. 1 (2013). doi:10.7191/jeslib.2013.1043.

Smith, Abby. "The Research Library in the 21st Century: Collecting, Preserving, and Making Accessible Resources for Scholarship." In *No Brief Candle: Reconceiving Research Libraries for the 21st Century*, 13–20. Washington, DC: Council on Library and Information Resources, 2008. http://www.clir.org/pubs/ reports/pub142/pub142.pdf (accessed February 27, 2014).

SPARC. "Campus-Based Open-Access Publishing Funds." http://sparc.arl.org/ resources/funds (accessed January 21, 2014).

Steinhart, Gail. "DataStaR: A Data Staging Repository to Support the Sharing and Publication of Research Data." *International Association of Scientific and Technological University Libraries, 31st Annual Conference*. West Lafayette, IN: Purdue University Libraries, 2010. http://docs.lib.purdue.edu/iatul2010/ conf/day2/8 (accessed February 27, 2014).

Steinhart, Gail, John Saylor, Paul Albert, Kristine Alpi, Pam Baxter, Eli Brown, Kathy Chiang, et al. *Digital Research Data Curation: Overview of Issues, Current Activities, and Opportunities for the Cornell University Library*. Ithaca, NY: CUL Data Working Group, 2008. http://hdl.handle.net/1813/10903 (accessed February 27, 2014).

Strauss, H. "Web Portals: The Future of Information Access and Distribution. *Serials Librarian* 44, no. 1–2 (2003): 26–35. doi:10.1300/J123V44n01_04.

Tenopir, Carol, Ben Birch, and Suzie Allard. *Academic Libraries and Research Data Services*. Chicago: Association of College and Research Libraries, 2012. http:// www.ala.org/acrl/sites/ala.org.acrl/files/content/publications/whitepapers/ Tenopir_Birch_Allard.pdf (accessed February 27, 2014).

Van Brakel, Pieter. "Information Portals: A Strategy for Importing External Content." *Electronic Library* 21, no. 6 (2003): 591–600.

Williams, Peter, and Ian Rowlands. *Information Behaviour of the Researcher of the Future*. A Study Commissioned by the British Library and JISC, 2008. http:// jdrulv01.jisc.ulcc.ac.uk/media/documents/programmes/reppres/ ggworkpackageii.pdf (accessed February 27, 2014).

Yang, Jie, and Liu Wanjun. "Cloud Computing in the Application of Digital Library." In *2010 International Conference on Intelligent Computation Technology and*

Automation (ICICTA), vol. 1 (2010): 939–41. http://doi.ieeecomputer society.org/10.1109/ICICTA.2010.39 (accessed February 28, 2014).

Zhou, Joe. "A History of Web Portals and Their Development in Libraries." *Information Technology and Libraries* 22, no. 3 (2003): 119–28. http://aaa.volospin .com/BT606B/zhou-history-of-web-portals.pdf (accessed February 27, 2014).

9

Skilling Up for eResearch: Core Competencies and Training Opportunities for Librarians

> Librarians may need to raise their profile, become "researchers" themselves; getting embedded in the research community; gaining credibility; and collaborating as equals.
> —Moira Bent, Pat Gannon-Leary, and Jo Webb (2007, 93)

By assuming new responsibilities as partners in eResearch, libraries are creating new expectations. Researchers, who rely on libraries for dissemination and preservation of knowledge, are placing a great deal of trust in the competence of library professionals and expect them to deliver eResearch support expertly and with confidence. The influential National Science Foundation report on cyberinfrastructure described the need not only for high-performance technological tools and networks, but also for skilled information professionals to facilitate their use (National Science Foundation 2003).

To ensure that libraries live up to these expectations, "re-skilling" (Auckland 2012) is essential for librarians who need to extend their skills and competencies beyond the scope of traditional library practices.[1] Traditional skills, such as subject knowledge, skills in vendor relations, and "liaisoning" (i.e., outreach activities in assigned academic departments and programs), can be layered inside these newer skills that represent both a profound change and a continuation of traditional practice.

SKILLS FOR eRESEARCH

While there is a clear trend in libraries toward providing eResearch support at their institutions, eResearch librarianship (also referred to as eScience librarianship) is still not a well-defined field (Alvaro et al. 2011). It is a field that evolves rapidly and has some ambiguity with regard to what skills and areas of knowledge are considered essential for eResearch librarians and how these skills and areas of knowledge can be applied appropriately to their services. Although librarians are used to "living without the comfort of expertise" (Lattuca 2001), meaning that they routinely research in unfamiliar fields and with unfamiliar terminology, it is essential to establish baseline eResearch knowledge and skills among librarians so that they can move beyond a vague awareness of eResearch to a more well-informed understanding of its key concepts, practices, and core technologies.

Several studies attempted to identify skills and competencies required for supporting eResearch (Choi and Rasmussen 2009; Kim, Addom, and Stanton 2011; Kim, Warga, and Moen 2013; Pryor and Donnelly 2009). Most of these studies, however, focused on identifying skills and competencies tightly connected to specific positions, such as those with "electronic," "data," "repository," or "digital" in the job title. These positions usually require advanced technological expertise related to high-performance and cloud computing, data management, data curation, digital repository maintenance, software development, remote communications, visualization, and computer programming. Not every librarian needs the same level of advanced technological expertise (or deep disciplinary knowledge) in order to provide eResearch support. Furthermore, technological skills and disciplinary knowledge cannot exist in isolation, and personal and business skills are equally important for eResearch. As Cribb and Schmidt (2011) observed, "high tech still requires the high personal touch." There are, however, requirements for fundamental proficiency in current technological applications for all librarians engaged in eResearch support as well as for knowledge of key eResearch concepts and familiarity with eResearch trends and practices.

A more comprehensive study, conducted by Mary Auckland for Research Libraries UK (RLUK), expanded the list of competencies required for research support. The goal of this study was to map the information needs and information-seeking behavior of researchers to the role of subject librarians and to determine what skills and areas of knowledge subject librarians needed or would need in the future to provide support the researchers require (Auckland 2012). The study was based on data from professional literature and questionnaire returns from participating organizations around the world that included libraries, organizations known to provide training for librarians, and library and information studies schools from Europe, Australia, and North America. The findings of the study, presented in the final report *Re-skilling for Research*, identified a set of 32 skills and areas of knowledge that the study participants described as essential for becoming trusted and competent partners in research. Although many of these skills fall within the scope of core competencies and a traditional mix of activities expected of any subject librarian (e.g., knowledge of their discipline/subject, information literacy skills, and proficiency in the use of information discovery tools), the study also uncovered a high skills gap in nine key areas, which were more directly related to supporting eResearch (as opposed to traditional research) and in which the participants felt they needed the most training. These nine key areas are:

1. Ability to advise on preserving research outputs
2. Expertise to advise on data management and curation
3. Knowledge to support researchers in complying with the mandates of research funders, including open access and open sharing requirements
4. Ability to advise on discipline-specific data manipulation tools
5. Expertise to advise on data mining
6. Knowledge to advocate, and advise on, the use of metadata
7. Ability to advise on the preservation of project records, such as research-related correspondence
8. Knowledge of sources of potential research funding
9. Skills for developing metadata and advising on discipline- and research project–specific metadata standards and practices (Auckland 2012)

Despite its value, this list is hardly comprehensive. As the field of eResearch continues to evolve, so do the skills required for research support. The following list expands the range of skills perceived to be central for effective eResearch support and groups them into seven major categories that emphasize core knowledge areas, competencies, and interpersonal skills over specialized technological skills. These seven categories are: (1) familiarity with key eResearch concepts; (2) knowledge of current eResearch trends and policies; (3) data literacy competencies; (4) technological skills; (5) competencies related to institutional research support; (6) personal skills; and (7) business skills.

Familiarity with Key eResearch Concepts

This includes knowledge and understanding of:

- The difference between eResearch and traditional research, between eResearch and eScience
- Research life cycle
- Types of research data
- Metadata standards and metadata tagging for research data
- Data life cycle
- Principles of data management and data curation
- Types of eResearch-enabling technologies and tools
- Role of collaboration in the eResearch environments

- Importance of scholarly communication in the research process
- Disciplinary differences with regard to eResearch practices

Knowledge of Current eResearch Trends and Policies

This includes the knowledge and understanding of:

- Sources of potential research funding
- Current research funder mandates and compliance policies with regard to data and research outputs
- Data management plan components
- Concept of open access, including open access publishing and open sharing requirements
- Copyright laws as apply to scholarly output, in order to be able to advise researchers on publishing options (in addition to open access), fair use rights, reuse of research data, and educational use
- Concepts of transdisciplinarity and open scholarship

Data Literacy Competencies

This includes knowledge and skills such as:

- Understanding concepts of data, data types, and diversity of data
- Knowledge of existing metadata standards and naming conventions
- Knowledge of commonly used data file formats
- Ability to advise on the preservation of project records
- Ability to conduct data interviews
- Ability to discuss funder compliance requirements with regard to research data
- Ability to instruct on developing a data management plan
- Ability to discuss data ownership, copyright and intellectual property, and confidentiality and privacy requirements
- Understanding of data identifiers such as the Data Object Identifier (DOI) system
- Ability to locate existing data
- Ability to cite data properly
- Ability to provide guidance on the handling and management of unpublished research data
- Ability to create data management research guides
- Awareness of major data analysis and data manipulation tools within specific disciplines
- Awareness of open source options for data repositories
- Ability to advise on depositing data in an institutional repository or in external repositories and data archives

- Ability to assist with finding relevant external data sets
- Ability to advise on data ethics issues such as intellectual property rights, issues of confidentiality and privacy, implications for sharing (or not sharing) data, and assigning attribution for one's work

Technological skills

This includes skills such as:

- Fluency with current computer technology and current software applications (e.g., Microsoft Office tools)
- Proficiency in the use of presentation software (e.g., PowerPoint, Apple Keynote for Mac, Prezi, and OpenOffice Impress)
- Familiarity with cloud-based storage systems (e.g., DropBox and Google Drive)
- Basic knowledge of collaborative technologies such as video-, tele- and Web-conferencing technologies; instant messaging; content management systems; and online workflow tools
- Knowledge of Web design and ability to produce blogs, wikis, websites, and other electronic methods of communication
- Proficiency in the use of bibliometrics tools and techniques (e.g., citation analyses and impact factors)
- Familiarity with bibliographic management software applications (e.g., EndNote, RefWorks, and Zotero)

Competencies Related to Institutional Research Support

This includes knowledge and skills such as:

- Knowledge of institutional policies with regard to research and research computing, including research data backup policy
- Knowledge of institutional policies on intellectual property
- Knowledge of institutional repository solutions for data and scholarly output
- Ability to advise on preserving research outputs
- Ability to refer researchers for assistance to appropriate research units and administrative offices
- Ability to provide grant writing support, including assistance with developing data management plans

Personal Skills

This includes skills such as:

- Flexibility
- Adaptability to change

- Research skills
- Active listening skills
- Interviewing skills
- Motivation
- Collaboration skills
- Perseverance
- Commitment to continual learning

Business Skills

This includes skills such as:

- Team building skills
- Training and train-the-trainer skills
- Change management skills
- Project management skills
- Negotiating, marketing, and advocacy skills
- Policy writing skills
- Time management and task prioritization skills

While assigning eResearch support tasks to subject librarians is not yet an established practice in many libraries, the future of eResearch librarianship may well depend to a significant degree on the acquisition and continuous updating of these skills and knowledge areas.

TRAINING OPPORTUNITIES

There is no single delivery mechanism for acquiring eResearch knowledge, skills, and competencies. Some of them are being covered, to a greater or lesser extent, by programs and courses in library schools (in cooperation with other disciplines and practitioners), while others are acquired on the job and supplemented by attendance at workshops and short courses, and still more others are gained through self-education and self-training.

Library and Information Science (LIS) Programs

The following list is a sample of programs and courses currently offered at American Library Association–accredited Library and Information Science (LIS) programs in North America. These programs and courses were identified through a content analysis of course descriptions and syllabi by using eResearch core competencies as a criterion for inclusion. Some of these programs were established through an Institute of Museum and Library Services (IMLS) Laura Bush 21st Century Librarian (LB21) grant (http://www .imls.gov/applicants/detail.aspx?GrantId=9).

Master's Level Programs and Courses

- Certificate of Advanced Study in Data Science, School of Information Studies (iSchool), Syracuse University
  http://coursecatalog.syr.edu/2013/programs/data_science
  Comprises two core courses in databases and data science and several elective courses from such areas as scholarly communication and collaboration, digital curation, digital libraries, research project management, statistics, technologies, and visualization.

- Data, Data Practices, and Data Curation, Department of Information Studies, University of California at Los Angeles (UCLA)
  http://polaris.gseis.ucla.edu/cborgman/Chriss_Site/Courses_files/IS289H-andoutWin2012Borgman.pdf
  This two-part course examines data practices and services, including data-intensive research methods; social studies of data practices; national and international data policy, comparisons between disciplines; management of data by research teams, data centers, libraries, and archives; technical standards for data and metadata; and data curation. Includes lectures (through videoconference) by researchers and practitioners from the National Academy of Sciences, the Library of Congress, and other prominent organizations.

- Data Curation Education Program (DCEP), Graduate School of Library and Information Science, Center for Informatics Research in Science and Scholarship, University of Illinois at Urbana-Champaign
  http://cirss.lis.illinois.edu/CollMeta/dcep.html
  Provides a strong focus on the theory and skills necessary to work directly with academic and industry researchers who need data curation expertise.

- Data Librarianship, Faculty of Information, University of Toronto
  http://current.ischool.utoronto.ca/course-descriptions/inf2115h
  Addresses "topics in the acquisition, management and retrieval of numerical information, both aggregated (statistics) and disaggregated (data)."

- Digital Curation and Data Management Graduate Academic Certificate (GAC), University of North Texas
  http://lis.unt.edu/digital-curation-and-data-management
  This four-course GAC is aimed at training new librarians and retraining experienced librarians in the area of digital curation and data management. It is also intended for graduate students in nonlibrary fields who may be responsible for managing and curating research data.

- DigIn Digital Information Graduate Certificate program, School of Information Resources and Library Science, University of Arizona
  http://sirls.arizona.edu/programs/digIn
  Combines intensive, hands-on technology exercises with learning the theoretical principles needed to manage large, complex digital collections.

- Introduction to Research Data Management, School of Library and Information Studies, University of Wisconsin–Madison
  http://www.slis.wisc.edu/continueed-DataMgmt.htm
  An introductory course intended for liaison librarians, scholarly communication librarians, systems librarians, and digital librarians.

Introduction to Scientific and Technical Data Collections: An Introduction to Management and Preservation of Scientific Data, School of Information Sciences, University of Texas at Austin
http://courses.ischool.utexas.edu/Anderson_Bill/2012/spring/INF382R/schedule.php
Examines communication patterns, data collection, and access methods for scientific and technical data.

Post-Masters Certificate (PMC) Programs

- Data Curation, School of Information and Library Science, University of North Carolina at Chapel Hill
  http://sils.unc.edu/programs/graduate/post-masters-certificates/data-curation
  Consists of two introductory courses, six online courses, and two project-oriented independent studies related to the student's current or desired work environment

- iCamp Project, University of North Texas (UNT)
  http://icamp.unt.edu/icamp/content/icamp-project
  A collaborative project between the UNT's College of Information and the UNT Libraries, funded by the LB21 grant. Develops curricula and programs in digital curation, digital librarianship, and digital preservation.

Doctoral-Level Programs

- eScience Librarianship @ Syracuse University, School of Information Studies (iSchool), Syracuse University (in partnership with Cornell University Libraries)
  http://eslib.ischool.syr.edu/wp/
  Funded by the LB21 grant, includes courses in scientific data management, cyberinfrastructure, and data services, as well as an eScience "lab" that focuses on such themes as institutional data policies, models for data publication and sharing, and scientific workflow tools.

Mentoring Programs

- EScience Librarianship Mentoring Program, Cornell University Library, and iSchool, Syracuse University
  A two-year mentoring program led by the Cornell University Library for students enrolled in the eScience Librarianship program at Syracuse University's iSchool. (More information about this program can be found at: http://escholarship.umassmed.edu/jeslib/vol1/iss3/1/.)

- LLAMA Mentoring Program
  http://www.ala.org/llama/llama-mentoring-program
  Developed by the American Library Association's Library Leadership and Management Association, this program "pairs librarians who are currently in leadership positions with librarians who are interested in becoming leaders."

Continuing Education

- DuraSpace/DLF E-Science Institute (ESI)
  http://duraspace.org/e-science-institute
  Sponsored by DuraSpace and Digital Library Federation (DLF). A six-month
  learning experience with three online modules and one in-person module
  designed to assist institutions in developing a sound strategic agenda for their
  support of eResearch in general, and eScience in particular.
- MANTRA: Research Data Management Training
  http://datalib.edina.ac.uk/mantra/
  A free self-paced online course developed at the University of Edinburgh and
  funded by JISC Managing Research Data program. Provides online learning
  materials reflecting research data management practices in three disciplinary
  contexts: social science, clinical psychology, and geoscience. Includes video
  interviews with leading researchers, quizzes, and practical exercises.

Self-Education and Self-Training

While degree programs, courses, workshops, and other formal ways of learning continue to have their value, it is equally important for librarians to take
advantage of less formal ways of being trained in eResearch skills, such as
keeping up with current literature and current news. Journals that regularly
publish papers related to eResearch librarianship include:

- *D-Lib* Magazine
  http://www.dlib.org
  Dedicated to digital library research and development.
- *Journal of eScience Librarianship*
  http://escholarship.umassmed.edu/jeslib/
  An open access, peer-reviewed journal. Focuses on services related to data-
  driven research in the physical, biological, and medical sciences.
- *International Journal of Digital Curation*
  http://www.ijdc.net/
  An open access journal that publishes articles and news items on digital
  curation and related issues.

Other helpful resources for self-education include the e-Science Portal for
New England Librarians: A Librarian's Link to eScience Resources (http://
esciencelibrary.umassmed.edu/index), CurateCamp (http://curatecamp.org/),
and Digital Curation Centre (http://www.dcc.ac.uk/training).

NOTE

1. BusinessDictionary.com (2014) defines a skill as "an ability and capacity
acquired through deliberate, systematic, and sustained effort to smoothly and adap-
tively carry out complex activities or job functions involving ideas (cognitive skills),
things (technical skills), and/or people (interpersonal skills)." A competency can be

described as knowledge of professional, technical, subject and other matters that individuals gain through education or experience.

WORKS CITED

Alvaro, Elsa, Heather Brooks, Monica Ham, Stephanie Poegel, and Sarah Rosencrans. "E-Science Librarianship: Field Undefined." *Issues in Science and Technology Librarianship* 66 (2011): 1–16. doi:10.5062/F46Q1V55.

Auckland, Mary. *Re-skilling for Research: An Investigation into the Role and Skills of Subject and Liaison Librarians Required to Effectively Support the Evolving Information Needs of Researchers.* Research Libraries UK (RLUK), 2012. http://hdl.voced.edu.au/10707/204093 (accessed on February 9, 2014).

Bent, Moira, Pat Gannon-Leary, and Jo Webb. "Information Literacy in a Researcher's Learning Life: The Seven Ages of Research." *New Review of Information Networking* 13, no. 2 (2007): 81–99. doi:10.1080/13614570801899983.

Choi, Youngok, and Edie Rasmussen. "What Qualifications and Skills Are Important for Digital Librarian Positions in Academic Libraries? A Job Advertisement Analysis." *Journal of Academic Librarianship* 35, no. 5 (2009): 457–67.

Cribb, Gülçin, and Janine Schmidt. "Online Space Displacing Physical Space in Libraries: The Impact of Online Use on the Transformation of Library Design." 2011. http://hdl.handle.net/10679/154 (accessed February 28, 2014).

Kim, Jeonghyun, Edward Warga, and William Moen. "Competencies Required for Digital Curation: An Analysis of Job Advertisements." *International Journal of Digital Curation* 8, no. 1 (2013): 66–83. doi:10.2218/ijdc.v8i1.242.

Kim, Youngseek, Benjamin K. Addom, and Jeffrey M. Stanton. "Education for eScience Professionals: Integrating Data Curation and Cyberinfrastructure." *International Journal of Digital Curation* 6, no. 1 (2011): 125–38. doi:10.2218/ijdc.v6i1.177.

Lattuca, Lisa R. *Creating Interdisciplinarity: Interdisciplinary Research and Teaching among College and University Faculty.* Nashville, TN: Vanderbilt University Press, 2001.

National Science Foundation. *Revolutionizing Science and Engineering through Cyberinfrastructure: Report of the National Science Foundation Blue Ribbon Advisory Panel on Cyberinfrastructure.* Arlington, VA: National Science Foundation, 2003, http://www.nsf.gov/od/oci/reports/toc.jsp (accessed on February 20, 2014).

Pryor, Graham, and Martin Donnelly. "Skilling Up to Do Data: Whose Role, Whose Responsibility, Whose Career?" *International Journal of Digital Curation* 4, no. 2 (2009): 158–70. doi:10.2218/ijdc.v4i2.105.

SUGGESTED READINGS

Marcum, Deanna B., and Gerald George, eds. *The Data Deluge: Can Libraries Cope with E-science?* Santa Barbara, CA: ABC-CLIO, 2010.

Morrison, Heather. *Scholarly Communication for Librarians.* Oxford: Chandos Publishing, 2009.

10

In Search of Unity: Toward New Modes of Knowledge Production

> The very use of the phrase "knowledge production" rather than
> "research" ... emphasizes that new knowledge can appear at every stage
> of the process by which information is generated, collected, processed,
> curated, distributed, and used.
>
> —Sandra Braman (2006, 6)

To some extent, the interdisciplinary collaborative eResearch practices and initiatives described in Chapter 5 reflect on the idea that eResearch is a more complex concept than traditional research inasmuch as it creates more extensive cross-disciplinary linkages than traditional research. At the same time, they also reflect on an emerging scholarship theme that research should not only transcend the boundaries of scientific and "nonscientific" knowledge and integrate different disciplinary perspectives, but also move beyond inter-disciplinary problem-solving toward transdisciplinary scholarship. While interdisciplinary research transcends the boundaries of scientific and "nonsci-entific" knowledge disciplines, transdisciplinary scholarship views research as a mutual, interdependent learning partnership between scholarship and society, and involves synergistic coalitions with policy makers, educators, practitioners, development agencies, and other stakeholders outside of aca-demia (Bunders et al. 2010; Hirsch Hadorn et al. 2008). This integrative pro-cess, referred to as "knowledge democracy," links scholarly and practical knowledge and reflects their mutual dependencies. The first involves problem identification and problem structuring; the second involves the application of research results to addressing and solving problems in the real world. This shift creates a demand for researchers and research organizations such as universities to modify their approach to knowledge production.

Although only time will tell whether this trend will prevail or whether new trends will emerge and become more prominent, the future of eResearch (and, consequently, of eResearch librarianship) is likely to see the following:

1. An emphasis on digital scholarship co-evolutionary with technological advancements
2. A fundamental shift toward transdisciplinarity of research
3. A continuing move toward "openness" at every stage of knowledge production and knowledge distribution

Collectively, these trends promise to strengthen and refine the link between research and society and, in so doing, accelerate both the knowledge production and knowledge distribution.

UBIQUITOUS COMPUTING IN A FLAT WORLD

> [T]he world is becoming flat. Several technological and political forces have converged, and that has produced a global, Web-enabled playing field that allows for multiple forms of collaboration without regard to geography or distance—or soon, even language.
> —Thomas L. Friedman (from an interview with *Wired* magazine, May 2005)

In 1993, scientists at Xerox PARC envisioned a future, in which computers would become pervasive, woven through people's daily lives and activities (Weiser 1994). Today, an ever more pervasive network connects computers and mobile technology in real time all over the world, giving rise to ubiquitous computing that impacts not only the daily lives of individuals and businesses, but also the way research is conducted and communicated.[1] The following technological trends are currently seeing significant development and will continue to shape eResearch practices in the near future:

- *Proliferation of mobile devices and sensors.* The widespread use of sensors and inexpensive local wireless connectivity creates opportunities for ambient data collection[2] and easy data sharing.
- *Data processing technologies.* A new generation of technologies address the challenges of processing large data sets such as MapReduce, Hadoop Distributed File System (HDFS), NoSQL (Not Only SQL) data stores, MPP (Massively Parallel Processing) databases, and in-memory databases processing systems.
- *Data-intensive computing.* With this form of computing, researchers are able to progressively filter, miner, and transform massive volumes of data

into information (which, in turn, is converted into knowledge) that can help the users make decisions more quickly and efficiently.

- *On-demand computing resources and services.* The advent of on-demand use of vast computing infrastructure (e.g., clouds and computing grids) enables researchers to analyze "big data" with low usage cost.

- *Visualization technology.* The visualization of data is becoming an increasingly important synthesis tool for exploration and analysis in a data-intensive research workflow.

- *Internet.* The Internet-enabled decentralized, globalized, mobilized information sharing is expanding the availability of information while lowering the participants' costs.

- *Availability of faster, more efficient computers.* Energy-efficient computers, which are built for processing complex software simultaneously and effectively, will enable researchers who face multiple demands on their time to access resources rapidly and conveniently and undertake increasingly ambitious projects.

- *Social networking.* Recent Web paradigms such as the Social Web and the Semantic Web combined with the capabilities of consumer technologies (e.g., smartphones, palmtops, and Personal Digital Assistants [PDAs]) provide new and creative ways to advance scholarly communication among researchers across disciplinary, institutional, and geographical borders.

- *Open source model.* An open source framework facilitates access to data, collaboration across organizational and geographical boundaries, and open rules for sharing that enable or mandate various forms of open scholarship.

Digital technology is, undoubtedly, one of the most powerful eResearch-driving forces that enable breakthroughs that might not be otherwise possible. At the same time, technological solutions are evolving faster than our understandings of their impacts and benefits for scholars and for the society in general. Although these technological solutions drive, to a certain extent, novel research methods, they also raise a number of nontechnological concerns, including legal, ethical, social, and disciplinary issues. In *The World Is Flat: A Brief History of the Twenty-First Century,* Friedman (2005) observed that digital technologies have contributed to the creation of a level playing field between nations, groups, and individuals. However, he argued, there was no guarantee that these technologies would be used for the benefit of humanity because the disempowered live in the "flat world" but "don't have the tools or the skills or the infrastructure to participate in any meaningful or sustained way" (382).

Recently, transdisciplinary research has been seen as a potentially effective means for solving, mitigating, or preventing a wide range of social, economic, and quality-of-life-related problems such as violence, unemployment, sustainability, or environmental pollution. Solutions to these problems rarely exist within orderly categories of academic discipline but are instead distributed across disparate disciplines.

BEYOND DISCIPLINES: LINKING RESEARCH AND THE "LIFE-WORLD"

The world has problems, but universities have departments.
—Garry D. Brewer (1999, 328)

Research has historically been detached from "practical life or the life-world"[3] (Hirsch Hadorn et al. 2008, 20). As research continues to become increasingly multidimensional, complex, and interdependent, it moves beyond inter- and multidisciplinary combinations of academic disciplines toward a new approach to understanding of the relationship between knowledge and society known as transdisciplinarity.[4]

Transdisciplinarity is neither a new discipline nor a new research methodology but rather a new mode of knowledge production that is "driven by the need to solve problems of the life-world" (ibid., 29) and "making academic research an authentic part of the globalized world it claims to study" (Leavy 2011, 14)—or what Giri has called "a new way of thinking" (Giri 2002, 103). All disciplines, when viewed separately, offer a limited, however unique, perspective of the society they attempt to study. Even inter- and multidisciplinary approaches to research, although having made an invaluable contribution to bringing diverse disciplines together, can go only so far in the integration and synthesis of scholarship and society. Transdisciplinarity, on the other hand, attempts to bridge the gap between academic research objectives and public needs in order "to create new conceptual, theoretical, methodological, and translational innovations that integrate and move beyond discipline-specific approaches to address a common problem" (Harvard School of Public Health 2014).

The concept of transdisciplinarity as a novel way of looking at the relationship between knowledge and society emerged in a seminar on interdisciplinarity held in Nice, France, in 1970. The idea is attributed to the Swiss philosopher and psychologist Jean Piaget, who stated that transdisciplinarity "will not be limited to the interactions or reciprocities between the specialized researches, but will locate these links inside a total system without stable boundaries between the disciplines" (Piaget 1973, 144).

The term "transdisciplinarity" (TD) was coined by the Austrian astrophysicist Eric Jantsch who envisioned a multi-level systemic coordination of research, innovation, and education. According to Jantsch (1972), "the essential characteristic of a transdisciplinary approach is the coordination of activities at all levels of the education/innovation system towards a common purpose" (114). From this perspective, transdisciplinarity can be seen as part of a social process, and transdisciplinary research can be seen as "public-good research" that is initiated by unsolved problems (Pohl and Hirsch Hadorn 2007).

In the ensuing decades, other perspectives on transdisciplinarity gained wide attention. In *The New Production of Knowledge* (1994), Gibbons et al. formulated the thesis that beside the traditional disciplinary production of knowledge (which they called Mode 1), there is another form (which they called Mode 2) that can be characterized by its transdisciplinary approach that is not circumscribed in any existing disciplinary field and is strongly sensible to social needs. Nicolescu in his *Manifesto of Transdisciplinarity* (2002) identified three pillars of transdisciplinarity: complexity, multiple levels of reality, and the logic of the included middle. Nicolescu argued that transdisciplinarity, in contrast to the one-dimensional reality of classical thought, acknowledges multidimensionality and that the logic of the included middle is capable of describing coherence among different levels of reality, inducing an open structure of unity (Nicolescu 2002). Thompson Klein (2004) states that "[t]ransdisciplinary vision, which replaces reduction with a new principle of relativity, is transcultural, translational, and encompasses ethics, spirituality, and creativity" (516). Pohl and Hirsch Hadorn (2007) argue that transdisciplinary research deals with problems in such a way that it can "(a) grasp the complexity of problems, (b) take into account the diversity of scientific and life-world perceptions of problems, (c) link abstract and case-specific knowledge, and (d) develop knowledge and practices that promote what is perceived to be the common good" (20). Further terms derived from studies relating to the interaction of research and policy emerged in the early 1990s such as "mandated science" (Salter 1988) and "regulatory science" (Jasanoff 1990).

Although the interpretations of transdisciplinarity vary from one author to the other (as would be expected with an emergent and complex concept) and are "fluid," they all have one assumption in common: the search for unity, the unity of multiple (possibly all) disciplines aiming to generate knowledge that is socially valuable, and the unity of knowledge and society. In starting research with "life-world" common problems as opposed to conceptual problems, researchers might be able to contribute to solving these problems in a more efficient manner.

The transdisciplinary approach to research has grown rapidly over the last few decades, particularly in health, environmental, educational, and social studies, due to several reasons, including the social justice movements of the 1960s and 1970s (such as the civil rights movement, the women's movement, and the gay rights movement), the rise of environmental concerns, the globalization of the world, and technological advancements. While the social justice movements and environmental concerns have exposed a range of widespread issues on the global level, globalization has transcended geographical and cultural limits and thus allowed for a multinational, multicultural exchange of ideas about addressing these concerns. Technology has further propelled advances in transdisciplinary research via the development of research collaborations that allowed researchers to work on "combined projects" (Ernst 2008) and make the global world problems a subject of scientific inquiry across disciplinary, temporal, and geographical boundaries. An example of such a transdisciplinary project is SEAD, the Network for Sciences, Engineering, Arts, and Design (http://sead.viz.tamu.edu/index.html). The SEAD Network, originating from a series of workshops sponsored by the National Science Foundation's (NSF) Computer and Information Science and Engineering (CISE) Information and Intelligent Systems (IIS) program in 2010–2011, aims to bring together scientists, engineers, artists, funders, policy makers, and representatives from nonprofit organizations to address the needs of the transdisciplinary research community, including the development of a digital archive of resources for its members.

OPEN SCHOLARSHIP: THE PRINCIPLE OF OPENNESS IN RESEARCH

> [T]he Open Scholar is someone who makes their intellectual projects and processes digitally visible and who invites and encourages ongoing criticism of their work and secondary uses of any or all parts of it—at any stage of its development.
>
> —Gideon Burton (2009)

Similar to the concept of transdisciplinarity, the principle of openness in scholarship has a strong ideological basis rooted in the pursuit for democratization of knowledge. The principle of openness means the move toward unrestricted access (or at least with only a few restrictions) to research data, processes, methodologies, and discoveries by anyone.[5] As Fuchs observed, scientific communication is in principle "open" because closing off communication would violate the scientific norm of an endless refinement of knowledge (Fuchs 2002). The principle of openness is, however, no longer restricted to scientific communication but applies to other disciplines, as well as to the way of conducting research in general.

Presently, the move toward openness has found the most resonance in the scholarly publishing paradigm, and was most prominently manifested by emergence of the open access publishing model discussed in Chapter 4. In addition to disseminating their research outputs through open access journals, researchers are using a number of other approaches to conduct research "in the open," such as sharing logs of research, data, and research proposals; contributing their data and manuscripts to institutional or national repositories; maintaining open digital presence through social networking sites (e.g., scientific blogs and wikis); and participating in open online conferences.

In education, the move toward open scholarship is gaining worldwide attention as a variety of governmental, institutional, and philanthropic organizations continue to adopt open educational resource (OER) policies and to support OER development.[6] OERs, enabled by digital technologies, are further acting to democratize the scholarship process in which "anyone can now learn anything from anyone at anytime" (Bonk 2009, 7–8). In addition, the practice of creating open courses, similar to MIT's OpenCourseWare project (http://ocw.mit.edu/index.htm), has taken root at universities that make their course materials (in the form of syllabi, video lectures, audio recordings, course notes, presentation files, and other learning objects) available to the public.[7] This evidence speaks to the evolving nature of open scholarship and the efficacy of openness as an inclusive approach, be it in conducting research, communicating research results, or in educating the "researchers of tomorrow."

AT THE KNOWLEDGE FRONTIERS: ROLES AND CHALLENGES OF FUTURE LIBRARIES

> Knowledge about knowledge has a peculiar multiplier or leverage effect on the growth of knowledge itself. The more we know about learning and the transmission of knowledge, and the more we know about the processes by which knowledge advances at the frontiers, the more efficient will be the use of resources, both in education and in research.
> —Kenneth Boulding (1968)

The value of knowledge, as expressed by Boulding's statement above, conveys one of the basic principles for libraries that support eResearch. Understanding how research works at the knowledge frontiers, how new knowledge is communicated and integrated with existing knowledge, and how it is consumed is key to fostering knowledge production and distribution. While developments in eResearch present significant challenges for libraries, they offer libraries a potential to further elevate their mission as knowledge managers and thereby raise their overall status and profile.

In the 2008 report, *No Brief Candle: Reconceiving Research Libraries for the 21st Century,* the Council on Library and Information Resources (CLIR) identified several key challenges for research libraries that are positioning themselves to support eResearch. The key challenges are:

- Ensuring the quality, integrity, and curation of digital research information
- Sustaining today's evolving digital service environments
- Bridging and connecting different worlds, disciplines, and paradigms for knowing and understanding
- Archiving research data in a data world (Council on Library and Information Resources 2008)

The report also highlighted three key roles of research libraries in the future, which are: (1) supporting knowledge creation at all its stages;

(2) connecting research communities by facilitating physical and virtual research spaces; and (3) digital curation, including preservation and management of knowledge and development of well-structured metadata. Although these library roles will likely evolve parallel to the evolution of research, the underlying principle of these roles reflects the fundamental nature of library services that are driven by and reflect the needs of the research communities they seek to support.

New responsibilities, in addition to expanded traditional roles, will likely become the norm in the libraries that support research activities. By combining their traditional and innovative roles, the libraries will not only find a unique niche as knowledge mediators who facilitate research needs of their patrons, but will also become more involved in the eResearch enterprise as potential collaborators in eResearch projects. The products of this collaboration can benefit both the research communities and the libraries and, in the process, advance further research and scholarship.

Even today, in the wired or wireless environment, Ranganathan's vision of the library as a growing organism continues to be one of the main incentives that drives librarians to stay abreast of evolving research and technological trends while maintaining the library's core values. These core values reinforce libraries' emphasis on growth and adaptability to change as traditional knowledge boundaries shift and the paths, which the research of tomorrow may embark upon, are never-ending.

NOTES

1. Ubiquitous computing has been described as computing that can "appear everywhere and anywhere ... and can occur using any device, in any location, and in any format" (Wikipedia 2014, http://en.wikipedia.org/wiki/Ubiquitous_computing, accessed February 28, 2014).

2. Ambient data refers to data stored in nontraditional computer storage areas and formats and lie in areas not generally accessible to the user.

3. The term "life-world" was brought into sociology by Austrian social scientist Alfred Schutz, who defined it as the "world of daily life" (1962).

4. Several authors explored the differences among inter-, multi-, and transdisciplinarity (Frodeman, Thompson Klein, and Mitcham 2009; Hirsch Hadorn et al. 2008; Ramadier 2004). Interdisciplinarity constructs a common model from a range of disciplinary perspectives by using the methods of one discipline to inform another; multidisciplinarity (also sometimes called pluridisciplinarity and polidisciplinarity) approaches a research problem from the perspective of a number of different disciplines; and transdisciplinarity breaks away from any fragmentary models typical of disciplinary thinking and combines inter- and multidisciplinarity "in order to rise above these forms of thought" (Frodeman, Thompson Klein, and Mitcham 2009, 434).

5. The concept of open scholarship has gained particular attention after Friedman (2005) argued that digital technologies and open source initiatives had helped to connect knowledge centers across the planet, thereby "flattening" the world, and had

contributed to the development of an "even playing field" between nations, groups, and individuals.

6. The Organization for Economic Co-operation and Development (OECD) (2007) defines Open Educational Resources (OERs) as "digitised materials offered freely and openly for educators, students and self-learners to use and reuse for teaching, learning and research." Examples of OERs include OER Commons (http://www.oercommons.org/), the Wikimedia Foundation (http://wikimediafoundation.org/), and Flat World Knowledge (http://catalog.flatworldknowledge.com/).

7. Open courses differ from Massive Online Open Courses (MOOCs). Although MOOCs are "free," they are offered by both for-profit and nonprofit organizations.

WORKS CITED

Bonk, Curtis J. *The World Is Open: How Web Technology Is Revolutionizing Education*. San Francisco: John Wiley and Sons, 2009.

Boulding, Kenneth Ewart. *Beyond Economics: Essays on Society, Religion, and Ethics*. Ann Arbor: University of Michigan Press, 1968.

Braman, Sandra. *What Do Researchers Need? Higher Education IT from the Researcher's Perspective*. Boulder, CO Educause Center for Applied Research, Issue 1, 2006.

Brewer, Gary D. "The Challenges of Interdisciplinarity." *Policy Sciences* 32 (1999): 327–37. doi:10.1023/A:1004706019826.

Bunders, Joske F. G., Jacqueline E. W. Broerse, Florian Keil, Christian Pohl, Roland W. Scholz, and Marjolein B. M. Zweekhorst. "How Can Transdisciplinary Research Contribute to Knowledge Democracy?" In *Knowledge Democracy: Consequences for Science, Politics, and Media*, edited by Roel Veld, 125–52. Berlin: Springer Berlin Heidelberg, 2010.

Burton, Gideon. "The Open Scholar." *Academic Evolution* 11 (2009). http://www.academicevolution.com/2009/08/the-open-scholar.html (accessed February 26, 2014).

Council on Library and Information Resources. *No Brief Candle: Reconceiving Research Libraries for the 21st Century*. http://www.clir.org/pubs/reports/pub142/pub142.pdf (accessed February 28, 2014).

Ernst, Richard. "Societal Responsibility of Universities, Wisdom and Foresight Leading to a Better World." In *A Vision of Transdisciplinarity: Laying Foundations for a World Knowledge Dialogue*, edited by Frédéric Darbellay, Moira Cockell, Jerome Billotte, and Francis Waldvogel, 121–35. Boca Raton, FL: CRC Press, 2008.

Frodeman, Robert, Julie Thompson Klein, and Carl Mitcham, eds. *The Oxford Handbook of Interdisciplinarity*. Oxford: Oxford University Press, 2009.

Fuchs, Stephan. "What Makes Sciences Scientific?" In *Handbook of Sociological Theory*, edited by J. Turner, 21–35. New York: Kluwer Academic/Plenum Publishers, 2002.

Gibbons, Michael, Camille Limoges, Helga Nowotny, Simon Schwartzman, Peter Scott, and Martin Trow, eds. *The New Production of Knowledge: The Dynamics of Science and Research in Contemporary Societies*. London: Sage, 1994.

Giri, Ananta Kumar. "The Calling of a Creative Transdisciplinarity." *Futures* 34, no. 1 (2002): 103–15.

Harvard School of Public Health. Transdisciplinary Research in Energetics and Cancer Center. "About Us: Definitions." http://www.hsph.harvard.edu/trec/about-us/definitions/ (accessed April 21, 2014).

Hirsch Hadorn, Gertrude, Susette Biber-Klemm, Walter Grossenbacher-Mansuy, Holger Hoffmann-Riem, Dominique Joye, Christian Pohl, Urs Wiesmann, and Elisabeth Zemp. "The Emergence of Transdisciplinarity as a Form of Research." In *Handbook of Transdisciplinary Research*, edited by Gertrude Hirsch Hadorn, Holger Hoffmann-Riem, Susette Biber-Klemm, Walter Grossenbacher-Mansuy, Dominique Joye, Christian Pohl, Urs Wiesmann, and Elisabeth Zemp, 19–39. Dordrecht: Springer, 2008.

Jantsch, Erich. "Towards Interdisciplinarity and Transdisciplinarity in Education and Innovation." *Interdisciplinarity: Problems of Teaching and Research in Universities*, OECD, Paris (1972): 97–121.

Jasanoff, Sheila. *The Fifth Branch: Science Advisers as Policymakers*. Cambridge, MA: Harvard University Press, 1990.

Leavy, Patricia. *Essentials of Transdisciplinary Research: Using Problem-Centered Methodologies*. Walnut Creek, CA: Left Coast Press, 2011.

Nicolescu, Basarab. *Manifesto of Transdisciplinarity*. Albany: State University of New York Press, 2002.

Piaget, Jean. *Main Trends in Interdisciplinary Research*. London: George Allen & Unwin, 1973.

Pohl, Christian, and Gertrude Hirsch Hadorn. *Principles for Designing Transdisciplinary Research*. Munich: Oekom, 2007.

Ramadier, Thierry. "Transdisciplinarity and Its Challenges: The Case of Urban Studies." *Futures* 36, no. 4 (2004): 423–39. doi:10.1016/j.futures.2003.10.009.

Salter, Liora. *Mandated Science*. Dordrecht: Springer Netherlands, 1988.

Thompson Klein, Julie. "Prospects for Transdisciplinarity." *Futures* 36, no. 4 (2004): 515–26. doi:10.1016/j.futures.2003.10.007.

Weiser, Marc. "The World Is Not a Desktop." *Interactions* 1, no. 1 (1994): 7–8.

SUGGESTED READINGS

Dewey, Barbara, ed. *Transforming Research Libraries for the Global Knowledge Society*. Oxford: Chandos Publishing, 2010.

Friedman, Thomas L. *The World Is Flat: A Brief History of the Twenty-first Century*. New York: Farrar, Straus and Giroux, 2005.

Hirsch Hadorn, Gertrude, Holger Hoffmann-Riem, Susette Biber-Klemm, Walter Grossenbacher-Mansuy, Dominique Joye, Christian Pohl, Urs Wiesmann, and Elisabeth Zemp, eds. *Handbook of Transdisciplinary Research*. Berlin: Springer, 2008.

Nicolescu, Basarab. *Manifesto of Transdisciplinarity*. Albany: State University of New York Press, 2002.

Veld, Roel, ed. *Knowledge Democracy: Consequences for Science, Politics, and Media*. Berlin: Springer, 2010.

Glossary

AJAX (Asynchronous JavaScript and XML): A set of Web programming techniques that enables a faster processing of information by exchanging smaller amounts of data with the server and thus makes it possible to update sections of a webpage without reloading the entire webpage.

Ambient data: Data that is stored in nontraditional storage areas, for example, as unused sections of a file and hidden segments of storage media, and thus not usually accessible to users.

Altmetrics: Alternative metrics, a method for measure engagement with research products. Altmertric.com and ImpactStory are examples of altmetrics.

Application Programming Interface (API): A specification for how software programs should interact with each other.

Artificial Intelligence (AI): A science and engineering field that explores how to simulate various aspects and functions in the field of human intelligence, such as perception, recognition, reasoning, learning, translating, etc.

ASCII (American Standard Code for Information Interchange): A code for representing numbers as letters in the Roman alphabet.

AWS (Amazon Web Services): The set of Web services that Amazon offers to help Web developers build Web applications and use Amazon's cloud computing environment.

Binary language (or binary code): Representation of information in computer form made of 0s and 1s.

Blog: An abbreviation of the term "weblog." An ongoing set of postings on the Web, such as commentary, diary, advice, and other types of information, with embedded hypertext links and often comments from readers.

Cloud computing: A model for making shared computing resources available through a network to the users without requiring them to purchase or own the equipment. These resources can be made rapidly available upon demand, and the user is usually charged for how much they use.

Consortium: A cooperative association among organizations to exchange and share resources and services.

Cutting-edge technologies: Leading and innovative technologies that represent the most advanced technological developments in the competitive market.

Cyberinfrastructure: A system of widely distributed computing equipment and facilities that can be used by researchers who need access to such resources to support their data acquisition, processing, storage, and handling requirements. These computing equipment and facilities are usually beyond the ability of a single organization to have under their own purview.

Dark data: Data that have not been carefully indexed and stored and thus cannot be easily found by potential users and are likely to remain underutilized or lost.

Data: Raw material used as a primary source for research; factual records that can be collected in the form of observations, images, computer program results, recordings, measurements, or experiments.

Data citation: A citation that provides attribution to research data sources to allow for easier access to research data within journals and on the Internet.

Data curation: The ongoing management of data through their life cycle.

Data deluge: The situation where the volume of new data and the speed with which the data are being generated are overwhelming, and often beyond the capacity of institutions to manage the data and researchers to make use of the data.

Data ethics: Refers to the issues of intellectual property rights, confidentiality, and privacy (especially with regard to research involving human subjects), and assigning attribution in order to gain recognition for one's work.

Data-intensive computing: A transformative computing approach that is designed to handle massive amounts of data (typically terabytes or petabytes in volume and are often referred to as "big data") from multiple sources. This usually requires the use of parallel processing techniques that allow for distribution of the processing load across many computers.

Data interview: An interview between a librarian and a researcher to draw out information needed to construct a data curation profile or data management plan.

Data life cycle: The phases that data progress through during the research process.

Data literacy: The ability to understand, read, and communicate data.

Data management checklist: A recording of all of the information items necessary in creating a successful data management plan.

Data management plan: A written supplement to a research or grant proposal outlining how research data will be handled during and after the research project.

Data migration: The process of transferring data from one format, storage type, or system of computers to another.

Data mining: A technique that allows researchers to discover new trends and patterns within data that researchers can then analyze and interpret to form new insights.

Data preservation: A series of activities to ensure continued access to data.

Data privacy: The need to anonymize or safeguard data in order to maintain privacy restrictions, particularly when dealing with data about human subjects or health information.

Data provenance: The process of tracking data origins and transformations during the research project.

Data repository: A place that organizes and holds data and makes the data available for use and reuse.

Data reuse: Reusing data for the same or different purpose by the same or different user.

Data sharing: The practice of making research data available to other investigators.

Data visualization: The visual representation of data, usually in a form that makes them easier to interpret and extract useful information.

Data set: A collection of data represented in a particular form.

Digital: A method of encoding, storing, processing, and transmitting information in binary form (i.e., in 1s and 0s), to enable the information to be handled and processed by computing devices.

Digital curation: A series of activities to ensure the preservation of digital data over the long term.

Digital data: Data represented in the form of numbers in order to facilitate their processing and storage.

Digital humanities (DH): A set of practices in humanities scholarship that uses advanced digital technology and computational techniques as the integral part of the research process.

Digital librarianship: Knowledge and skills needed to design and implement digital information services.

Digital library: A virtual library providing access to part or all of its collections that have been digitally converted and made accessible via the Internet.

Digital object: Kahn and Wilensky (2006) defined a digital object as "a data structure whose principal components are digital material, or data, plus a unique identifier for this material, called a handle" (116).[1] The object is usually a document but can also be an article, a database, an image in digital form, an audio or video file, etc.

Digital object identifier (DOI): A unique persistent identifier for a published digital object such as an article or a study.

Digital repository: A database for archiving digital content in the form of digital objects.

Digital Rights Management (DRM): The practice of controlling and limiting the usage of protected digital products.

Digitization: The process of electronically converting information resources into a digital format.

E: A prefix for "electronic," such as in e-mail or e-journal, i.e., existing in computer readable form.

Elasticity: The ability of a computing resource to expand or shrink in size in real time based on the immediate need.

Electronic book (eBook): A full-length book publication in a digital format that can be read via a computer or via handheld devices called eBook readers.

Electronic journal (eJournal): A periodical publication produced in electronic format.

E-mail (electronic mail): Messages that are sent electronically from one computer to another.

Emerging technologies: New evolving technologies with significant market potential.

ePrint: A digital version of a document, such as a research journal article, book chapter, thesis, or dissertation.

eResearch: A highly collaborative, data-driven, and networked research process that relies on the use of advanced information and computational technologies such as the Grid computing, the Internet, cloud computing, visualization software, and scholarly communication and collaboration online tools.

eScience: A computationally intensive, data-driven science research carried out in highly collaborative and distributed research environments.

eSocial science: A field of study that uses advanced information and computational technologies to generate and analyze human data.

File format: A standardized way of encoding data for storage in a computer file. The format specifies both how the data is organized and the types of data contained in the file.

Folksonomy: The collaborative approach to creating and managing tags to describe and classify digital content. Also known as "social tagging."

Fourth paradigm: A concept based on the idea that computational science constitutes a new set of research methods beyond the three other traditional paradigms: empiricism, theory, and simulation.

Geographic Information System (GIS): A collection of tools and approaches for capturing, storing, analyzing, managing, and viewing geospatial data.

Grid: A massive distributed computing power; the hardware, software, and standards necessary for coordination of geographically distributed computing and data resources and making them available to researchers over the Internet.

Grid computing: Computing model that makes use of multiple computing resources that are distributed across various locations to run a single application. The resources used in a grid are typically loosely coupled and are not of the same kind or nature.

High-performance computing (HPC): The use of parallel-processing computers and programs in a manner that delivers much higher performance than one could get out of a typical computer or workstation.

High-throughput computing (HTC): The use of many computing resources for a very large computing task that typically takes a long time to complete.

HTML (hypertext markup language): A code invented by Tim Berners-Lee in 1991 to serve as a means to encode webpages, i.e., to standardize how the webpage looks and behaves on the computer screen regardless of what kind of computer is being used.

HTTP (hypertext transport protocol): A standard way for Web browsers to link and transmit data over the World Wide Web. HTTPS is a version of the protocol that uses encryption to keep the data secure while traveling between computers.

Human-computer interaction (HCI): The study of the exchange and transfer of information between computers and human beings.

IaaS (Infrastructure as a Service): A cloud service that includes computing resources, associated software, and facilities owned by a cloud vendor but offered to users as a "service" that allows them to run their own applications using the vendor's computing resources. The user is billed based on how many resources are being used and for how long.

IDEF0 (Integration Definition for Function Modeling): A modeling technique based on the SADT (Structured Analysis and Design Technique) that was developed in the 1970s by Douglas T. Ross and SofTech, Inc.

In-memory database processing systems: The systems that utilize main memory of a server to store and manage data.

Information: Data that have been processed and organized in such a way that they "inform" people, or give them access to the meaning of the data.

Information and communication technology (ICT): The technology used to handle information and aid in its communication.

Information visualization: Visualization of multidimensional data in order to provide an intuitive and/or simplified view on complex issues.

Infrastructure: In information technology, infrastructure includes basic computer hardware, storage devices, associated networks, operating systems, and other software that the application relies upon.

Institutional repository (IR): A series of services that an academic institution offers to its community for the management, preservation, and dissemination of digital scholarly materials authored by the institutional members.

Intellectual property rights (IPR): Rights acquired over any work created or invented with the intellectual effort of an individual. Common types of IPR include copyrights, patents, trademarks, industrial design right, and design layouts.

Interdisciplinarity: A form of coordinated and integration-oriented collaboration between researchers from different disciplines.

Internet: A global network linking computers around the world and enabling them to communicate via standard protocols and data formats.

Internet Protocol (IP): The standard that determines the format and methods of sending and receiving data between computers on the Internet.

Invisible colleges: Informal methods of scholarly communication, such as e-mail, blogs, wikis, discussion lists, and society and professional hubs.

Learning object (LO): A digital object or collection of digital objects that can assist in the teaching and learning process (e.g., a module, a course, or a quiz).

Learning object repository (LOR): A digital collection intended for storing, managing, and sharing educational content (i.e., "learning objects") for reuse.

Linked data: The practice for exposing, sharing, and connecting data on the Semantic Web using Unique Resource Identifiers (URIs) and the Resource Description Framework (RDF).

Mashup: A website, or Web application, that combines content from different resources or services into a single website or application.

Metadata: Also known as "data about data." The description of all aspects of data and software components used for the collection or creation of data.

Middleware: Software that lies in between two separate applications that helps link the applications together. Middleware can also lie between an application and a database that enables the application to have access to that data.

Multidisciplinarity: An approach to addressing an issue using the different perspectives from a range of disciplines.

Multimodality: the combination of audio, video, and textual media modes, or modalities, to create a single cultural object.

Network: A system of computers linked together through wired or wireless connections for the purpose of transmitting data between those computers.

Networked environment: An interconnected system of networks that connects computers around the world via the Internet protocols.

Open access (OA): Availability to anyone. In the context of scholarship, open access is the idea and practice of providing free, unrestricted access to research findings and other research materials, e.g., research data.

Open access publishing: The practice of making research papers freely available on the Web immediately after their publication.

Open source: Software source code that is available for use to the public free of charge and that can be modified from its original design.

Optical Character Recognition (OCR): The process of a digital translation of printed or written text characters by a computer.

PaaS (Platform as a Service): A cloud service that includes hardware and operating software along with a development environment owned by a cloud vendor but offered to users as a "service" that allows users to develop and run their own applications using their computing resources. The user is billed based on how many "platform" resources are being used and for how long.

Personal Digital Assistant (PDA): A handheld device that facilitates the use of such tools as calendars, clocks, calculators, address books, memos, and alerts.

PDF (Portable Document Format): A standardized file format developed by Adobe Systems that captures all the elements of a printed document.

Peer review: A practice in scholarly journal publishing and in the review of proposals for grants, in which external peers, who share disciplinary expertise, impose stringent criteria on acceptance of contributions for publication or proposals for research funding. There are two traditional types of peer review: blind peer review, a process in which the identity of the reviewers is concealed from the reviewee; and double-blind peer review, a process in which the identity of the reviewee is also concealed from the reviewers.

Private cloud: As opposed to a public cloud, which is available to the general public, a private cloud is a computing infrastructure established within the boundaries of a corporate firewall that allows only authorized users in the corporation to use these cloud resources.

Public cloud: A set of cloud computing resources available to the general public over the Internet.

Refereeing: A practice in scholarly journal publishing, in which external referees, an editor, or members of an editorial board impose strict criteria on acceptance of contributions for publication.

Research data management: The practice of managing, sharing, and archiving of research data.

Research life cycle: The different stages that a research project might progress through from its inception to its completion.

RSS (Really Simple Syndication): Originally, RDF Site Summary. A method by which Web content (such as news and updates) can be easily and quickly distributed when it is changed or newly entered into a website or blog.

SaaS: Software as a Service. The providing of a self-service application based on a cloud infrastructure.

Scalability: The ability of a hardware or software system to increase the amount of computing or networking resources made available to a user based on immediate demand.

Scholarly communication: A social process in which scholars share ideas, data, resources, methodologies, innovations, and discoveries with their peers and with the public.

Semantic Web: A segment of the Web incorporating semantic information that allows machines to understand the information contained on the Web.

Sensors: Devices that measure movements of structures such as bridges, buildings, and airplane wings; vital signals of humans; atmospheric conditions; and fluctuations in power and water networks.

Social networking site (SNS): A website designed to create relationships among people who share common interests, activities, and other social connections.

Social Web: A new approach of the Web, also known as Web 2.0, that emphasizes user-generated content and user interactions in Web applications.

Spatial computing: A set of technologies that utilizes the concepts of space and time in computation.

Spatial data: Data related to locations on the earth's surface.

Structured data: Highly organized data retrieved from databases or other sources.

Tag: A keyword assigned to a piece of information that describes and categorizes that piece of information.

Tag cloud: A visual depiction of user-generated tags.

Text encoding: The process of adding codes to text to make that text computer-readable.

Text mining: The process of extracting by computer of new information from text.

Transdisciplinarity (TD): A new mode of knowledge production that is driven by the need to solve problems of the real world.

Ubiquitous computing: An advanced computing concept according to which computing can occur using any device, in any location, and in any format.

Unstructured data: Raw data directly extracted from online applications without being organized into effective formats.

Videoconferencing: A technology that enables users to see each other in the monitor through cameras on or connected to the computers on each end.

Virtual Research Environment (VRE): An online platform dedicated to supporting research collaborations.

Virtual reference service: A real-time online library reference service offered via an Internet-based software application.

Visualization: The process of representing abstract ideas or data as images.

Web 2.0: Web applications that enable the creation or sharing of resources by a group of users, for example, blogs, wikis, and social networking sites.

Webometrics: A field of quantitative social science research that uses data from the World Wide Web such as hyperlinks between webpages in order to identify, among other factors, the visibility of websites.

Wiki: A collaborative Web space, to which anyone at any time can add content or edit the existing content.

World Wide Web (WWW): A segment of the Internet that enables the accessing and distributing hypertext documents via Web browsers and Web servers running over the Internet platform.

NOTE

1. Robert Kahn and Robert Wilensky, "A Framework for Distributed Digital Object Services," *International Journal on Digital Libraries* 6, no. 2 (2006): 115–23, doi:10.1007/s00799-005-0128-x.

Index

About the Author

VICTORIA MARTIN is the life sciences librarian at the University Libraries of George Mason University, a position she has held since 2001. During this time, she has served as a liaison librarian for graduate-level bioscience programs, including bioinformatics, molecular biology and microbiology, biodefense, and neuroscience. Her publications include journal articles, book and electronic resource reviews, literary works, and a book chapter. Martin holds a master of library science degree from Texas Woman's University and a master of fine arts degree in creative writing from George Mason University.